S0-EWX-513

LITERATURE AS HISTORY
FROM EARLY TO CONTEMPORARY TIMES

LITERATURE AS HISTORY
From Early to Contemporary Times

edited by
CHHANDA CHATTERJEE

PRIMUS BOOKS

PRIMUS BOOKS
An imprint of Ratna Sagar P. Ltd.
Virat Bhavan
Mukherjee Nagar Commercial Complex
Delhi 110 009

Offices at CHENNAI   LUCKNOW
AGRA   AHMEDABAD   BANGALORE   COIMBATORE   DEHRADUN   GUWAHATI   HYDERABAD
JAIPUR   KANPUR   KOCHI   KOLKATA   MADURAI   MUMBAI   PATNA   RANCHI   VARANASI

© *Editorial selection and Introduction Chhanda Chatterjee 2014*
© *Individual contributors for their essays 2014*

All rights reserved. No part of this publication may be reproduced or transmitted, in any form or by any means, without permission. Any person who does any unauthorized act in relation to this publication may be liable to criminal prosecution and civil claims for damages.

First published 2014

ISBN: 978–93–84082–03–1

Published by Primus Books

Laser typeset by Digigrafics
Gulmohar Park, New Delhi 110 049

Printed and bound in India by Replika Press Pvt. Ltd.

This book is meant for educational and learning purposes. The author(s) of the book has/have taken all reasonable care to ensure that the contents of the book do not violate any existing copyright or other intellectual property rights of any person in any manner whatsoever. In the event the author(s) has/have been unable to track any source and if any copyright has been inadvertently infringed, please notify the publisher in writing for corrective action.

Contents

Preface	vii
Introduction: Literature as History: From Early to Contemporary Times CHHANDA CHATTERJE	1
1. 'Historicality in Literature': A Case Study of the Classical Tamil Text, the Patiṟṟuppattu GANAPATHY SUBBIAH	17
2. Mystical and Eclectic Traditions as Reflected in Persian Sources of Medieval India AMIT DEY	27
3. Naturalization of the Nation and Nationalization of Nature: A Study of the Nationalist Literature of Bengal ANURADHA ROY	49
4. The Radical Rabindranath: 'The Red Oleanders (*Rakta Karabi*)' and Dreams of a New World CHHANDA CHATTERJEE	81
5. Reading Tagore's *Letters from Russia* in the Twenty-first Century SOBHANLAL DATTA GUPTA	95
6. The Evolution of Indian English Language and Literature: A Socio-Historical Survey SOMDATTA MANDAL	109
7. 'Tagore Syndrome': A Case Study of the West's Intercultural (Mis)readings IGOR GRBIĆ	139
8. The Politics and Poetics of Translating Indian Women's Fiction in English SWATI GANGULY	151
Notes on Editor and Contributors	165
Index	167

Preface

THIS IS A book which hopes to illustrate that the literature of a particular period of time can also be read to understand its history. The quality and definition of this literature has changed over time. In ancient days it was often a dynastic chronicle, or the eulogy of some great royal personage. And yet even this kind of literature could contain glimpses of the lives of the common people as the article on the Tamil text *Patirrupattu* by Ganapathy Subbiah would show. As we progress from early India to the days of Islamic hegemony we can trace the cultural transition through the literature of the new phase. Here Amit Dey introduces us to the ideas of the Sufis, who not only assigned an honoured place to the women of the faith, but also tried to begin an inter-faith dialogue through a translation of the canonical literature of the conquered.

The onset of a new phase of colonial rule, beginning with the East India Company's regime and transforming itself into a new dispensation of the British Queen's sovereignty in the wake of the outbreak of 1857, brought new influences. The literature of the colonial period was marked by these new ideas. Contact with the West introduced the ideas of nationalism and the resentment of the colonized against foreign domination began to reflect in a prolific outcrop of nationalist literature. Nationalist writers began to look upon their country as a distressed woman, who had once been bedecked with precious jewels. But the very richness of her possessions had proved to be her undoing. It attracted the greed of robbers from across the seas, and the country, which had once been famed for its wealth, stands despoiled of all her prize possessions. Ravaged by repeated famines and disease, her villages are now marked by underdevelopment. Anuradha Roy has shown how nature, nation, mother and country all became one in the nationalist imagination. The great poet and dramatist of this period, Rabindranath Tagore, tried to portray the exploitation of mine-workers under the capitalist dispensation in one of his seminal dramas, *The Red Oleanders*. It was an indictment of the contemporary materialism, of which imperialism and capitalism were the off-shoots. Tagore seemed to have found a way out of this imbroglio in a system of free education reaching to the lowest strata of the population, such as he had seen during his visit to Russia. Narrated in the form of letters, the *Letters from Russia* emphasized the contrast between the growth of underdevelopment in colonial India and the Bolshevik government's care and concern for the well-being of the members of the state. Chhanda Chatterjee's essay tries to read the workings of Tagore's mind in the context of the changes in the world system by linking up the train of thoughts from the *Red Oleanders* to the *Letters from Russia*. In Sobhanlal Datta Gupta's writings, however, we find a reference to Tagore's subsequent disillusionment with this system. Tagore's angry interview to the *Izvestia* before his departure from Russia (referred to in his Bengali original but carefully left out from Sasadhar Sinha's English translation, widely circulated by Visva-Bharati) regarding the repressive face of Bolshevism, perhaps represented the retreat of the entire world from the first flush of enthusiasm about the radical revolution in the lot of all wretched of the earth expected from the Bolshevik experiment.

The kind of awareness of the problems of the world that informed the writings of Tagore touched a new high in the post-colonial period with the splurge of Indian writing in English originating from the Indian diaspora dispersed in different corners of the world. They succeeded in investing local concerns like the resurgence of the malaria fever in Bengal or the proneness of the coastal areas of the Indian sub-continent to repeated attacks of cyclones, with global importance in a manner typical of post-modernist thinking.

Somdatta Mandal's deft pen has traced the growth and development of this Indo-Anglian writing. Such writings were perhaps an illustration of what Jean Paul Sartre called 'novels of situation,' where 'man plays or wins or loses in the womb of universal history' (Jean Paul Sartre, *What is Literature*, tr. Bernard Frechtman, Northhampton: Methuen and Co. Ltd., 1st pub., 1950, repr. 1967).

Feminism—yet another off shoot of post-colonialism—is the subject of Swati Ganguly's essay on the biased translation policy of big publishing houses. Ganguly argues convincingly that new and comparatively less known women writers never get the attention of translators engaged by well-known publishers and their voice therefore remains unheard among the slowly, but definitely, crystallizing feminist literature in the world.

Igor Grbić's piece analyses Western attitude towards the East in general. Igor's enquiry into the fate of the writings of Tagore enables him to advance a few hypotheses. War-weary West had worshipped Tagore as a new prophet in the inter-war years. But the infatuation passed off as the world settled down to a humdrum existence and allowed Tagore to fade into insignificance. Grbić fears a recurrence of the same phenomenon for Indo-Anglian literature too. Grbić thus discerns a close connection between the emotions of an age and the kind of literature that it produces.

The essays also have a lot to say about the linguistic development that had been taking place during the period in which the literature dealt with in each of these essays had flourished. The *Patirrupattu* represents a decisive break for Tamil out of 'the Sanskrit cosmopolis'. Sufi literature began a new journey in vernacular writing. Nationalist writing in Bengal coincided with a period of linguistic renaissance for the regional language, with authors like Michael Madhusudan Dutta and Rabindranath Tagore experimenting with new ways of using the rhetoric. Indian writing in English, which made its debut in the colonial period as a modest effort, has now embarked on a conquest of the world in the post-colonial times. Indian words are slowly making their way into the English lexicon in larger numbers. Award winning diasporic writers are using more and more Indian words while writing English to create a genuine *desi* ambience. They have thus launched a 'conquest of English' in the cultural sense.

Our volume grew out of a national seminar on the 'Linguistic and Literary History of India' in the Department of History in Visva-Bharati in December 2008. Experts on languages from all corners of the country had been invited. Delegates came from Punjab, Bihar and Tamil Nadu. The Indian Council of Historical Research generously contributed money to supplement the University Grants Commission's SAP seminar funds. But when it came to contributing their papers for publication most of the delegates developed cold feet. Only a few angels (I cannot think of a better term, otherwise I would have no hesitation in using it) took pity on me and it is out of their contributions that the present volume could take shape. Professor Datta Gupta joined us in a later international conference but he permitted me to use his paper in this volume. Dr. Grbić was a new acquaintance from another international conference in Edinburgh, who kindly agreed to write for us.

This publication would not have been possible without the blessings of our Vice Chancellor, Professor Sushanta Dattagupta, who entrusted me with the responsibility of looking after the Special Assistance Programme of the University Grants Commission. The Department is deeply indebted to him for his active encouragement and cooperation with generous contribution of funds for international delegates. The Department is also equally indebted to Professor Suranjan Das, Vice Chancellor, University of Calcutta and External Member, appointed by the University Grants Commission to the Advisory Board of the UGC SAP DRS II of the Department of History, Visva-Bharati for his advice and cooperation. Thanks are also due to Professor Kaushik Roy, Guru Nanak Professor of Indian History, Jadavpur University, for the assistance that he has generously provided me in bringing out this volume.

I am heartily grateful to Uma Bali, Under Secretary UGC and members of the staff in the UGC office for the timely release of funds for our programme. Members of the Finance, Audit and Accounts departments in Visva-Bharati were equally helpful in the processing and release of funds. Our Registrar, Professor Gunasekharan, had always been very prompt and willing regarding the required approval for the project. Kamal Halder and

Utpal Hazra in the Registrar's office and Dr. Shyamala Nair in the Vice Chancellor's office had always been very kind to me. I had to rely heavily on Dr. Amarendra Kumar, Deputy Coordinator, UGC SAP DRS II for his friendly assistance in making the programme work. Finally I must thank my husband for having lent his generous assistance in expediting the publication. Without the cooperation of his P.S., Sreedharan Nair, it would not have been possible for me to follow up the work in New Delhi.

CHHANDA CHATTERJEE

INTRODUCTION

Literature as History: From Early to Contemporary Times

CHHANDA CHATTERJEE

LITERATURE IS SAID to fulfil its true purpose only when it is able to mirror life. It is able to offer rare insights into the lives of people which are beyond the reach of 'dry as dust historians'. Ashin Dasgupta had pointed out in the course of a lecture that journalists and historians can merely narrate an event, whereas literature reserves the right to enter into the heart of an event.[1] The emotions and mentalities of a people are therefore increasingly becoming the concern of historians.[2] The German historian Ranke, who had been a very strong proponent of the objectivity of History, had confessed to drawing inspiration from the historical novels of Sir Walter Scott in his writings.[3] Historical writing in pre-colonial India was often associated with the narrative or *Purana* and *Kavya* tradition[4]—very far from the objective, rational and scientific historiography that came into vogue in the nineteenth and early twentieth century under the influence of colonial projects of deriving power from knowledge about the colonized. Rabindranath Tagore would have liked literature to fill the gaps in academic historiography by bringing in the tales of the lives of people as they were lived in reality.[5] Our volume hopes to be such an exercise in literary historiography, where each paper has made use of the literature of a particular age to bring forward the mentality of that age before the historian's gaze.

In the first essay in this volume 'Historicality in Literature': A Case Study of the Classical Tamil Text, the Patiṟṟuppattu', Ganapathy Subbiah tries to show from an analysis of the ancient Tamil text Patiṟṟuppattu (the dates may be from the second century BC to second century AD or from the second century AD to the fourth century AD), that classical Tamil literature could be said to contain 'historicality' in Ranajit Guha's sense of the term.[6] Subbiah refers to the lamentation of K.A. Nilakantha Shastri that while in other countries literature was taken to be the 'bedrock of history,' in India it was often regarded as a 'snare'.[7] Texts were very often in the nature of a 'fable' acquiring many irrational accretions through the passage of time. Thus they were rarely of much worth to historians in unravelling the mystery of the past. Even a veteran authority like Vishwambhar Sharan Pathak worried that the susceptibility of ancient literature to the values and mentalities of the days of yore might make them incomprehensible to the historian of the present generation with his widely divergent conceptual tools.[8] It therefore only adds further to the credit of Subbiah that he undertook the onerous task of delving deep into the ancient Tamil text Patiṟṟuppattu and tried to trace through it 'the life lived by the people in their everyday contentment and misery'.[9]

Patiṟṟuppattu was one of the eight anthologies (*ettuttokai*) which formed part of the classical Tamil texts known as *caṅkam* literature. The name Patiṟ ruppattu denoted Ten Tens or ten poems, one for each of the ten kings of the Cēral family, by a particular poet. Of these 100 poems only 80 could be traced; the first and the last bunch of ten poems each could not be found in the text. The last could, however, be retrieved from references by commentators. The editing and publication of Patiṟṟuppattu along with an old commentary for the first time by Mahamahopadhyaya U.V. Swaminathan Aiyar in 1904 came about as part of a wave for the rediscovery and printing of lost Tamil classics. Vasudha Dalmia would view such moves as an attempt at a 'new articulation of nationhood' which wanted to derive strength from a recovery of the past.[10] The publication ran into two more editions, one in 1921 and another in 1940. In 1950 the Saiva Siddhanta Works Publishing Society (SSWPS) brought out a new edition with a modern commentary by Vidvan Avvai Su. Duraiswami Pillai. The composition of one hundred poems in praise of a single dynasty (the Cēralar) endows them with the character of a chronicle of Kerala. Added to the Ten Poems as a suffix is the *patikam* or an epilogue of 10 to 21 lines summarizing the achievements of the hero and his lineage. These lines seem to be composed by later writers who could draw on sources not available to the early composers. The authenticity of the Patiṟṟuppattu is further corroborated by the mention of some of the kings eulogized in the text as donors in the Pugalur Tamil-Brahmin inscriptions.

As in most ancient texts, the concern of the Patiṟṟuppattu poems was also the singing of the heroic and martial achievements of the Kings. Thus nearly two-thirds of its contents can be classified as *pāṭāntinai* or praise for the hero. The *tinai* is concerned with the King's specific acts of valour. But in *pāṭān* is found greater details of the king's character, his various acts in relation to his subjects. The poet's attempt to elaborate not merely the physical prowess, but every other act of benevolence by the king, enables him to contextualize the various aspects of the lives of the inhabitants of the kingdom in their everyday 'contentment and misery.' Subbiah's enquiry into and analysis of the classical Tamil text thus elevates the status of ancient texts of this genre, juxtaposing them alongside modern day literature which is increasingly being viewed as an index of contemporary mentalite and contemporary life.

While Subbiah's study points to the efficacy of classical Tamil literature for an overview of the weal and woes of the people in those days, Amit Dey has made use of Persian literature in his paper 'Mystical and Eclectic Traditions in Medieval India: A Study of Persian Sources' to trace the position of honour and reverence accorded to women in Sufi mystical literature. The second part of his paper is concerned with the tradition of tolerance and respect for other religions running parallel to Islamic orthodoxy in medieval times. In spite of an ingrained prejudice in certain Islamic circles against the moral and intellectual capability of women for religiosity and virtue, such as is seen in Abu Talib's *Qutal Qulub* or even in the poet Jalal-ud-din Rumi (1207–73) (who would not even spare his own mother for having brought him to this cruel world just as Eve, the world's first woman, had brought about the banishment of mankind from the Garden of Eden), Dey could cite an impressive array of Islamic literature to demolish such orthodoxies.

Dey could trace abundant instances of the high place assigned to women even in pre-Sufi literature. He quotes *Sura* 12 of the holy Koran which points to the Prophet's sympathy for women. The Prophet held his four daughters in great esteem and of them Fatima was greatly venerated in Shia circles. The Prophet's mother Amina and his daughter Fatima came to be regarded as saints. In fact, the Islamic community could be held together over the ages through the strong faith of Muslim women. An echo of this belief can be found in the holy Koran's equal concern for *al muslimin wa al muslimat, wa al-muminin wa al-muminat* (all believing Muslim men as well as women). Koranic principles did not obviate the attainment of the highest inner spiritual experience by women. On the contrary, the first true saint of Islam was a woman—Rabi'a al-Adawiyya. The great importance of woman saints made Abdul-Haqq Muhaddis Dihlawi (AD 1551–1642) devote a separate chapter in his Persian work *Akhbar'ul-Akhyar* on them.

Veneration for women reached a new high with the advent of the Sufis. The role of women in the first religious instruction of men was recognized by the Prophet when he pronounced the words: 'Paradise lies at the feet of the mother.' Bibi Zulaykha, the mother of Sk. Nizam-ud-din Auliya, Ganj-i-Shakar, the mother of Shaikh Farid, and Bibi Sara, mother of Sk. Nizam-ud-din Abdul Muid formed the subject of Sufi literature—as can be found in the *Fawa'id-u'l-Fu'ad* of Amir Hasan. Shaikh Nizam-ud-din Auliya always visited his mother's tomb during times of trouble. He ignored Sultan Qutb-ud-din Mubarak Shah's orders to attend Friday prayers at the Sipri Fort and paid his *ziyarat* (usual visits) to his mother's tomb. In fact, his reply to the Sultan was *Masjid nazdik darem wa in ahaqq ast,* that is, 'There is a mosque nearby and it is more worthy.' Curiously enough, he was saved from the Sultan's wrath and retaliation for such defiance, as the latter was assassinated soon after. The saintly woman's *Baraka* (charisma), according to contemporary observers, must have acted as a protective shield for her devout son.

Shaikh Farid-ud-din's daughter Bibi Sarifa had all the spiritual attributes of a saint and the Shaikh openly declared that she had the competence to be a Khalifa (spiritual deputy of a Sufi saint). The *malfuzat* or conversations of Shaikh Nizam-ud-din Auliya and Shaikh Farid refer to Bibi Fatima Sam, a renowned Sufi woman of Delhi. Her famous saying about how, feeding the hungry, giving water to the thirsty and distributing money amongst the poor on festive occasions were more meritorious than hundreds and thousands of *namazes* and many days spent in fasting, is still celebrated in Sufi circles. Shaikh Nasir-ud-din's *Chirag-i-Dihlawi* makes mention of Bibi Fatima, who died praying after a 40–day fast as she believed in the transcendence of human life.

In Bengal, Hazrat Sayeda Zainub Khatun, also known as Raushan Bibi (either a celibate or married to an ancestor of Titu Mir), was a popular female saint. She has her grave on the western bank of the river Ichamati in the Basirhat subdivision. Maharaja Krishnachandra of Nadia granted 65 bighas of land in the name of the Pirani probably to extend his influence among the lower orders of the population.

Shaikh Abdul-Haqq Mahaddis Dihlawi mentions Bibi Auliya, a contemporary of Sultan Muhammad-bin-Tughluq, mediating in her *hujra* (chamber) for many hours and fasting continuously. In the month of *Muharram,* she would open a *langar* for the distribution of free food.

Yet another female saint of the Qadiryya order during its formative period in the Punjab who is worthy of mention was Bibi Jamal Khatun (d. AD 1639) who happened to be a sister of the famous Sufi saint, Hazrat Mian Mir, the mystical guide of the Mughal Prince, Dara Shikoh.

Jahan Ara or Fatima, the sister of Prince Dara Shikoh, was also a seeker of God. A follower of the Chishti Order, she herself was the author of *Munis-ul-Arwa* (The Comforter of Souls)—a biography of Khwaja Mu'in-ud-din Chisti. The Princess also had contacts with other Sufi saints like Mulla Shah. She addressed certain queries to him, and so impressed was Mulla Shah by her sincerity that the saint agreed to her initiation into the Qadiryya order. Her journey into mysticism, experience of ecstasy and attainment of pure union with God through mystic revelations has been recorded in her *Risala-i-Sahibiyya*.

Mulla Shah admitted that Jahan Ara had the intellectual abilities to be his *khalifa* (deputy) just as Shaikh Farid had recognized the talents of his daughter Bibi Sharifa to have similar honours. However, even Sufis would not allow women to become *sajjada nashins* and women were never incorporated into Sufi monasteries or *khanqas*. They could only become lone hermits and the spiritual and material resources commanded by *Pirs* remained beyond their reach. But a few such incapacities notwithstanding, Dey's deft use of Sufi literature can successfully establish how the position of women and the outlook of society towards women were being revolutionized during these times.

Dey also tries to demonstrate how Sufism was fostering multiculturalism, inter-faith understanding and mutual appreciation of the local culture of the subcontinent and Islamic culture, which had entered India in the train of the invading Muslim armies of Mahmud of Ghazni, Muhammad of Ghur and the Arab settlers of Sind. The Sufi attempt at the dissemination of religious knowledge among the common people through the use of the vernaculars, promoted the vernacularization of languages. Persian was not discarded but it was mixed with vernaculars. Hindawi and Punjabi thus came into prominence. Amir Khasrau experimented by the intermingling of Persian with *Brajabhasha*. This process of intermingling of languages was known as the *majma-ul-zabanat* and was facilitated by the interaction of the *Bhakti* movement and Sufism.[11]

Islam's interest in Indian culture was as old as Al Beruni's, who had translated Patanjali's *Yogasutra* to aquire knowledge of Indian mysticism. *Yogis* had free access to Sufi hospices and *jamat khanas*. Their mutual understanding had been made possible through the acceptance of the doctrine of *wahdat-ul-wujud* (the unity of existence as the manifestation of God) and *Hama Ust* (God is everywhere). Once this doctrine became accepted, even Hindus could not be regarded as *kafirs*. Mulla Daud, who is remembered along with the fourteenth century Sufi saint, Nasir-ud-din, *Chiragh-i-Delhi*, praised the Prophet Muhammad as the beloved of everyone. Yet the same person was also the author of *Chandayan*, where he referred to the Vedas and the Puranas as revealed books just like the Koran. The same views were shared by Mirza Mazhar Jan-i-Janan, a Naqshbandi Sufi poet. Idol worship was equated to *Tasawwur-i-Shaikh* or concentration on the mental image of the preceptor.

An avid interest in the thoughts and culture of the local people was shown by a number of Muslim rulers like Zainul Abedin of Kashmir, Sultan Sikandar Lodi and several others. Akbar, the Great Mughal, took the initiative to get the Hindu epics, *Ramayana* and *Mahabharata* translated in *Maktabkhanas*. Abul Fazl wrote a preface to the *Mahabharata*, where he invited everyone to study the book with an open mind. Akbar employed learned men of different faiths to engage in inter-faith debates and was convinced that all religions contained various elements of truth.

Akbar's liberal predilections had been inherited by Prince Dara, the heir designate to Emperor Shah Jehan. Like his illustrious great grandfather, Dara attached great importance to *aql* or reason and believed in *ijtihad* or the right of the learned to interpret scriptures according to changing circumstances. He felt that a composite culture was needed to control a multicultural country like India. He had resolved to bring back the realm of *aql* which had made Islam a world religion as against the dominance of *ilm* (literally knowledge, but virtually fundamentalism). Dara authored the *Safinat-ul-Awaliya* or lives of Sufi saints and had learnt of *tauhid* (monotheism) and *irfan* (divine knowledge). Knowledge of Sanskrit enabled him to study Upanishadic monotheism, which he discovered to be not far different from Koranic monotheism. Dara's Persian version of the Upanishads was translated into Latin. Dara also studied the Bible and tried to find out the common points of Islam, Hinduism and Christianity.

Dey concludes with a hopeful note, that the same liberal tradition and interest in the culture of the other continued in the heteroglossal scholarship of Rammohun Roy and Keshab Chandra Sen in the nineteenth century and was carried forward into the twentieth century by a man of universalist vision such as India had been fortunate to have in Maulana Azad (AD 1888–1958). Dey's study of medieval Sufi and Islamic literature thus brings alive the liberal and syncretist strands in Islamic thinking and opens up a new horizon of mutual understanding and co-existence.

The third essay in this volume 'Naturalisation of the Nation and Nationalization of Nature: A Study of the Nationalist Literature of Bengal' by Anuradha Roy takes us from the threshold of the medieval to the heart of the modern or *Nava Yuga*.[12] This was the period when the introduction of the rule of law, the spread of print culture, the linking of the far-flung regions of India through the railways and the formation of voluntary associations between individuals, irrespective of their birth, into specific castes and communities ushered an age of awakening among the people of India.[13] Anuradha Roy has devoted her familiarity with nationalist literature to demonstrate how nationalist poets and essayists had made use of the natural landscape of the country in their writing, to create a sense of bonding with the country, to evoke a sense of belonging and identification, to share the pride of the country's prosperity, which attracted foreign invaders down the ages to rob her of her wealth and to hope for the end of the dark days which had clouded her fabled prosperity before her subjection to foreign rule. This kind of romantic equation of nature and nation can be linked up with the eighteenth century intellectual shift born of the European Enlightenment from which the Romantic nationalism in Europe can be said to have emerged.[14]

The literary nationalism of the nineteenth century which began to identify the nation with the natural environment of the territory inhabited by it, according to Roy, reinforced the 'process of historicizing the nation'.[15] In a multicultural country like India, where it was difficult to decide upon a 'single ethno-linguistic criterion'[16] for the nation, landscape could serve as an important marker of cultural identity. Oneness with one's natural surroundings came much more spontaneously to men than any artificial social and legal ties. The Hindu Aryan imagery of India conjured up in the Vedas and the twin epics *Ramayana* and *Mahabharata,* speak of a huge territory capped by the Himalayas, girdled by the Oceans and straddled by the rivers Ganga, Jamuna, Narmada and Kaveri. In a later period in Kalidasa's *Shakuntala* or *Meghadootam,*[17] which covers a sprawling geographical canvas from Ramgiri to Alka, comes back the same image of the country over a wide geographical expanse. Nature was a site which the colonized could still claim as their own in the face of the colonizers. The country was conceived of as the mother, nourishing her children.[18] Not far from the mother was the mother-Goddess in the matricentric psyche indigenous to the people of the subcontinent. The Aryans had been worshippers of Mother Nature (*Prakriti*). With all his Brahmo abhorrence for image-worship, Tagore had set the tune for Bankim Chandra's *Bande Mataram,* first published in his *Anandamath* in 1881. While Tagore could view this equivalence of the country with a mother Goddess with equanimity as a 'subjectless practice', the Muslims later resented this idolatrous imagery and shied away from it.

For the poets and writers of Bengal, the Himalayas, the oceans and the rivers Jamuna, Narmada and the Kaveri often lay in the realm of imagination rather than within everyday experience. Yet Michael Madhusudan wrote *Parichay* (1866), Bhudev Mukhopadhyay wrote *Adhibharati* in his anthology *Pushpanjali* (1876), Gobinda Chandra Ray wrote *Jamunalahari* (The Flowing Jamuna) and Kamini Ray wrote in *Ashar Swapan* (Dreams of Hope) of rivers resonating with hymns to Gods. Visions of the Aryan hermitage (*tapovana*) came back with Tagore's denunciation of Western materialism since the onset of the First World War. In many of his *Santiniketan Essays*, in *Sadhana: The Realization in Life*, in the 'City and Village (1924),' and in the 'Religion of the Forest' in *Creative Unity* he held up an idyllic view of the village as the core of Indian life.[19]

However, towards the end of his life Tagore too had discovered how Indian villages had suffered a decay due to the concentration of wealth in the cities and the consequent neglect of the villages by the colonial administration.[20] A familiar theme with such landscape poets was their lament at the degradation of the country through foreign conquest. Kumudini Basu gave words to the heartburns of her countrymen in the poem *Janmabhumi* where she compared the country with a crematorium, without a sign of life. The analogy of the crematorium came back in Atulprosad, who prayed for green bowers enlivened with cooing of cuckoos in place of the deathly gloom that had gripped the country. In Rajkrishna Ray once again there is the reference to the rain of grief, ending with romanticization of the village as a place of tranquillity, purity and security reminiscent of the Russian Slavophiles' adoration for the peasant commune.[21] There were also realistic poems like Sabitri Prasanna Chattopadhyay's *Byarthabodhan* or Sarat Chandra Chattopadhyay's *Palli Samaj* which reflected an awareness of the evils of village life like superstitions, caste consciousness and group rivalry.

The reordering of society is also the theme of the article 'The Radical Rabindranath: "The Red Oleanders (*Rakta Karabi*)" and Dreams of a New World' by Chhanda Chatterjee. Chatterjee tries to trace how Tagore's *Rakta Karabi*, a literary text, tries to bring alive a new phase in the history of India under colonial domination—the extraction of surplus from human labour by capitalists under imperial protection. The *Sardars* were the labour contractors in the pay of the foreign capitalists who served to intimidate the workers into submission, while the *Gosains* acted as the clever accomplices of the surplus extractors and helped to lull the spirit of protest in the hearts of the exploited labourer. The misery of the mine workers in 'the city of the Djinn' represented the misery of the plantation labourer in tea gardens, of the indentured labourer and agricultural labourers—all those who had been wrenched from their home in the villages to a life of misery, repression and squalor. Tagore ended his play with the arousal of the mine workers and the breaking of the prison walls in the dead city of the Djinn. Chatterjee endeavours to link up the 1923 play with Tagore's dreams of a new world, which had found expression in an essay of 1918 in the *Modern Review* 'At the Crossroads'. Gnatyuk Danil'Chuk saw in it a subdued statement of Tagore's enthusiasm for the dawn of a new world in Russia.

As a poet and philosopher from a British colony Tagore was not free to express his enthusiasm for the Soviet experiment all too vociferously. The last paragraph of his 1918 article 'At the Crossroads' merely voiced a muffled hope for an alternative way of life.[22] The colour red in *Rakta Karabi* pointed to rebellion against the repression of the human soul. Nandini's red flowers came as a wake up call from the lifeless stupor of work in the pit of the earth. It was only in 1930 that Tagore could physically visit the Soviet Union and get a first-hand idea of what had predominantly been a romantic vision in 1918. The Soviet emphasis on strengthening the village economy as the core of the republic and their attempt to spread education to the remotest parts of the country were much to his liking as he himself had initiated steps towards these reforms in his own international university at Santiniketan. His letter of 25 September 1930, recounting his experience in Russia gave the clarion call 'The time is come for us to proclaim that there is no salvation for man if the power of the weak is not awakened at once'.[23] This was the same language that Nandini had spoken in *Rakta Karabi* in 1923.

Sobhanlal Datta Gupta's essay 'Reading Tagore's *Letters From Russia* in the Twenty-First Century' examines how the hope of the world for the ushering of a new age expressed in Rabindranath Tagore's 1918 essay changes to repugnance for the repressive regime that the Soviet experiment ultimately turned out to be. This change of tenor was particularly noticeable in letter no. 8 in Tagore's original Bengali version of *Russiar Chithi*. Datta Gupta has put his command of the Russian language, the rare opportunity to visit the Russian Archives and his intimate knowledge of the working of the Soviet regime to good use to deconstruct Tagore's 1930 letters from Russia. He has taken special care to explain Tagore's early enthusiasm for visiting the Soviet Union and the subsequent dampening of spirit reflected in some of these letters. Unlike Tagore's other travel letters his missives from Russia later turned into a critique of the Russian system, which persuaded Datta Gupta to call them a political rather than a literary text. Tagore's translator Sasadhar Sinha in fact carefully avoided translating his letter no. 8 for the negative image of Russia conveyed in it. Similarly his interview to *Izvestia* of 25 September 1930 could not see the light of the day; it was later published in the *Manchester Guardian*. Amongst the complaints from Tagore that Datta Gupta had mentioned were serious charges like coercion, summary trial of the people, compulsion to act in compliance with the authorities, unilinearity of programmes as the Soviet ideologues did not recognize the notions of diversity and difference, and stereotyped education system. To add insult to injury, the rebuff administered by the Soviet authorities was taken seriously to heart when Tagore inadvertently mentioned his appreciation for Anton Chekov, a writer whose views were not found to be consonant with the Soviet system. Tagore failed to appreciate the sort of class hatred and revengefulness against those not sharing the Soviet ideals that was inculcated by the Soviet intellectuals.

In 1918 Tagore had viewed the political experiment in Russia as a welcome alternative to the 'prosperity built upon moral nihilism',[24] that characterized the scramble for power by the imperialist West during the First World War. But between the period in 1925 when Lev Karakhan, the Russian Ambassador to China (1923–6), had extended an invitation to him to visit Russia, and his actual visit in 1930, the political situation in Russia had changed drastically. The invitation to Tagore in 1925 to visit Russia had been engineered by the VOKS (All Union Society for Cultural Relations with Foreign Countries) in which Anatoly Lunacharsky, the Minister of Education and Culture, the leading intellectuals Meyerhold and Stanislavsky and Orientalists like Oldenburg and Pavlovich had taken a very prominent part. But the situation was changing very fast.

Triumphant in the face of a worldwide conspiracy against the communist experiment in Russia, communist intellectuals grew wary of the non-communist world outside as the workers of the world showed no immediate interest in getting united and the prospect of a 'Permanent Revolution' held up by revolutionary intellectuals like Trotsky proved to be a chimera.[25] Opinion in Russia was turning against Tagore through the machinations of Indian Communist intellectuals like M.N. Roy, who had been opposed to the spiritualism of Tagore and Gandhi. It was Roy's writings which biased Orientalists like Veltman and Georg Lukacs, Leader of the KPD (Communist Party of Germany) against Tagore. Lukacs criticized *Ghare Baire* (the Home and the World) in the *Rote Fahne* (Red Flag).[26] A recent article by Imre Bangha draws attention to the criticism of the Hungarian poets of Tagore's preference for the Western path of development as against Gandhi's opposition to Western ways.[27] The Sixth Comintern (1928) had ceased to look upon the nationalist bourgeoisie in the colonial countries as a progressive force. The Glavlit (Directorate of Literature) at its meeting of 7 March 1927, had decided against fostering literature on problems of philosophy and sociology of a vividly idealist tendency. Tagore's visit to the Soviet Union was thus marred by an atmosphere of condescension on the part of the Soviet authorities. Despite his initial favourable impression of Russian efforts to spread literacy to the remotest parts of the country, efforts to arrange for the care of children, the realization of the ideas of humanity and measures for the upliftment of peasants, Tagore could soon see through the smokescreen of official camouflage and consequently gave expression to his disappointment in his unpublished interview to the *Izvestia*. The Tagore letters are illustrative of a very important phase in the world's history, which had roused immense hopes in the heart of mankind. They end with a note of disappointment which must have choked all hopeful hearts with tears at the overpowering of this great promise with a phase of repression, brief though it may have been.

Unlike the five preceding essays, which engaged in the analysis of specific literary texts in their historical contexts, Somdatta Mandal's 'The Evolution of Indian English Language and Literature: A Socio-Historical Survey' tries to trace the course of Indian literary initiatives in English, from the early days of British contact with India till the present times, trying to portray different historical situations.

English had originally been promoted in the subcontinent to fill up the lower rungs of the administration and meet the pressing need for scribes with local elements, who could substitute their likes from across the sea at a much lower cost. Added to it was the belief that Christianity would be easier for the missionaries to preach among English educated inhabitants. Macaulay had proposed a total cultural transformation of the country on the model of the Albion to strengthen the roots of British rule in India, and he won the day in 1835 at the peak of the Orientalist-Anglicist controversy. Yet the number of Indian writers in English till the early twentieth century remained few. Both Bankim Chandra and Michael Madhusudan Dutta tried their hands unsuccessfully at it and later opted for their vernacular.

Among the early writings were very old tracts like Shaikh Din Muhammad's *Travels of Dean Mahomet* published in 1794 from Ireland, which portrayed the social and political conditions in India from a sojourner's perspective. Other publications of the period like Revd Krishnamohan Banerjee's *The Persecuted* (1831) had the avowed purpose of painting Hindu society in a lurid light. Subsequently, Lal Behari Dey and Govinda Samanta took up their pen to describe Bengal peasant life, which has proved to be good fodder for agrarian historians in present times.

Among the most important Indo-Anglian writers mentioned by Somdatta three deserve particular mention. Raja Rao's *Kanthapura* (1938) brought forward a fictional representation of Mahatma Gandhi's work on popular consciousness in a remote village. Mulk Raj Anand's *Untouchable* (1935) brought into focus the raging controversy over caste during this period and Mahatma Gandhi's efforts to alleviate such sufferings through the life of a young sweeper Bakha. R.K. Narayan's *Swami and Friends* (1935) too had Gandhi's Civil Disobedience Movement towering over small vignettes of middle class life in the south Indian town of Malgudi.

Since 1947, English was no longer viewed as the language of the colonizer. It had become a link language among the various provinces, and authors like Nirad C. Chaudhuri, Khushwant Singh, Anita Desai and Kamala Das became quite popular among the English literates. The numbers involved were, of course, few. But their numbers were far outweighed by their social, economic and political importance.

However, Indo-Anglian literature assumed its current status of prestige especially since the 1980s. Rushdie called it 'perhaps the most valuable contribution India has yet made to the world of books'. This popularity boom was made possible by several developments on the political horizon. The collapse of the Soviet bloc gave rise to a unipolar world and increasing hegemony of the US. The major part of the world now began to be dominated by English. The success of Rushdie's *Midnight's Children* (1981) brought a host of writers on the literary scene like Amitav Ghosh, Vikram Seth, Allan Sealy, Upamanyu Chatterjee, Shashi Tharoor, Furrukh Dhondy, Rohinton Mistry and Firdaus Kanga—all of whom were called 'Rushdie's children' by *The New York Times*. They included 'cultures that will not stay in place' and were carried forward by migrants and diasporas. Sheldon Pollock calls it the emergence of a 'new cosmopolitanism' made possible by 'capitalist globalization—a form of transregional cultural change far more powerful and coercive than what marked the age of empires'.[28]

Some of these writers made use of landmark incidents in historical and contemporary times to weave interesting tales which could enthral people across the continents. Amitav Ghosh, for example, wrote the history of the discovery of the malaria virus and its transmission through the agency of mosquitoes of the anopheles variety by the scientist Ross in his *The Calcutta*

Chromosome, when interest in these questions were at their heights due to a rising incidence of malaria in Calcutta and its suburbs through the breeding of the anopheles in the metro ditch in Calcutta in the early nineties. Similarly *The Hungry Tide,* also by him, had the disaster suffered by the people of the Sunderbans through the invasion of the mangroves, which were a natural safeguard against the ravages of the sea as its subject. These historical situations were, however, so deftly woven into the lives of ordinary middle class people that the unwary reader could rarely sense that he was being made to live through a period in the country's history while poring over the pages of Ghosh's book. Ghosh's masterpiece was the *Sea of Poppies* which had for its subject matter the history of opium cultivation and processing of opium in the so-called opium factories, its export to China, the involvement of small middle class investors and bigger zamindars like the Halders of Raskhali in the financing of this trade and finally the bursting of the bubble leading to the opium war in China. This book would give far better insights into the entire mechanism of opium production and export and how it affected the lives of the various classes of people connected with the process much better than any book of economic history. With this book one could enter the lives of the *girmitiyas* forcibly indentured for service across the seas, the ruthlessness of fortune hunters like the Burnhams and even the lives of the sailors and their small weals and woes.

The language of this genre of literature was not always the Queen's English, but rather it was an amalgam of pidgin English, Baboo English and Hinglish, where Hindi words had invaded the English dictionary. It was marked by the emergence of an 'Asian English' or 'Englishization of vernaculars'. Some like Amitav Ghosh had done meticulous research to study the language of the mariners before using them in his writings. Amit Chaudhuri used Bengali words to create a truly Bengali ambience with glossaries at the end, which Ruchir Joshi calls 'the foot note school' in a light vein. This downright invasion of the Queen's English has been called 'our conquest of English' by Rushdie.

The remaining two articles in this collection by Igor Grbić and Swati Ganguly are essays in literary criticism rather than a recapitulation of historical literature. The optimism projected in the article of Mandal has been put under a question mark in Igor Grbić's '"Tagore Syndrome": A Case Study of the West's Intercultural (Mis)readings' where Grbić writes of the fickleness of Western appreciation for non-Western writings, the case of Rabindranath Tagore being a glaring example. Western attention to non-Western writings, according to Grbić depends on favourable reviews by critics. Whenever such media hypes are lacking, the appreciation of the Western public is also apt to decline. Grbić has highlighted Rabindranath Tagore as a case in point. In 1913 Tagore could reach the pinnacle of public appreciation in the West, leading to the award of the Nobel to this eastern poet. This had been made possible through Yeats' introduction to his

Gitanjali or 'Song Offerings', a collection of 103 poems translated from Bengali by the poet himself. The approbation was soon carried to the continent and Tagore found many translators, the poet Andre Gide and Boris Pasternak topping the list. But Tagore's lectures series of the inter-war years often so peeved Western critics that their initial enthusiasm eventually turned into hostility. Anna Akhmatova's translation of Tagore in the mid-1960s was an exception. The situation had not changed much till 2011, when a perusal of the Oxford and Penguin Books of Quotations did not throw up a single entry from Tagore.

Grbić fears the same kind of oblivion and going out of vogue for the Indian English literature, which has been catapulted into intense popularity through the awarding of the Booker for Rushdie in 1981 and then again the Booker of Bookers in 1993, Booker for Arundhuti Roy's *God of Small Things*, Kiran Desai's *The Inheritance of Loss*, and Aravind Adiga's *White Tiger*. Grbić has a premonition that the West's curiosity for the non-Western 'exotic, juicy, wild' might soon pass away. Once the West tires of these writings, the interest in the country of the writer's origin would also gradually recede. This is to happen because the popularity of such writings depend on the *pizza effect*, a term coined by Agehananda Bharati and here elaborated upon by Grbić.[29]

Grbić wants the non-West and East Europe to be heard by the West for what they really are. Comparisons with their Western counterparts, like Kalidasa with Shakespeare and looking at Kalidasa through the prism of Goethe, or Tagore through Yeats, could not be a respectable solution.

Swati Ganguly's 'The Politics and Poetics of Translating Indian Women's Fiction in English' laments how many promising women writers in *Bhasha* literature fail to come to the limelight. They fail to get included in the University syllabi and cannot achieve popularity among the English-educated monolingual readers since English translations are not available. The actual process of getting translated or getting included in the curriculum is, however, fraught with a good many hurdles. Publishing houses are business establishments keen on ensuring the commercial viability of a book. They would therefore look to the academia, from among whom come the reviewers, to base their choice of material for publication. Ganguly therefore stresses 'visibility' as a very important factor in arriving at such decisions. The interest shown by a noted US based academician Gayatri Chakravarty Spivak in Mahasweta Devi and her annotated translation of the latter's *stanadayini* (the wet nurse) ensured great publicity for all works by Mahasweta and no anthology of translations would be complete without a piece from her. But lesser known writers of *Bhasha* literature like Sabitri Roy, Sulekha Sanyal and Chhabi Basu failed to make their entry into anthologies despite the originality of their theme and the strong inner message contained in their writings. Ganguly attributes this to the lack of availability of good translations of such authors.

But the decision as to which author would get a translation was also governed by the same calculations of acceptance by the market and commercial viability. Third world intellectuals working in metropolitan academies, who decide upon translation policies are influenced by post-colonial theories generated in Anglo-American academics for the consumption of the West. Such policies are thus often oblivious and negligent of values and messages contained in *Bhasha* literature. Ganguly here underwrites Igor Grbić's strong plea to get a hearing from the world through good translations.

Sheldon Pollock wrote in one of his articles that the 'creation of a vision of power and culture (could be) made possible only by the elaboration of a literary corpus'.[30] The articles in this volume try to create such a vision by emphasizing the writings of different ages. Subbiah takes us to an age, otherwise long lost to the historian, which comes alive through the rediscovery of its literature and even fulfils certain criteria of historicality. Amit Dey delves into Persian Sufi literature to show how Islam had assigned a position of honour and respectability to women. He also traces an influential and important section of Islamic opinion which looked for peace and co-existence with other communities. Anuradha Roy has dicussed the complexities of identifying the nation with nature or landscape, a theme varying between the country as mother and the country as Goddess. Sobhanlal Datta Gupta and Chhanda Chatterjee have shown new ways of reading Tagore. Somdatta Mandal attempts to trace the new developments in Indian literature, which has created a new genre of its own by using a language which is not really Queen's English but a new cosmopolitan language of its own. Thus the historicist logic that everything new (like modernity, Enlightenment, capitalism or nationalism) can originate 'first in the West and then elsewhere'[31] has been utterly reversed. Igor Grbić, however, has fears that this honeymoon of Indo-Anglian literature with the West may not last very long, just as the West's initial enthusiasm with Rabindranath Tagore had declined after a time for various reasons. Swati Ganguly gropes for ways to combat such unpredictable popularity by trying to look into the norms of translation policies and the various factors that influence such policies. The volume is thus expected to chart out a new path in looking at the evolution of literature through different ages which could form the core of history.

Notes

1. Ashin Dasgupta, *Itihas O Sahitya,* Kolkata: Ananda, 1st pub., 1989; 3rd repr., 2006.
2. Emmanuel le roy Ladurie, Theodore Zeldin, Tapan Raychaudhuri, Ashis Nandy and Rajat Kanta Ray are among the most prominent of authors, who have written history based on human emotions.

3. Amales Tripathi, *'Aitihashik Ranke'* in his *Itihas O Aitihashik*, Kolkata: West Bengal State Book Board, 1986, p. 80; Also see Georg G. Iggers and James M. Powell, *Ranke and the Shaping of the Historical Discipline,* NY: Syracuse, 1990.
4. Romila Thapar, 'Society and Historical Consciousness: The Itihasa-Purana Tradition', in *Situating History: Essays in Honour of Sarvepalli Gopal,* Romila Thapar and Sabyasachi Bhattacharya, eds., New Delhi: OUP, 1986, pp. 353–83.
5. Rabindranath Tagore, *'Itihashkatha'* in *Itihas,* comp. Prabodh Chandra Sen and Pulin Behari Sen, Kolkata: Visva-Bharati Granthan Vibhaga, BY 1362, AD 1955.
6. Ranajit Guha, *History at the Limit of World History*, Delhi: Oxford University Press, 2003.
7. K.A.N. Shastri, *The Colas,* Madras: OUP, 1955, cited by G. Subbiah.
8. Vishwambhar Sharan Pathak, *Ancient Historians of India: A Study in Historical Biographies,* Bombay: Asia Publishing House, 1966, cited by G. Subbiah.
9. Ranajit Guha, op. cit.
10. Vasudha Dalmia and Stuart Blackburn, *India's Literary History: Essays on the Nineteenth Century*, Introduction, Ranikhet: Permanent Black, 3rd impression 2010.
11. Shahabuddin Iraqi, *Bhakti Movement in Medieval India: Social and Political Perspectives,* Centre of Advanced Study, Department of History, Aligarh Muslim University and Manohar, 2009.
12. The term *Nava Yuga* was first used by Shibnath Shastri in his *Ramtanu Lahiri O Tatkalin Bangasamaj* (Ramtanu Lahiri and Bengali Society in His Time) published in 1903. Tagore had earlier used this term in 1895 while reviewing Shibnath Shastri's novel *Yugantar* (From One Age to Another). The term is found once again in Tagore's polemical essay *Satyer Ahban* (The Call of Truth) during his debates with Gandhi in 1921. See Rajat Kanta Ray, 'The Indian Awakening and the Bengal Renaissance', in *Exploring Emotional History: Gender, Mentality and Literature in the Indian Awakening,* Delhi: OUP, 2001, pp. 29–36.
13. R.K. Ray, *Exploring Emotional History,* p. 33.
14. Vasudha Dalmia and Stuart Blackburn, *India's Literary History,* Introduction.
15. Anuradha Roy.
16. Ibid.
17. Roy refers to Buddhadeb Bose's translation of Kalidasa's *Meghadootam* in Bengali, which was published in 1957.
18. Sugata Bose, 'Nation as Mother: Representations and Contestations of "India" in Bengali Literature and Culture', in *Nationalism, Democracy and Development: State and Politics in India,* Sugata Bose and Ayesha Jalal, eds., Delhi: OUP, 1997.
19. *Santiniketan Essays* 1–10 and 11–17 in *Rabindra Rachanavali,* vols. VII and VIII, Low priced edition published by Visva-Bharati on the occasion of 125th anniversary of the Poet. 'City and Village (1924)' in Letters and Addresses in Sisir Kumar Das, ed., *The English Writings of Rabindranath Tagore,* vol. III, New Delhi: Sahitya Akademi, 1996, pp. 623–5; 'The Religion of the Forest', in *Creative Unity,* Sisir Kumar Das, ed., *The English Works of Rabindranath Tagore,* vol. II, New Delhi: Sahitya Akademi, 1996, pp. 511–19.

20. Rabindranath Tagore, *Letters From Russia*, 1st pub., 1960, repr., Kolkata: Visva-Bharati, January 1984, tr. Sasadhar Sinha, *Sabhyatar Samkat* (Crisis of Civilization) in *Rabindra Rachanavali*, vol. III.
21. Martin Malia, *Alexander Herzen and the Birth of Russian Socialism*, New York: Grosset and Dunlap, 1965.
22. A.P. Gnatyuk Danil'Chuk, *Tagore, India and the Soviet Union: A Dream Fulfilled* translated from Russian by Harish Chandra Gupta, Kolkata: Firma KL, 1986.
23. Rabindranath Tagore, *Letters From Russia*, Kolkata: Visva-Bharati, 1st pub., 1960, repr., 1984, p. 109.
24. Rabindranath Tagore, 'At the Crossroads', 1st pub., *Modern Review*, 1918, in Sisir Kumar Das, ed., *The English Works of Rabindranath Tagore*, vol. III, pp. 380–4.
25. The theory of a 'Permanent Revolution' had been professed by Leon Trotsky in 1906 in a book called 'Results and Prospects'. It hoped for the revolution in Russia to touch off the smouldering discontent of workers all over the world, and for the rest of the world to follow the Russian example.
26. See Ashis Nandy, *The Illegitimacy of Nationalism*, OUP, 1989, for a discussion of Lukacs' review of the *Home and the World*.
27. Imre Bangha, 'Rabindranath Tagore and Hungarian Politics', *Parabaas*, September 2008.
28. Sheldon Pollock, 'India in the Vernacular Millennium: Literary Culture and Polity 1000–1500', *Daedalus 127*, no. 3, 1998, pp. 41–74.
29. A. Bharati, *Hindu Views and Ways and the Hindu-Muslim Interface*, New Delhi: Munshiram Manoharlal, 1981.
30. Sheldon Pollock, 'The Sanskrit Cosmopolis and the Vernacular Revolution', in *Rethinking Early Modern India*, Upinder Singh, Delhi: OUP, 2011, pp. 269–92.
31. Dipesh Chakravarty, *Provincializing Europe: Postcolonial Thought and Historical Difference*, Princeton University Press, 2000; New Delhi: OUP, 1st pub. in India 2001, Introduction, pp. 3–23, 42–6.

CHAPTER ONE

'Historicality in Literature': A Case Study of the Classical Tamil Text, the Patiṟṟuppattu

GANAPATHY SUBBIAH

> These (medieval) interpretations may appear grotesque to modern historian as history viewed from the modern angle would have been to the medieval man. . . . It will be readily agreed that both these viewpoints represent the historical mentality of the respective ages and neither of them is final. They are the different stages in the evolution of the historical ideas. Is it, therefore, historical to call these medieval explanations unhistorical in absolute sense?
>
> —VISHWAMBHAR SHARAN PATHAK, *Ancient Historians of India: A Study in Historical Biographies*, 1966, pp. 148–9.

'LITERATURE IS IN other countries,' wrote K.A. Nilakanta Sastri, 'the bedrock of history; in India it is often a snare'.[1] While expressing such a viewpoint with regard to Indian literature, Sastri was not speaking for himself alone. For, it is a point of view that has been, and still is, shared by a large number of historians working on Indian history. Having thus condemned and reduced the vast body of literary texts in Indian languages to the level of a 'snare', historians, particularly those working on early Indian history, have seldom bothered to work out modes of analysing the texts that might help us in deciphering the message of the past contained in them. This apathy of historians towards using literature as a source for history, is matched in inverse proportion by the importance they attach instead to archaeological sources such as inscriptions, coins and monuments for reconstructing the past. The reliability of archaeological sources is held so high by them that these sources are simply assumed to display 'facts' from

---

*The first part of the title is taken from Ranajit Guha's translation of Rabindranath Tagore's essay in Bangla, *Sāhitye Aitihāsikata*. See Ranajit Guha, *History at the Limit of World-History*, New York, 2002, pp. 76, 95.

the past, while the literary texts are perceived to contain more of fable than fact. Consequently the contents of literary texts are usually kept at a respectable distance in historical discourses until and unless those are 'corroborated' or 'authenticated' by archaeological sources—particularly from the realm of epigraphy. The sceptical attitude of modern historians towards literary texts is well encapsulated in the following quote from V.S. Pathak:

... the modern historian is disinclined to accept the forms of ancient Indian *itihāsa* as historical. Conditioned by the language and ideas of modern historiography, historians viewed them rather as the monsters of the fable, who callously tortured and disfigured the fairy princesses of history, and from whose clutches the historians as gallant knights were duty-bound to liberate them; at the best these texts were thought to be full of irrational accretions which should be removed before the pure gold of history could be seen.[2]

This differential treatment meted out by the historians, to the early Indian literary texts as a source for history, was not simply the result of a concern for objective and scientific approach to the study of the past. There appear to be far more serious and subtle reasons behind such an attitude. In one of his recent works, titled *History at the Limit of World-History*, Ranajit Guha provides an illuminating analysis of the issue. Tracing the root of the inadequate importance given to the contents of literary texts in Indian historiography to the 'dominance exercised by a mode of colonialist knowledge', he says:

Sponsored and propagated by the Raj, it has had the effect of replacing the indigenous narratologies of precolonial times by ones that are typically modern and western. . . . We work within the paradigm it has constructed for us and are therefore far too close and committed to it to realize the need for challenge and change. No wonder that our critique has to look elsewhere, over the fence so to say, to neighbouring fields of knowledge for inspiration, and finds it in literature, which differs significantly from historiography in dealing with historicity.[3]

In the same work he also explains how the 'prose of history' ('historiography powered by statehood') of pedantic or academic historians has become insensitive to the events and sentiments that inform the 'prose of the world' (the 'wide open fields of historicality beyond the precincts of statist narrative') and 'how schooled academic writing on the Indian past had cut itself off from the prose of the world and the stories it had to tell'.[4]

Not that there were no dissenting voices against this 'poverty of historiography'. According to Guha, the creative voice of Rabindranath Tagore constituted one of the vocal protests against the dull and pedantic historiography. In Tagore's view, as Guha reminds us, literature made up for the failure of historiography 'by addressing the life lived by people in their "everyday contentment and misery"'.[5] In short, Tagore's was a powerful plea to historians to drop their 'statist blinkers and emulate literature to look afresh at life in order to recuperate historicality of what is humble and habitual'.[6] Life lived by people in their 'contentment and misery' formed the subject matter of the literary texts not only of the recent times but of the early times as well. There is therefore enough justification to look afresh upon the early literature in order to understand and appreciate the creative manner in which the poets presented before us the contentment and misery of their time.

Against this analytical backdrop then, we venture to make a preliminary study of one of the early Tamil texts called, the *Patiṟṟuppattu*. The classical Tamil texts, popularly known as *caṅkam* literature, have come down to us in two large collections, namely *eṭṭuttokai* ('eight anthologies') and *pattuppāṭṭu* ('ten songs'). The *Patiṟṟuppattu* (literally 'Ten Tens', hereafter *PṟP*), is one of the eight anthologies (*eṭṭuttokai*) of the classical Tamil texts. This anthology and another anthology in the same group, called the *Puṟanāṉūṟu* ('*puṟam* four hundred') contain poems on *puṟam* ('heroic' or 'martial') themes involving a number of early Tamil kings and chieftains. These two anthologies are therefore generally regarded as valuable source for the reconstruction of the early history of Tamiḷakam. The anthology *PṟP* was first edited and published with an old commentary by Mahāmahopādhyaya U.V. Swaminatha Aiyar in the year 1904 and the second and third editions of the text were brought out by him in the years 1921 and 1940 respectively. The Saiva Siddhānta Works Publishing Society (SSWPS) brought out its edition of the text in the year 1950 with a detailed modern commentary by Vidvan Avvai Su. Duraiswami Pillai.[7]

The anthology, as indicated by its name, consisted of a hundred ('Ten Tens') laudatory poems on ten kings of the Cēral family, each decade having been composed by one poet in honour of each king.[8] The name of neither the editor who compiled it nor the patron who caused its compilation is available to us. The first and the last decade poems were found missing in all the available manuscripts and, consequently, the text has now only eight decade poems.[9] The missing decades are generally taken to be the first and the tenth decade.

As pointed out by Swaminathan Aiyar, in his introduction to the third edition, the anthology is unique among the classical Tamil texts in many ways. It is exclusively devoted to the praise of the kings of a single ruling family, i.e. Cēralar. Although verses glorifying the deeds of kings of different lineages are found in other anthologies too, it is only in this anthology that we find a set of ten separate poems in praise of each Cēral king, rendering the text almost like a 'chronicle of the early kings of Kerala'.[10] At the end of each verse are found notes indicating the *turai* ('poetic situation'), *vaṇṇam* ('rhythm') and *tūkku* ('pause in metrical recitation'). The 'poetic situation' is given in the colophons of poems in other anthologies also, but details such as rhythm and metrical pause are found only in the *PṛP.*

Above all, each decade poem in the *PṛP* is accompanied by an 'epilogue' or *patikam*, consisting of two parts, one in verse and the other in prose. The verse part of the *patikam* elaborates on the lineage and exploits of the hero praised in the decade poems, in addition to what is already found in the poem itself; the prose part on the other hand consists of the name of the poet, the name of each poem in the decade (which is nothing but a striking phrase taken from the respective poem itself), the *paricil* (reward) the poet received from the king who is the hero of the poem and the span of years of reign of the king. The length of the decade poems varies from five lines to fifty-seven lines and the average length of a whole decade is found to be two hundred and eleven lines. The length of the *patikams* too varies from ten to twenty lines. As the *patikams* are found only in those manuscripts, which also included the old commentary, it is taken to mean that these were not authored by the poets who composed the decade poems but rather, were composed and added to the text at a later time. However there are reasons to believe that the *patikams* were appended to the decades before the time of the old commentator, and the author of the *patikams*, whoever he/she was, had drawn on early sources that were perhaps not available to the poets of anthology.

Drawing our attention to the fact that the *patikams* in the *PṛP* are, to some extent, akin to the Tamil *meykkīrtti* section of the Chōḷa inscriptions of the time of Rājarāja I and his successors, T.V. Sadasiva Pandarattar, in his historical introduction to the SSWPS edition, has also pointed out the crucial difference between the two. The *meykkīrtti* is a typical historical introduction set in the inscriptions as a prefix whereas the *patikam* is found suffixed to the decade poems in the *PṛP*. Rājarāja I introduced the *meykkīrtti* format in his inscriptions a few years after his invasion of the southern part of Kerala—which leads Pandarattar to suggest that the Chōḷa king was perhaps induced to do so after his acquaintance with the region as well as the composition of the *patikams*.[11]

The serial number of the decade, the hero praised in the decade, and the poet who composed it are as follows:

Decade	Name of the hero	Name of the poet
II	Imayavarampan Neṭuñcēral ātan	Kumaṭṭur-k-Kaṇṇanār
III	Palyānai-c-Celkeḻu Kuṭṭuvan	Pālai-k-Kautamanār
IV	Kalaṅkāy-k-Kaṇṇi Nārmuṭi-c-Cēral	Kāppiyārru-k-Kāppiyanār
V	Kaṭal pira-k-kōṭṭiya Cenkuṭṭuvan	Paraṇar

Decade	Name of the hero	Name of the poet
VI	āṭukoṭpāṭṭu-c-Cēralātan	Kākkaipāṭiniyār Naccellaiyār
VII	Celva-k-katuṅkō-v-āli-y-ātan	Kapilar
VIII	Peruñcēral Irumpoṛai	Aricil Kiḷār
IX	Ilañcēral Irumpoṛai	Perunkunrur Kiḻār

The genealogical data contained in the *patikam* indicate that the eight kings mentioned above belonged to two lineages of the Cēralar, namely, the Utiyan line (five kings from serial nos. II to VI) and the Irumpoṛai line (three kings from nos. VII to IX). In *patikam* II, Utiyan Cēral is mentioned as the father of Netuñcēral ātan, and it could be assumed that he was perhaps the hero of the now missing decade no. I. In *patikam* VII, Antuvan (Cēral Irumpoṛai) is mentioned as the father of āli-y-ātan. Marr has suggested that the other missing decade could well have been what was originally no. VII, and that Antuvan, who is mentioned as the father of āli-y-ātan in the *patikam* of the existing seventh decade, 'may have been the hero of a decade now lost that preceded the one now numbered VII'. Therefore, the missing decades, according to him, are the first and 'the one that preceded the extant decade VII. The extant decades VII to IX may have actually formed decades VIII to X of the original complete *Patiṟṟuppattu*'.[12]

The sixties of the last century witnessed a remarkable turning point in the study of classical Tamil texts in general and of *PṟP* in particular. The names of the kings of the three successive generations of the Irumporai line, who are the heroes of the decade nos. VII to IX in the *PṟP*, were compared and identified as one and the same with the names of three successive generations of rulers of the same lineage, who appear as donors in two near identical early Tamil-Brāhmi inscriptions from Pugalur.[13] This has resulted in the following identifications:

Pugalur inscriptions	Heroes in *PṟP*	
1. Kō ātan Cel-Irumpoṛai	VII	Celva-k-katuṅkō-v-āli-y-ātan
2. Perunkaṭuṅkōṉ	VIII	Peruñcēral Irumpoṛai
3. Kaṭuṅkōṉ Ilaṅkaṭuṅkō	IX	Ilañcēral Irumpoṛai

The Pugalur inscriptions have been dated by I. Mahadevan to *c.* second century AD, and thus these records have become not only the 'sheet-anchor of the Sangam chronology,'[14] but also 'one of the most important synchronisms found so far to determine the dates of the contemporary princes and poets of the Cankam age from about the middle of the first century to the middle of the third century AD'.[15] Peruñcēral Irumpoṛai, the hero of the eighth decade, is hailed in the text for his decisive victory over Atiyamāṉ Neṭumāṉ

Añci, the lord of Takaṭūr. One Satiyaputo Atiyan Neṭumāṉ Añci appears as donor in an inscription found from Jambai, and he has been identified with the one who was defeated by Peruñcēral Irumpoṟai.[16] Thus the historicity of the three Cēral kings and Añci, the ruler of Takaṭūr, stand 'corroborated' by inscriptional evidences.

Chronologically, I. Mahadevan assigns all the Tamil-Brāhmi inscriptions to two phases namely, the early phase (second century BC to second century AD) and the late phase (second century AD to fourth century AD). According to him, the Pugalur inscriptions belong to the late phase and are datable to the beginning of the second century AD. But the chronology suggested by him for Tamil-Brāhmi inscriptions has not been accepted by all scholars. According to at least some scholars, the so-called Tamil-Brāhmi inscriptions should properly be called *Damili* inscriptions, and the earliest among them may well be assigned to a period earlier than that of the inscriptions of the Mauryan king Asoka.[17] This would mean that the date of the kings mentioned in the Pugalur and Jambai inscriptions may have to be pushed back by a century or two. We are, however, concerned here more with the structure and contents of the poems in the *PṟP* than with the issue of whether the kings mentioned in the text should be assigned to a couple of centuries earlier or later.

Let us turn our focus again to the text. Nearly two-thirds of the poems in the *PṟP* have been classified under *pāṭāntiṇai*, which is one of the seven 'poetic situations' in the *puṟam* ('heroic') poetry. The term *pāṭāṇ* may be taken to mean 'praising a hero'. As a poetic situation, it was perhaps the most popular one among the classical Tamil poets and yet it was also the most unusual one. The reasons for this have been laid out after interrogation: a careful study of the statements of Tolkāppiyar in his celebrated grammar book reveals that he regarded *pāṭāṇ* not just as another of the seven divisions of heroic poetry but as an inclusive and open-ended poetic situation. In other words, unlike the other poetic situations (*tiṇai*) in *puṟam* in which a specific act of valour of the hero is extolled, in *pāṭāṇ*, not only the physical prowess but every trait that makes him stand out can singly or collectively form the theme of the poem. In short, it is a mode of praise of the total personality of the king. It has therefore been suggested that *pāṭāṇ* is to be seen not as a separate, but as an 'associative' poetic situation.[18]

The decade poems in the *PṟP* do not follow any structural or sequential order in narrating the traits of the hero-king.[19] Yet, they include a wide range of themes such as the hero's brilliance, physical prowess, munificence, compassion and other qualities of head and heart. All this no doubt fall within what is called heroic or court poetry, which is eulogistic and hyperbolic in nature. The poems of *PṟP* are no exception. Even then, what sets the text apart, is that it contains a number of references to events in the personal life of the poets, their interpersonal relationships and the life lived in general by people in their 'contentment and misery'.

This we propose to illustrate by taking a closer look at one of the decades, no. VII, which is composed in praise of Celva-k-katuṅkō-v-āli-y-ātan (who is identified with Kō ātan Cel-Irumporai of the Pugalur inscriptions) by Kapilar, one of the most celebrated and prolific classical Tamil poets. There are a total of 235 poems attributed to Kapilar among the classical Tamil texts and these are found in seven of the *eṭṭuttokai* works, while one of the poems, *kuṟiñcippāṭṭu*, in the *pattuppāṭṭu* collection is also attributed to him.[20] The poems of Kapilar in other anthologies reveal that he had strong emotional ties with his patron, Pāri, one of the seven legendary *vallal* (donors) in early Tamil literary tradition, who was the Chieftain of the Parampu hills.[21] He identified himself so fully with Pāri and his family that, after the demise of his patron, he acted as the guardian of his daughters.[22] This background is necessary to appreciate the very first poem of the decade that he addressed to Celva-k-katuṅkō-v-āli-y-ātan:

He was the lord of the (Parampu hill) region where the northern winds carry the fragrance of honey that oozes out of the fresh, ripe and cracked jackfruit; he was the husband of the fine-looking lady endowed with all virtues; he lived in a house that had been decorated like a beautiful painting (ll. 1–4).

He was our king, the great Pāri, who stood with his wide shoulders, smeared with sandal paste, and who was famous for his undiminishing generosity; He has left us and gone to the world from where no one ever returns. The outer layer of the drums in his palace is dried up, unattended and uncared for. And, the suppliants are all sad. But, do not think that I have come to you for begging (because my patron is no more). I shall sing your glories without exaggeration or understatement. I have come to you because I heard that you never ponder over what you gave to the suppliants and you are never carried away by the fame that accrues to you on account of your generosity (ll. 7–14).[23]

We quote below two segments from the third poem of the decade where the poet is virtually declaring that the people get the ruler they deserve:

Modesty is unknown to you except when you are in the company of the brahmans. You are endowed with a fearless head and heart that bows to none, but you yield readily to the demands of your friends. Your broad shoulders that carry fragrant garlands resembling the curved bow are exposed only to your consorts. Owing to the vagaries of seasons, landscape may lose its nature for a long period, but the words you utter are never belied (ll. 1–7).

Therefore, O! the king Celva, the descendent of the lineage of Ceralar! If people of this wide world, which is surrounded by sea where the winds cause constantly roaring waves, have done any thing good in their life, then Ata! May you live for ages and ages (ll. 16–21).

Like the *patikams*, the material contained in the decade poems has also been viewed as belonging to the category of *prasasti*. As eulogistic compositions, these poems no doubt fit the description. But, at the same time, one cannot ignore the crucial differences between the two literary compositions. Unlike the *prasasti*, in all the poems in the *PṛP* the poets address the king in second person and, as in the example quoted above, poets do talk about their interpersonal relationships, the pains and pleasures that they have gone through, and how they, as individuals of high creative talent, demanded and commanded respect from the patrons. It is equally important to note that a number of these poems contain 'information of sociological and cultural interest that does not pertain to any particular Cēral'.

We close our discussion with a translation of the *patikam* appended to the decade VII. As noted above, it was not authored by the poet who composed the decade poems but added to it at a later date. It was also noted that the verse part of it gives some information on the genealogy as well as on other traits and achievements of the king who is praised in the decade:

Antuvan, who was known for deep learning, turned his foes into allies with unrelenting determination. His chief queen, who was the daughter of Orutantai, bore him a son. That son created (new) settlements and eliminated all enemies within the country; performed a number of sacrifices and other righteous acts; vanquished his opponents with his frightening army; set his mind and heart on the black-coloured (māyavannan) god (Visnu?) and gifted to the god the village of Okantūr famous for the cultivation of high quality paddy (*ottiranel*); outshone his own preceptor by displaying flawless knowledge and conduct. He was Celva-k-katunkō-v-āli-y-ātan, and Kapilar composed the above ten poems in praise of him.

At the end of the prose section, it is stated that the king bestowed upon the poet *cirupuṟam ena* (a 'small gift') of one hundred thousand *kānam* (gold coins) and took him up the hillock and there gifted him all the land that was visible to the eye. Celva-k-katunkō-v-āli-y-ātan ruled for twenty years.

One may conclude by suggesting that there is the need for making a conscientious effort to listen to these voices of the past lying still unheard in the vast literary wealth which constitutes our extraordinary inheritance. It may be fitting to close the essay with a quote from K.A. Nilakanta Sastri, who we commenced with. While commenting on the importance of the classical Tamil literary tradition as a source for history, he wrote:

The truth is that we now know so little of the technical conditions which governed the propagation and preservation of literature and literary tradition in the distant past that it is unprofitable to hazard surmises against which may be pitted other surmises not less plausible. But this we do know: that in some manner that seems to us such a marvel, the ancients commanded the means of handing down from generation to generation, orally or otherwise, a considerable literature with exceptional accuracy....[24]

The method of working in data drawn from it in a restoration of the past, and the pattern resulting from their disposition offer limitless scope to the talent of the individual historian.[25]

Notes

1. K.A.N. Sastri, *The Cōḷas*, Madras, 1955, p. 11. However, Sastri himself was more considerate to the contents of the literary texts, particularly the classical Tamil texts. Pointing out that the colophons to the poems in the *Puranānūṛu* may after all embody a correct tradition, he wrote: '... then we must recognise in these poems a quantity of literary evidence of unique value: because then, no other part of India can be said to provide such sober and realistic pictures of contemporary life and politics as these early Tamil classics furnish.' K.A.N. Sastri, *Studies in Cōḷa History and Administration*, Madras, 1932, p. 1.
2. V.S. Pathak, op. cit., p. 138.
3. Ranajit Guha, op. cit., p. 5.
4. Ibid.., pp. 72–3.
5. Ibid., p. 92.
6. Ibid., p. 94.
7. The *Canka Ilakkiyam (Pāṭṭum Tokaiyum)*, containing only the texts including the *PṛP*, was compiled and edited by S. Vaiyapuri Pillai and others and published by the Saiva Siddhānta Mahā Samājam in 1940. In 1957, Murray S. Rajam brought out the texts of all the Cankam classics including the *PṛP.*
8. J.R. Marr had cogently argued (in his doctoral dissertation titled 'The Eight Tamil Anthologies with special reference to Purānānūru and Patiṟṟuppattu' submitted to the University of London in 1958) that the name for the ruling family in the classical texts is Cēral in singular and Cēralar in plural, and the name Cēra is therefore not valid in the context of the anthologies. This outstanding work was published by the Institute of Asian Studies in 1985. J.R. Marr, *Eight Anthologies: A Study in Early Tamil Literature*, Madras, 1985, p. 263. Also see K. Kailasapathy, *Tamil Heroic Poetry,* 1966, p. 28
9. Apart from an Invocatory verse, a few verses from among the last decades have been found and restored from the writings of the medieval commentators and appended to the published text.
10. Ibid., p. 262
11. *Patiṟṟuppattu* with commentary, SSWPS edn., 1973, pp. 47–8.
12. Marr, op. cit., pp. 273–4.
13. R. Panneerselvam, 'An Important Brāhmi Tamil Inscription: Reconstruction of the Genealogy of the Chera Kings', in *Proceedings of the First International Conference-Seminar of Tamil Studies, I*, Kuala Lumpur, Malaysia, 1968, pp. 421–5.

I. Mahadevan, 'Tamil-Brāhmi Inscriptions of the Sangam Age', in *Proceedings of the Second International Conference-Seminar of Tamil Studies*, I, Madras, 1971, pp. 73–106.. If we accept Marr's suggestion that Antuvan, who is mentioned as the father of āli-y-ātan in the *patikam* of the existing seventh decade, was the hero of one of the two missing decades, it would then mean that the text originally had four successive decades lauding four successive generations of rulers of the Irumporai family.

14. Mahadevan, op. cit., p. 96. Also see, Mahadevan, *Early Tamil Epigraphy: From the Earliest Times to the Sixth Century AD*, Chennai and Harvard University, 2003, p. 117. For the text of the Pugalur and Jambai inscriptions, see pp. 405–6, 399.
15. Ibid., p. 117.
16. Ibid. On the controversy over the 'authenticity' of the inscription, see, ibid., p. 23.
17. K.V. Ramesh, *Indian Inscriptions: A Study in Comparison and Contrast*, ICHR, Bangalore, 2006. pp. 4, 13. Also see K. Rajan, 'Situating the Beginning of Early Historic Times in Tamilnadu: Some Issues and Reflections', in *Social Scientist*, vol. 36, nos. 1–2, January and February 2008, pp. 40–78.
18. For a detailed discussion on the importance of *pātān* poetry for an understanding of early Tamil culture and thought, see G. Subbiah, *Roots of Tamil Religious Thought*, Pondicherry, 1991, pp. 116–29.
19. Only the decade IV is somewhat special in the sense that it is composed in *antāti* (Skt. *anta+ādi*) in which the phrase or word in the last line of a poem forms the first line of the succeeding poem.
20. Kapilar's authorship of *kuriñcippāṭṭu* is however doubted by some modern writers, see K. Kailasapathy, op. cit., p. 48.
21. For an account of the celebrated seven donors (*vallal*) of the early Tamil literary tradition, see G. Subbiah, op. cit., pp. 146–52.
22. For a brief discussion on the close ties and mutual regard that existed between Pāri and Kapilar and other pairs of poets and their patrons in classical Tamil society, see, Kailasapathy, op. cit., pp. 57–60.
23. The translations are all mine. While rendering the classical poetry in prose form, I have tried to be as faithful as I could to the original.
24. K.A.N. Sastri, *Studies in Cola history* ..., p. 9.
25. Ibid., p.18.

CHAPTER TWO

Mystical and Eclectic Traditions as Reflected in Persian Sources of Medieval India

AMIT DEY

THE PRESENT ESSAY is divided into two parts. In the first part efforts have been made to explore feminine elements in Indian Sufism. The second part is an endeavour to focus upon India's eclectic traditions as manifested in the writings and thinking of Prince Dara Shukoh. To the purpose of fulfilling both aims, we have mainly consulted Persian sources—although at times we have also had to rely on a few non-Persian sources to provide a more comprehensive picture.

Many Muslim writers speak with contempt of women's incapacity for religion and of their lack of intelligence and morals; an early writer in fact claims, 'The majority of women are lacking in religion and virtue and that which prevails in them is ignorance and evil desires.'[1]

Even the famous Persian poet Jalalu'd-Din Rumi (1207–3) says, 'My first and my last fall were caused by woman, since I was spirit—and how have I become body?'[2]

However, the sect of the Sufis were different in this very respect. They were well aware of the positive aspects of womanhood. Some of the Koranic tales serve as beautiful illustrations of the role of women in religious life. The most famous example is that of Potiphat's wife as told in *Sura* 12: the woman completely lost in her love of Joseph is a fine symbol for the enrapturing power of love, expressed by the mystic in the contemplation of divine beauty revealed in human form. It can even be said that Sufism was more favourable to the development of feminine activities than were other branches of Islam. The sympathy of the Prophet for women, and his four daughters, excluded the feeling of dejection so often found in medieval Christian monasticism. In medieval Europe, after the collapse of the Roman Empire, several Christian monastic orders emerged and played a significant role in philanthropic activities. They provided peace and solace to the people of Europe during crises and they were often venerated for the simple and austre lifestyle. But they were not necessarily free from orthodoxy, and like the large medieval European society, they were also not favourably disposed towards women. The veneration of Fatima in *Shia* circles, on the other hand, is indicative of the important role assigned to the feminine element in Islamic religious life.[3]

In fact, the strong, untiring faith of Muslim women has played, and still plays, an important role in the formation of the Muslim community. The Koran speaks repeatedly of the *Al-muslimin wa al-muslimat, wa al-muminin wa al-muminat* or—'For Muslim men and women,' and 'For believing men and women'.[4] The same religious injections are valid for both sexes. We see, therefore, that in spite of the general contempt among several Muslim writers for her, the Muslim woman was, theoretically at least, on a plane of spiritual equality with the Muslim man and was held to be of equal worth in the sight of God, and that, as a matter of fact, no obstacle was created great enough to prevent her from rising to that full experience of the inner spiritual life and to that devoted exercise of faith which was possible for man and which proved to be equally possible for her.

The very fact that the first true saint of Islam was a woman—the great lover Rabi'a al-Adawiyya (d. 752 AD or 801 AD)—certainly helped to shape the image of the ideal pious woman who could be praised in the most glowing terms. To call a virtuous woman 'a second Rabi'a' was, and still is, a common practice among the Muslims.[5]

History shows however, that Rabi'a was no exception, though she was credited with introducing the concept of pure love into the austere ascetic outlook of early Sufism. There were other women of her time and many after her, who were revered as saints and had some contribution to make. Even before Sufism arose, there were several women who were recognized as saints, such as Amina, the mother of the Prophet, and Fatima, his daughter, who enjoy the veneration of all Muslims because of their relationship to Muhammad.[6]

Therefore it is not surprising when Shaikh Abdul-Haqq Muhaddis Dihlawi (AD 1551–1642), a staunch critic of Akbar's religious policy, devotes a separate chapter to women saints in his famous Persian work, entitled the *Akhbar'ul-Akhyar.*[7]

In fact, women continued to play an important role in the Sufi movement of India, both as Sufis and as mothers of leading Sufis. In Shaikh Nizamu'd-Din Auliya's words: 'When the lion emerges from a jungle, none raises question about its sex. The descendants of Adam should adopt piety and obedience to God whether they be men or women.'[8]

It would be relevant to study the role of mothers in Sufi biographies. Many religious leaders admitted that they received their first religious instruction, and even their preliminary training in the mystical path from their mothers. The Prophet himself declared: 'Paradise lies at the feet of the mother.'

Whether it be Baba Fariduddin Ganj-i-Shakar's mother or Shaikh Nizamu'd-Din Auliya's mother, there is no doubt that many elderly women in the families contributed to the spiritual formation of some of the great sufi saints.

Bibi Sara was one of the earliest women saints mentioned in the *Akhbar'ul-Akhyar*. She was the mother of Shaikh Nizamu'd-Din Abu'l Mu'id, an important contemporary of Khwaja Qutbu'd-Din Bakhtiyar Kaki.[9] The *Akhbar'ul-Akhyur* (in Persian) provides an interesting story involving Bibi Sara. People used to visit Shaikh Nizamu'd-Din Abu'l Mu'id to get rid of their problems, both spiritual and material in nature. On one occasion there was an *imsake baran* (drought) in Delhi. Everybody began to pray for *baran* (rain) and the Shaikh was requested to do likewise. Consequently the Shaikh then took a *rishla* (thread) from a *daman* (garment) worn by his mother, and holding it in his hand, began to pray: 'Oh God the chastity (*hurmat*) of my mother is well-known. She had never unveiled her face before the strangers, and I am praying on behalf of this pious lady, please send rain for us.'[10] *Az Shaikh in haraf guftan, az Khuda baran ferestadan*. It is said that upon hearing the Shaikh's appeal God sent rain for them.[11]

Equally pious and venerated was the mother of Shaikh Fariduddin Ganj-i-Shakar. Her influence on the Shaikh was great. She used to absorb herself in *zikr* (recollection of God) for untold hours. The *Fawa'id-u'l-Fu'ad* (by Amir Hasan, in Persian) provides an interesting story reflecting her spiritual power.

One night a thief (*duzdi*) entered the house of Baba Farid's mother when all were sleeping except the Shaikh's mother. She was deeply absorbed in the thought of God. When the thief glanced at the praying woman, he became blind (*knr shud*) and could not go out. He began to cry, and addressing the men of that house as his father and brothers, and the women as his mother and sisters, implored them to restore his eyesight. The repentant thief vowed that he would abstain from stealing for the rest of his life. Hearing this appeal, the Shaikh's mother restored his eyesight, and he went away. She, however, did not disclose this story (*hekayet*) to the members of her family.' After a few days, a man with a pot (*sabu*) on his head, appeared before the Shaikh's family. They asked who he was. He (thief) then told them the whole story, how the spiritual dignity (*haibat*) of an old lady (*aurate buzurg*) had blinded him that night, and how she ultimately removed his blindness. He along with his family, then received the blessing (*barakat*) of Baba Farid's mother and embraced Islam.[12]

This was undoubtedly an instance of one of the rare conversions through early *Chishti* influence, although the event which prompted it, according to the story, was a *karamat* (miracle).[13]

The *Fawa'id-u'l-Fu'ad* also offers a strange story in connection with the passing away of Baba Farid's mother.

When Baba Farid settled (*sukunat sakht*) at Ajodhan, he sent his brother, Shaikh Najibu'd-Din Mutwakkil, to bring their mother to Ajodhan to live with him. Whilst travelling, Shaikh Najibu'd-Din and his mother rested under a tree (*dirakht*), and the Shaikh went to fetch some water (*ab*). When the Shaikh came back, his mother could not be seen anywhere. He made a desperate search, but it proved futile. The Shaikh came back, and told this tragic story (*qissa*) to Baba Farid and the latter prayed appropriately before asking his brother to distribute food (*ta'ami*, funeral banquet) among the poors for the repose of his mother's soul. After sometime Shaikh Najibu'd-Din again passed along the same route and came under that tree, where they had stopped . . . and found some human bones. He said to himself, *Bashad ki hamchunin ustukhwan walida-e ma ast, sher-e ya januar-e digar wu ra halak kardah bashad.* 'May be this is our mother's bone, who had fallen prey to a lion or some other beast.' The Shaikh then collected the bones, put them in a small bag and returned to his brother Baba Farid. Hearing the story from Shaikh Najibu'd-Din, Baba Farid asked him to open the bag (*kharita*). The bag was opened, but to the astonishment of the two brothers, it was empty.[14]

Baba Farid had three daughters, among whom Bibi Sharifa was considered the most pious. She had become a widow at a very early age and did not remarry. Her father would say that if women could have become *khalifas* (spiritual deputy of a *Sufi* saint), he would have made her one without hesitation. His third daughter was married to one of his own *murids* (disciple of a *Sufi* saint), Shaikh Badru'd-Din Ishaq—from which marriage a number of children were brought up by Shaikh Nizamu'd-Din Auliya.[15]

Yet another venerated name of a woman saint, as mentioned by Shaikh Abdul-Haqq Dihlawi, is that of Bibi Zulaykha, the mother of Shaikh Nizamu'd-Din Auliya; *Bibi Zulaykha walida-e Shaikh Nizamu'd-Din Auliya ast.*[16] Nizamu'd-Din Auliya had deep respect for his mother, pronouncing: *Walida mara ba Khuda Ta'ala asna'i bud*[17] (My mother was the way towards the Kingdom of God). If the Shaikh's mother encountered any dilemma, she could find the solution to it in her dream. According to *Sufi* belief, such power is exclusively reserved for *Sufi* saints. In this context, it is not difficult to get an impression about her *maqam* (place) in the history of Sufism. Shaikh Nizamu'd-Din had to pass his early days in abject poverty; when the house would be bereft of *ghalla* (food) his mother would console him by saying: *Imroz ma mehman-e Khudayem*[18] (Today we are the guests of God).

One day, while in a similar situation, the Shaikh's mother uttered the same words; suddenly the Shaikh observed that a man appeared in front of their house with *ghalla* worth one *tanka* (silver coin). This experience brought immense spiritual satisfaction to the Shaikh, all the more reinforcing his faith in his mother. In subsequent years whenever he was in need, the

Shaikh would visit his *khake walidai-e khud* (mother's grave) and offer prayers.[19]

Poverty and near-starvation failed to dampen Bibi Zulaykha's enthusiasm for making provisions for her son's learning. Being endowed with great foresight, she selected two of the most gifted teachers for her son's education. Shadi Muqri of Bada'un was his first instructor, who was known for his expertise in reciting the Koran. One understands that miraculous power is attributed to Sufis to enhance their position in Sufi hierarchy or to legitimize their position in mystical traditions. His students used to consider Shadi Muqri's teaching just as miraculous which enabled them to master the Koran perfectly.[20] Maulana Ala'u'd-Din Usuli, a saintly and erudite man of Bada'un, was the other *ustad* (teacher) of Shaikh Nizamu'd-Din.[21] One day, the Shaikh's mother took him before his teacher Maulana Ala'u'd-Din, when Ali Maula, another great saint of Bada'un was also present. The simplicity and piety of young Nizamu'd-Din impressed them so much that they predicted his future prominence as a saint: *In mard buzurg khwahad shud*.[22]

We have already referred to the *ziyarat* (religious visitation) of Shaikh Nizamu'd-Din Auliya to his mother's tomb. In this context, the *Akhbar'ul-Akhyar* provides an interesting anecdote, the importance of which, for a better understanding of the nature of relationship between the state and Sufism, cannot be ignored. Sultan Qutbu'd-Din Mubarak Shah (AD 1316–20) was jealous of Shaikh Nizamu'd-Din's popularity, and expected that along with all the Shaikhs and Ulema, Shaikh Nizamu'd-Din should also visit the mosque in the *qilae Sipri* (fort of Sipri) for the *juma* (Friday) prayer. But the Shaikh replied: *Masjid nazdik darem wa in ahaqq ast*[23] (There is a mosque nearby, and it is more worthy). Now, according to the Sultan's order, the entire religious community of Delhi, assembled at the palace on *darghurra har mahi* (the first day of the lunar month) to offer *tahni-at* (congratulations) to the Sultan. The Shaikh further antagonized the Sultan by sending in his place an *iqbal-e khadim* (a loyal servant) as his deputy. The *gharur-e badshahi* (vainglorious Sultan) at once made it clear to the Shaikh that if he did not personally come to pay homage to the Sultan, he would be forced to do so. Ignoring the threat, the Shaikh quietly prayed at his mother's tomb and returned home. It was *qaza'i Ilahi* (Divine dispensation) that led to the assassination of the Sultan by his favourite and protege Khusraw Khan before the *ghurra mahe ayanda* (first day of the next month) and consequently the Shaikh was saved from humiliation.[24] Thus the mother of Shaikh Nizamu'd-Din, not only contributed significantly to the later brilliance of her son, but even after her death, she continued to remain a constant and powerful source of peace, solace and inspiration to the greatest fourteenth century Sufi (d. 1325) in India.

Another great woman Sufi was Bibi Fatima Sam of Delhi. Baba Farid (d. AD 1265) often referred to her piety and sanctity. Her spiritual qualities were required as equal to those of the greatest male sufis of her time, which is why Baba Farid would say of her *Fatima Sam marde ast*.[25] She regarded Baba Farid and his brother, Shaikh Najibu'd-Din Mutwakkil, as her own brothers. Some important information about Bibi Fatima can be found in the *malfuzat* (conversations or discourses)[26] of Shaikh Nizamu'd-Din Auliya (b. AD 1238 and d. AD 1325). The latter had heard her saying: *Az berai anke para'e nan wa kuza 'e ab bakase dehand neyamathaye dine wa duniya wai nisar'e yu kunand ke sad hazar roza wa namaz na' tuwan yaft*[27]—which implied, that feeding the hungry, giving water to the thirsty, and distributing money amongst the poor on festive occasions, were far more meritorious than hundreds and thousands of *namazes* and many days spent in *roza* (fasting). After her death, Shaikh Nizamu'd-Din Auliya would often visit her *rauza* (tomb) to offer prayers, and would always experience immense spiritual satisfaction in doing so—*Sultan-ul-Mashaikh* (Shaikh Nizamu'd-Din) *dar rauza'e Fatima Sam bisiyar mushghul bud'e*.[28]

The Chishti attitude to manual labour and prayer has been revealed through a story related by the Shaikh.

One day the Shaikh visited the tomb of Bibi Sam which was near a pond (*hauz*). A man appeared with a basket filled with *khiyar* (a vegetable resembling a cucumber) and dropped them near the tank where he performed *wazu* (ablution) and then calmly said his prayers (*du rak'at-namaz*). After that, he washed the *khiyars* one by one (*yagan yagan khiyar'e shust*) and then recited three blessings for the Prophet Muhammad. Being deeply impressed with the man's piety, the Shaikh offered him a silver *tanka* but this was refused. The Shaikh asked the man, who was a lowly-paid labourer, how he could afford to refuse the offer. The man replied that his father was also a vegetable seller who died leaving him very young. After that his mother was able to teach him the most elementary rules for formal prayers. When she was dying, she advised him: *Tu niz khiyar'e wa sabze ba-faroshi* (You should also continue as a vegetable seller).' In short, his dying mother instructed him not to depend on any thing or anyone else for his living.[29]

After the man stopped talking, it appeared to the Shaikh as if he was listening to the words of a saint. From this it is clear that manual labour was not looked down upon by the *Chishtis;* on the contrary, they were prepared to appreciate the qualities of a common man or woman if he or she might have been aware of the value of self-reliance and followed some basic rules for formal prayers. This was one of the reasons behind the popularity of the *Chishti silsilah* among the common people.

It is evident from the *malfuzat* (conversations or discourses) of Shaikh Nizamu'd-Din Auliya that the *nazms* (verses) of Bibi Fatima Sam were of exquisite beauty, delicate but full of spiritual thought. Shaikh Nizamu'd-Din had memorized a famous *misra* (hemistich) composed by her: *Ham ishq talab kuni wa ham jan khuahi, har du talbi wale mir nashawad*[30] (A person, who is a seeker of 'Divine Love' (*ishqe ilahi*), but at the same time concerned with the safety and security of his personal life, cannot become a true lover).

Bibi Fatima's tomb was in the old Indraprastha. After a long time, it became a *kharabah* (deserted place). The memory of Bibi Fatima also fell into obscurity and she became known to the local people only as Bibi Sa'ima or Bibi Sham.[31]

Celebrated Sufi Saint Shaikh Nasiru'd-Din Chiragh-i-Dihli (AD 1276–7–1356) mentions a female sufi, Bibi Fatima, who became famous for constant fasting: *Hargiz. rozae iftar nakardi*.[32] She had a *kanizak* (female slave) who worked as a *muzdur* (labourer) and from these earnings, the slave girl used to prepare for her lady, two cakes of *nan'e jau* (barley) each day. Along with this, the slave girl used to place *yek kuza aab* (a pot of water) beside the *sajjada* (prayer carpet) of Bibi Fatima. These were the only items of food she took between fasts. One night Bibi Fatima believed she was dying, so she gave her bread to local dervishes, and deeply absorbed herself in prayer: *nan ba-darwesh dad wa khud ba-ibadat mushghul shud*.[33] For forty days and nights she remained without bread: *Ta chihal roz wa chihal shab nan na-khurd*.[34] She ultimately died on the fortieth day. Shaikh Nasiru'd-Din concluded the story by saying that Bibi Fatima's life was a true example of the belief that a real Sufi was one who was an *ibnu' l-waqt*,[35] that is, one who understood the real value of human life through a constant awareness of its transience.[36]

Mention should be made of Hazrat Sayeda Zainab Khatun of Bengal, who became famous as a female saint. She was born in Mecca in AD 1279 and died in Bengal in AD 1342.[37] Celebrated Pir Hazrat Gorachand Razi of Balanda was her elder brother. She came to India to preach Islam along with Syed Shahdali, another of her brothers. Her grave is situated on the western bank of the Ichamati River in the Taragunia village of the Basirhat subdivision, West Bengal. She is more popularly known as Raushan Bibi or Raushan Ara among the local people.[38] It is thought that she was most probably a celibate; however, according to one view, Pir Gorachand Razi gave his sister Raushan Bibi in marriage to Syed Sadu'llah, an ancestor of Titumir.[39] Pir Gorachand came to India before his sister to preach Islam, though it is not known whether the brother and sister could ever meet each other after their arrival in India. Therefore, the view about Raushan Bibi's marriage is not corroborated by facts. A short family tree of Raushan Bibi is available to us:[40]

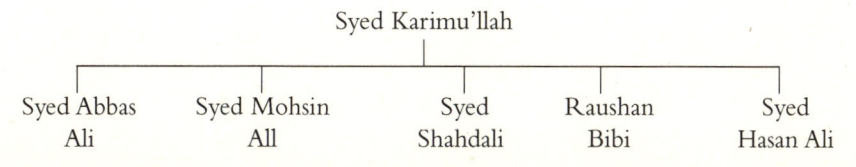

Syed Karimu'llah

| Syed Abbas Ali | Syed Mohsin Ali | Syed Shahdali | Raushan Bibi | Syed Hasan Ali |

The devotees of Raushan Bibi have built a beautiful dargah near her grave as a mark of their devotion, very neat and clean by one that has been kept the *zimma-dars* (trustees)[41] of the dargah. Incense is also burnt regularly at the dargah, while sometimes her devotees offer flowers, fruits and sweets at the dargah as *minnat*.[42] Every year, in the Bengali month of *Chaitra*, *Urs* (the death-anniversary of a *Pir*) is celebrated here with much enthusiasm. On this occasion, a fair is also held here which lasts for nearly ten days. More than one lakh people visit this fair, and they are entertained by the bandsmen, *qawwal-singers* and the sight of the resplendent night sky, beautifully decorated with *atish-bazi* (fireworks). It is said that Raja Krishna Chandra Roy had donated 365 bigha (1 bigha is equal to 1/4 ha.) of lands in the name of *Pirani* (fem. of Pir) Raushan Ara. Only a small portion of that land now remains under the supervision of the *khadimdars* (a person who has charge of a tomb).[43] If this view is taken for granted, then perhaps it can be deduced that Raja Krishna Chandra Roy being aware of the fact that thousands of devotees regularly thronged to the dargah of Raushan Bibi, wanted to secure the loyalty of the attendants and leader of the dargah by donating lands in the name of Raushan Bibi, which might have enabled the king to extend his influence among the lower population. By doing so, the king probably hoped to deepen the roots of his own authority throughout his kingdom. This hypothesis is supported by the fact that it was mainly the major dargahs, to which thousands of devotees regularly thronged, that enjoyed such land grants.

The existence of some popular stories in Taragunia about Raushan Bibi are indicative of her venerated image in the area. According to one such story, Pir Hazrat Gorachand Razi and his sister Raushan Ara died many many years ago. In spite of that Pir Gorachand would visit Raushan Bibi's dargah on some particular days of the year to converse with his sister. According to local belief, a few years ago, some local residents had actually heard this conversation after midnight.[44]

Pirani Hazrat Raushan Bibi's dargah is a place of pilgrimage for Muslims and Hindus alike and both offer *shirni* (votive sweets) and *chiraghi* (votive lamp) to the dargah with great devotion. After the *Urs*, the devotees receive sacred water from the dargah, akin to the Hindu tradition. Customarily, Hindu ladies often hang bricks after fastening them with cords at the temple of the Goddess *Shashthi* with the expectation of having children; such a practice is also common among the female devotees at Raushan Bibi's dargah.[45]

We have already referred to the fair held near the dargah of Raushan Bibi in the month of *Chaitra*. It is significant to note that a temple of Goddess *Kali* is also situated at the northern end of the dargah, and a large number of Hindus assemble there to worship their deity during the same month. During such a large and spontaneous gathering, both Hindus and

Muslims forget their religious differences and become one in a large ocean of humanity.[46] Thus the dargah, though an inanimate object itself, has been found to play the role of a syncretizing element in the social history of India.

Shaikh Abdu'l Haqq Muhaddis Dihlawi mentions the name of Bibi Auliya, a female Sufi who lived at the time of Sultan Muhammad bin Tughluq. Shaikh Abdul'l Haqq says: *Bibi Auliya az salihat waqt'e khud bud*[4] (Bibi Auliya was one of the most pious ladies of her time). She led a withdrawn life, meditating in her *hujra* (chamber) for untold hours. She was also known for her constant fasting. However, her reclusive life did not make her indifferent to the sorrows and sufferings of the common people. In the month of *Muharram* she actively engaged herself in charitable works which included the establishment of *langar* (an alms house) for the distribution of free food among the poor. It is said that Sultan Muhammad bin Tughluq had deep faith in her.[48] In Shaikh Abdu'l Haqq's writings, once again, we discover the location of her grave: *Qabr'e wu birun qula'e Ala'i ast*[49] (Her (Bibi Auliya's) grave is situated outside the fort of Sultan Alau'd-Din Khalji (Ala'i)). Her sons and grandsons apparently also became saints. When Shaikh Abdu'l Haqq Muhaddis Dihlawi (AD 1551–1642) was writing his *Akhbar'ul-Akhyar*, the descendants of Bibi Auliya were still alive and were popularly called *himams* (high-minded).[50] Among them, Shaikh Ahmad probably became the most famous. The latter was also well informed of many Sufi saints.[51]

It is a well known fact that Mian Mir was the first mystical guide of Dara Shukoh, the favourite son of emperor Shahjahan. Mian Mir's sister Bibi Jamal Khatun (d. AD 1639) was one of the exceptional saints of the *Qadiriyya* order during its formative period in the Punjab.[52]

We find a very interesting figure, among the women saints of Islam, of a type distinct from those already mentioned. This was Fatima, best known as Jahanara, the eldest daughter of the Mughal Emperor Shahjahan. Her luckless brother Dara Shukoh wrote a biography of Sufi saints, called *Safinatu'l-awliya* (The Ship of The Saints). The brother and the sister were bound together not only by the tie of strong affection, but also by a common seeking after God and a desire for union with him.

The house of Akbar was greatly devoted to the *Chishti* order. Initially, Dara Shukoh and Jahanara were also devoted to this sufi order—in fact Jahanara was a *murida* or disciple of this order and as an act of piety wrote a biography of Khwaja Muin-ud-din Chishti, entitled *Munis-ul-arwa* (the Comforter of Souls).[53] But the magnetic personality and piety of Mian Mir and the reputation of Maulana Shah drew Dara to the *Qadiriyya* fraternity. Unfortunately, the venerable saint Mian Mir passed away in AD 1635 without having had time to make Dara a *murid* or disciple. Ultimately Dara became a novice in the Sufi way under the spiritual guidance of the famous teacher and Saint Mulla Shah (d. 1661) who himself was a disciple of Mian Mir.[54] Being impressed by Dara's account of Mulla Shah, Princess Jahanara also expressed her desire to become a novice in the *Qadiriyya* way. An account of Mulla Shah's relationship with the princess is given by his biographer, Tawakkul Beg, himself a disciple of the saint.[55]

Jahanara wrote several letters to Mulla Shah expressing her desire to renounce the world and enter upon the mystic Path. The saint read those letters, but left them unanswered for a time. At last, being convinced of her sincerity and determination he consented to her initiation, though he had not even seen her.[56]

The princess herself wrote an account of her initiation in a work entitled, *Risala-i-Sahibiyya,* from which Tawakkul Beg quotes. She vividly describes how she had offered her faith to the saint, Mulla Shah and begged him to be her *murshid* or spiritual guide. The princess also describes how he had consented to her initiation according to the rule of the *Qadiriyya* order. When Mulla Shah was paying a visit to Emperor Shahjahan—who was at the time staying in Kashmir—she saw the *Shaikh* for the first time, from her hiding place behind the *purdah*, and immediately after that an inexplicable ecstasy filled her soul. The following day she was initiated by her brother acting for the saint. During her initiation she had to recite the order of Mulla Shah along with the formula of the Qadir dervishes. She goes on to relate how she returned to her apartments after that experience and became absorbed in contemplation. There she had a vision, as she believed, of the Prophet and his four friends. When she came to, she prostrated herself before the throne of the Absolute Being and poured out her soul in thankfulness to God for the 'immeasurable happiness'. He had accorded to a 'weak and unworthy woman'.[57] She offered thanks for having been allowed to conceive of the Absolute Being in the most complete manner which she had always ardently desired.

Those who do not possess the knowledge of the Absolute Being are not worthy to rank as human beings, they are still brutish. Every man who has attained this supreme felicity becomes, through this fact itself, the most accomplished and the most noble of beings and his individual existence is lost in the absolute existence; he becomes like a drop in the ocean, a mote in the sunshine, an atom amidst totality. Arrived in this state of exaltation, he is above death and future punishment. Whether he is man or woman, he is always the most perfect being.[58]

Jahanara became a mystic in the true sense of the term and it is said that she reached such a degree of perfection that she attained to pure union with God as also the knowledge of spiritual mysteries which came from the vision of God.[59] Though Mulla Shah was very affectionate towards all his disciples he felt a special attachment to the Mughal Princess and even said that her mystical knowledge was so extraordinary that she was worthy of being his representative.[60]

We have discussed about some outstanding female Sufis of medieval India whose lives have been documented. Unfortunately a large number of female Sufis have failed to get entry into the official annals. Most of the female Sufis mentioned above achieved great spiritual heights; the *dargah* of Raushan Bibi still enjoys enviable popularity—enviable from the point of view of her male counterparts. *Pirani* (fem. of *pir*) Raushan Bibi is venerated along with the famous *pirs* of Bengal. Bibi Auliya was renowned for plunging herself into humanitarian activities whenever the situation so demanded. There were also female saints who preached the value of self-reliance among the common people in the most lucid manner. The impact of such women on the Sufi movement cannot be denied. Theoretically, the Muslim woman was on a spiritual equality with man, but in practice, the female sufis had to face a number of obstacles. Jahanara's *murshid* (spiritual guide) Mulla Shah himself admitted that she was worthy of being his deputy. But she could never become a deputy. Equally pious and worthy was Bibi Sharifa, a daughter of the famous Sufi saint Baba Farid (d. AD 1265). But she was never allowed to become the spiritual successor of her father. In fact Baba Farid often stated: *Agar aurat ra khilafat wa sajjada'e mashaikh dadan rawa bude Man Bibi Sharifa midadam*[61] (If women could have become *khalifas* (deputies) or *sajjada nashin* (spiritual successors) I might have made Bibi Sharifa so). In other words the spiritual post of *khalifa* was reserved only for pious men, and pious women had no access to it, nor could the latter become *sajjada nashins*. Moreover, female mystics were never incorporated into *khanqahs* or Sufi monasteries. Circumstances often forced them to become hermits or lone dervishes who were bereft of spiritual and material comforts provided by the pirs and the *khanqahs*. However, these hardships and lack of encouragement from their male counterparts could not erode their profound commitment to mysticism and asceticism.

Prince Dara Shukoh and India's Eclectic Traditions

In the contemporary world of today, multiculturalism and secularism are facing a serious threat from resurgent religious fundamentalism. Systematic efforts to homogenize human behaviour and thinking are superficial acts, capable of destroying the importance of cultural pluralism. There should be respect for different views and cultures. Mughal Prince Dara Shukoh was the symbol of cultural pluralism. However, it is useful to remember that many saints and thinkers in India, before and after this liberal and eclectic prince, made sincere efforts to promote mutual understanding between different communities which in its turn created an environment of mutual appreciation. Thinkers are increasingly realizing the importance of meaningful dialogue between different communities which is the *sine qua non* for human progress. The present essay aims at understanding the ideas and works of Dara Shukoh in this broader context.

Rigid Periodization of History Should be Avoided

Those who talk about the Indian Renaissance generally speak about the nineteenth century Renaissance which according to them was the outcome of India's exposure to Western civilization and culture. There is no denying that India's interaction with the west was extremely significant. But the reluctance to trace the history of enlightenment in India before the advent of colonial rule is very unfortunate.[62] For a proper understanding of the history of enlightenment in India it is useful to study the events during the Sultanate and Mughal period or even earlier. Modernizing trends could be visible in the so-called medieval period whereas backwardness is noticeable in the so called colonial/post-colonial period. Intermingling and admixture of different traditions characterized Indian civilization even before Kabir and Dara Shukoh; for example, Kabir was influenced by both the *astika* (theistic) and *nastika* (atheistic) traditions. Whereas his philosophy and faith were soaked in the *astika* spirit, the vitality and freedom of his individual reasoning was a clear manifestation of the *nastika* tradition.[63] While the rationalist Mut'azilites were persecuted in West Asia, popular devotion and rationalism found acceptance in eleventh- and twelfth-century India. So it is not surprising that India emerged as a favourite destination for Sufis from Central and West Asia.

Linguistic Intermingling and Vernacularization

The appropriating nature of Sufism made Islam a world religion. Instead of promoting the process of Persianization, the leading Sufi saints in India often encouraged vernacularization of religious knowledge in order to reach out to the common people. This did not mean that they discarded Persian, but alongside that classical language, local languages such as Hindawi or Punjabi also got importance. Amir Khusrau's experimentation with Persian and *Brajabhasha* is well known. Like the Sufis, the Bhakti saints by writing in the vernacular also encouraged this process of vernacularization.[64] This linguistic intermingling which we can call *Majma-ul-Zabanat* actually preceded Dara's *Majma-ul-Bahrain* or intermingling of two oceans, Hinduism and Islam. In this way a liberal and healthy environment was created in many parts of India even before the advent of Dara. Acceptance of local languages has shown that the Sufis were prepared to respect indigenous culture. Recognition of diversity is essential for meaningful and peaceful coexistence.

Spirit of Mutual Understanding

Scholars such as Satish Chandra, Amalendu De and others have pointed out that the spirit of mutual understanding and mutual appreciation was strengthened by the interaction between the Bhakti and Sufi movements in the Indian subcontinent, and this process started earlier than the age of Dara. This spirit of interaction was also reflected in Indian literature, arts and music. The great scholar Al Biruni, a forerunner of Dara, translated Patanjali's *Yoga Sutra* into Arabic. Yogis used to visit *khanqahs* (sufi hospices) and *Jamat Khanahs* run by the Sufis,[65] as a result of which there was a lot of scope for interaction. It is a well known and interesting fact that some of the Sufis, including the illustrious Shaikh Nizamuddin Auliya, had adopted some breathing exercises; this was apparently the influence of the Yogis. In this context it would be appropriate to discuss the Sufi doctrine of *Wahdat–ul–wajud* or pantheism. The Sufis use a term *Hama Ust,* meaning everything is 'He'—which implies that God is reflected in everything. Using this doctrine some Sufis went to the extent of claiming that God is also reflected in a heathen or a Hindu and under such circumstances therefore a Hindu cannot be denounced as a *kafir* or infidel.[66] Mulla Daud, the author of *Chandayan,* who was linked to the famous fourteenth century Sufi Nasiruddin Chiragh-i-Delhi, praised Muhammad as the beloved of everyone. At the same time he also referred to the Vedas and the Puranas as revealed books, just like the Koran.[67] Mirza Mazhar Jan-i-Janan, a naqshbandi (a Sufi order) Sufi poet came to the same conclusion as Mulla Daud: that the Vedas were revealed books, and hence Hindus could not be identified with the *Kafirs* of Arabia. He even argued that there was little difference between idol worship and *tasawwar-i-shaikh* (common among those who venerate a Sufi saint), i.e concentration on the mental image of the preceptor.[68] Interestingly, in spite of sharing their views with Dara, these people were not persecuted. At the same time one has to remember that they were not Dara's contemporaries. What would have been their fate if they had flourished during the same period is a different question.

The translation of various Sanskrit works into Persian was undertaken by Sultan Zaynul Abidin of Kashmir, Sultan Sikandar Lodi and several other Muslim rulers, not only 'to satisfy their own intellectual curiosity' but also 'to increase Muslim understanding of Hinduism'. This process acquired a new direction under Akbar. The Ramayana and the Mahabharata were translated into Persian in the *Maktab Khana* set up by Akbar. The preface to the Mahabharata was written by Abul Fazl who 'urged his Muslim readers to study his account of Hindu learning with open minds'. The theological debates transformed Akbar's spiritual life. He came in contact with other religions and was convinced that 'all religions contained some truth and that this was not the prerogative of Islam'. He also 'believed that constant self-examination was a spiritual exercise of prime importance and that no action should be taken without sound reason'. In this way Akbar 'sought to heal the religious differences among his subjects'.[69]

Like his great forefather Akbar, Shahjahan's favourite elder son Prince Dara probably realized the fact that religious exclusivity of the ulama would not be helpful in running a vast multicultural empire like India, and deliberately tried to strengthen some institutions such as Sufism, which celebrated the composite nature of Indian culture. If we accept this hypothesis, it would imply that there was a political agenda behind the eclecticism of both Akbar and Dara. An interesting case in point is when Akbar had to overcome the political crisis of Rajasthan by making the Mughal Empire acceptable to both Muslims and Hindus who used to visit the Sufi Shrines. So he presented gigantic cauldrons to the shrine of Muinuddin Chishti of Ajmer. Thus he portrayed himself as the patron of Chisti shrines in Rajasthan, which were popular among both Muslims and Hindus.

Whatever may be the prime reason there is no denying the fact that their ideas and activities nourished the inclusive and composite nature of Indian society and polity. Indeed, present day statesmen have much to learn from them.

Dara Shukoh: A Renaissance Personality

Dara was a sound scholar, poet and calligrapher with an artistic bent of mind. But unlike his great forefather Akbar, he was not adept in the art of statecraft. It is said that Emperor Shahjahan advised his eldest son Dara to acquire the knowledge of history and philosophy available in the Greek, Roman and Persian worlds alongside the knowledge prevalent in India. After completing this process, Dara should, according to his father, launch his career like a second Alexander (Sikander Sani). However, it was not Dara's desire to be another conqueror, he rather wanted to be a thinker.[70] It appears from his famous work *Majma-ul-Bahrain* that he believed in *Ijtihad*, or the right of the learned to interpret scriptures according to changing circumstances. In other words, he placed emphasis on *Aql* or reason, like his predecessor Akbar and his cultural successor Raja Rammohun Roy. The clash in fact, appears not to be between different civilizations, but rather within Islam; it is between *Ilm* (here the term *Ilm* or knowledge has been used in a narrow sense, meaning scriptural knowledge) and Aql (Reason). The door of Ijtihad being partly closed today, Aql appears to have taken a back seat within Islam. But, till the tenth century, when the Mu'tazila (rationalist school) was still around, the term *Ilm* was used in the broad sense as it allowed Aql (Reason) to be its integral part. Through different phases, spanning several centuries, Islam experienced the reassertion of orthodoxy, which reduced the term *ilm*, virtually to the status of literal fundamentalism or scripturalism. Eminent historian Muzaffar Alam has implied in his scholarly work 'The Languages of Political Islam in India', that with the advent of Western political dominance since the late eighteenth century, the nervousness of the ulama increased, and they renounced and denounced the spirit of experimentation which actually made Islam a world religion. In this way, the door of *ijtihad* was partly closed during the colonial milieu, culminating in the decline of *Aql* (Reason) in Islamic societies.[71] A majority of the Muslim theologians still believe, that if experimentation is allowed to continue, Islam could be overwhelmed by the 'other'—the 'other' that is Christianity and Western thought and culture. This situation is posing a serious threat to India's eclectic traditions.

Dara was only twenty-five when he produced his very first work in Persian, entitled *Safinat-ul-Awliya* (The Notebook of The Saints). He mentions in the introduction to this work that he used to venerate the Sufis and the religious divines, and had studied their lives closely but was disappointed to find that the details of their lives were scattered in the pages of so many different manuscripts. This in fact, had made him decide to produce this work in order to provide, within a very small canvas, the details regarding the dates of birth and death, the place of burial and other important particulars of the saints of Islam.[72] Without being sectarian, Dara in this book wrote about various Sufi orders. However, the most significant part of this work is the author's focus on women as he deals with the wives and daughters of the Prophet and some female mystics. Some scholars on gender issues often imply that the gender discourse is simply the direct outcome of India's exposure to the West. Yet, one is inclined to suggest with all humility, that if time and energy were employed instead to understand the Indianness of this discourse as prevalent in pre-colonial India, it would provide a new dimension to gender related research. Consulting Indian Sufi literature available in Persian it can be proved that this legacy actually preceded Dara. For example the great Chishti Saint Nizamuddin Awliya (d. 1325) said: 'If a lioness emerges from the forest, no one raises any question about its sex. . . .' The implication in this context is that a learned woman can acquire the same spiritual status that her male counterpart can. Abdul Haq Dehlawi, a contemporary of Jahangir who was a shariat—centred scripture oriented pious scholar, devoted an entire chapter in his famous work *Akhbar-ul-Akhyar* to female mystics (see my book, *Sufism in*

India, Calcutta, 1996). Inclusion of such an issue in the work of a theologian indicated that unlike many of their modern counterparts, they reflected a liberal attitude to the female sex. Bikrama Jit Hasrat in his scholarly work *Dara Shikoh: Life and Works* (1979, repr. 1982) has shown that Dara was not only respectful to female mystics, he was also in favour of his talented sister Jahanara acquiring spiritual knowledge (also, A Dey, *Sufism*).

In *Majma-ul-Bahrain*, there is clear evidence to prove that Dara acquired knowledge about *Tauhid* (monotheism) and *Irfan* (Divine knowledge). The latter is a Koranic word. The selection of such a word by Dara is significant but not surprising since Dara did not renounce Islam officially. However, his rivals did try to denounce him as an infidel, which served their narrow political interests. I share my views with American scholar Professor Brian Hatcher, noted for his research on the Brahmas, pundits and Vidyasagar, that many Hindus in colonial Bengal such as Raja Rammohun Roy and Raja Radhakanta Dev, were well versed in Persian. In order to study India's composite culture, it is equally important to carry out research on Muslims in colonial and pre-colonial India who were well versed in Sanskrit. One ideal example in this line is indeed Dara Shukoh. His Sanskrit learning enabled him to explore and appreciate Upanishadic monotheism, which according to him was not different from Koranic monotheism. From AH 1065 (?) onwards, he was more deeply interested in the study of Hinduism. In AH 1066 he got the *Jug Bashist* translated into Persian. Shortly after, he himself translated the Upanishads into Persian prose. Most probably, he had *Bhagvat Gita* translated by one of his courtiers (*Majma*, p. 28).

In his *Hasanat-ul-Arifin*, which he completed in AH 1064 Dara included the name of Baba Lal—the only Hindu whose aphorisms he has quoted. In the *Majma-ul-Bahrain* also, Dara has put down the name of this saint, whom he calls Baba Lal Bairagi, by the side of those Muslim saints and divines who have been the best representatives of Islamic mysticism. The inclusion of the name of a Hindu in such an exclusive list of Muslim divines shows unmistakably the high esteem in which this devotee was held by Dara (*Majma,* p. 24). Dara in fact invited the saint and had conversations with him. It appears that Dara's private secretary, Chandar Bhan, was present on the occasion of these interviews and was perhaps, acting as an interpreter between them. It is also useful to note that Dara's eclectic mind was so broad that he did not confine his efforts only to exploring the commonalities between Hinduism and Islam. He was also thinking about including other religions in his project such as Christianity. Apparently this inclination of Dara was manifested in the year 1640–1, when he carefully studied the Bible (De, *Dara Shukoh O Rammohun Roy*).

It will be appropriate to wind up the discussion with a few examples from the *Majma*. This book begins with an interesting verse: 'Faith and Infidelity, both are galloping on the way towards Him….' Apparently Abul

Fazl had this verse inscribed on a building which Akbar had built for the common use of the Hindus and the Muslims (*Majma,* p. 37). It was a clear manifestation of the fact that Dara derived inspiration from the eclectic spirit which was sustained and enhanced by the policy undertaken by his great grandfather. In the pages of *Majma* (p. 38), Dara portrayed himself as a *faqir* and an *llm-I-Batin*—one who was endowed with esoteric knowledge. With this knowledge he aspired to know the tenets of religion of the Indian monotheists, and he was in fact elated to find that the difference between Indian monotheism and Islamic monotheism was only verbal.

Legacy of Eclecticism During the Nineteenth and Twentieth Centuries

Dara Shukoh's Persian version of the Upanishads entitled *Sirr-i-Akbar* was translated into Latin in AD 1800. At a later period Arthur Schopenhauer (1778–1860), the famous German philosopher, was influenced by this work. Dara Shukoh should rightly be called a propounder of the concept of modernism based on universalism, which was more visible in the ideas and activities of Rammohun Roy since the beginning of the nineteenth century. Roy, in his various works such as *Manazaratul Adian* (in Arabic, no longer available), *Tuhfat–ul–Muwahhidin* (in Persian, 1803–4), *Vedanta Sara* (1815) and other works on the Upanishads, expressed his ideas on theological issues, which he had analysed from the liberal–humanist–rational viewpoint. Much like Dara, Roy's religious ideas were also helpful to the growth of a new consciousness in a multi-religious country like India.[73]

The charismatic Brahmo leader Keshab Chandra Sen (1838–84) wanted to build a new human society by bringing the people of different faiths closer to each other. With this aim in view, he instructed some of his closest disciples to study Hinduism, Buddhism, Christianity and Islam. Bhai Girish Chandra Sen studied Islam, and to aid that study also learnt Arabic, Persian and Urdu. Besides the Koran, he translated several books on Islam from Arabic, Persian and Urdu into Bengali (De, '*Theological Discourses…*' and Amit Dey, *The Image of the Prophet in Bengali Muslim Piety; 1850–1947*, Kolkata, 2005, chap. 3). Picking up the eclectic thread from Dara Shukoh, nationalist leader and theologian Maulana Abul Kalam Azad (1888–1958) interpreted Islam from a different perspective. His own outlook was marked by a universal Islamic humanism very much in tune with the liberal Sufi traditions; he tried to build an Indian society on the basis of the country's cultural pluralism (De, '*Theological Discourses…*').[74] In an era when the forces of religious extremism are moving from strength to strength, it has become increasingly important to reassess the role of personalities like Dara Shukoh, Rammohun and Azad in the context of the ideal of 'multiculturalism' that they wanted to foster for the building of our nation.

Notes

1. Abu Talib, *Qutal-Qulub,* II, p. 238. Cited in Margaret Smith, *Rabia the Mystic and Her Fellow Saints in Islam,* Cambridge, 1928, p. 133.
2. *The Mathnawi of Rumi,* ed. and tr. by Reynold Alleyne Nicholson, vol. 6, London, 1934, p. 413. Here Rumi indicates that Eve was responsible for his first fall while his (Rumi's) last fall was caused by his own mother who brought him to this world.
3. Annemarie Schimmel, *Mystical Dimensions of Islam,* North Carolina, 1975, p. 426.
4.

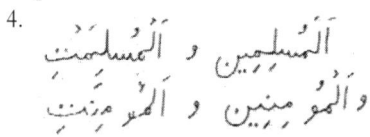

اَلْمُسْلِمِين و اَلْمُسْلِمَٰتِ
وَالْمُؤْمِنِين و اَلْمُؤْمِنَٰتِ

   Abdullah Yusuf Ali, The Holy Qur'an: Text, Translation and Commentary, new revd edn., Maryland, U.S.A, 1989, 33: 35. But in social terms women are subordinate to men, as indicated in the following Koranic verse:

   Men are the protectors and maintainers of women, because Allah has given the one more (strength) than the other, and because they support them from their means. Therefore the righteous women are devoutly obedient, and guard in (the husband's) absence what Allah would have them guard. As to those women on whose part ye fear disloyalty and ill-conduct, admonish them (first), (next), refuse to share their beds, (and last) beat them (lightly): but if they return to obedience. (ibid., Sura 4:34)

5. A. Schimmel, op. cit., p. 426. Rabi'a flourished in Basra, and was popularly known as Rabi'a Basri (AD 752 or 801). For details about Rabi'a, see Faridu'd-Din Attar (d. AD 1220), *Tadhkirat al-auliya,* edited in the original Persian by R. A. Nicholson, London, 1905, vol. I, pp. 59–73.
6. M. Smith..., op. cit., p. 137.
7. Shaikh Abdu'l Haqq Muhaddis Dihlawi, *Akhbaru'l-Akhyar* (in Persian), The Asiatic Society, Calcutta, pp. 280–3.

    After the death of Akbar, Shaikh Abdu'l Haqq (d. AD 1642) cherished a hope that Jahangir would start a new policy by reinvigorating the sharia. The Shaikh wrote a short treatise, the *Nuriya-i Sultaniya,* in order to show Jahangir some aspects of Sunni polity. In AD 1619–20 the Mughal Emperor honoured him with an audience, and the Shaikh presented him with his biogragphical dictionary of Indian Sufis, entitled, the *Akhbaru'l-Akhyar.*

    Jahangir, tr. Rogers and Beveridge, vol. II, p. III, cited in S.A.A. Rizvi, *The Wonder That was India,* vol. II, 1200–1700, London, 1987, p. 264.
8.

شیر از پستر برون آید کسی پر سیر که آن شیر نر است یا ماده
فرزندان ادم را طاعت و تقوی باید خواه مرد باشد و خواه زن

Sher az busha birun ayed kase pursid ke an sher nar ast va mada farzandane Adam ra ta 'at wa taqwae baid khua mard bashad wa khua zan.
Abdu'l Haqq, op. cit., p. 280.

9. بختیار کاکی خلیفہ بزرگ خواجہ معین الدین چشتی است

Bakhtiyar Kaki khalifa-e buzurg Khwaja Mu'inn 'd-Din Chishti ast.
Bakhtiyar Kaki (d. AD 1235) was the famous spiritual deputy of Khwaja Mu'inu'd-Din Chishti (d. AD 1236). Ibid., p. 28.
'Nizamu'd-Din Abu'l-Mu'id was a contemporary of Khwaja Qutbu'd-Din Bakhtiyar Kaki.' Ibid., p. 280.

10. Ibid.
11. Ibid.
12. Amir Hasan Sijzi, *Fawai'du'l-fu'ad* (in Persian), Lucknow, 1885, pp. 121–2.
13. S.A.A. Rizvi, *A History of Sufsm in India*, vol. 1, repr., New Delhi, 1986, p. 401.
14. Amir Hasan Sijzi, op. cit., pp. 122–3. Also see Abdu'l Haqq, *Akhbar...*, op. cit, pp. 281–2.

   The *Akhbaru'l-Akhyar* is a seventeenth century work. So it seems that the story of Baba Farid's (d. AD 1265) mother, her piety and miraculous power was very much alive in the minds of the devotees for several centuries. When two major Persian sources on Sufism mention her name, any question about her venerated image in the history of Sufism hardly arises.

15. Amir Khwurd, *Siyaru'l-Auliya* (in Persian), Dehli, 1302/1885, p. 191.
16. Abdu'l Haqq, *Akhbar,* op. cit., p. 282.
17. Ibid.
18. Ibid.
19. Ibid.
20. Amir Hasan Sijzi, *Fawai'd,* op. cit., pp. 154–5.
21. Ibid., pp. 165–6. Also see Hamid Qalandar, *Khayru'l-Majalis* (in Persian), Aligarh, 1959, pp. 190–1.

   The *Khayru'l-Majalis* by Hamid Qalandar was a significant work containing discourses by Shaikh Nasiru'd-Din (d. AD 1356). Like the *Fawi'du'l-Fu'ad,* its accounts are not dated. It is even more voluminous than the latter, consisting of one hundred chapters and an appendix.

22. Hamid Qalandar, op. cit., pp. 190–1.
23. Abdul'l Haqq, *Akhbar,* op. cit., p. 282.
24. Ibid., pp. 282–3.
25. فاطمہ سام مردی است

'Fatima Sam is a man.' Ibid., p. 280.

26. The discourses delivered by a leading Sufi to a select gathering of Sufi disciples and visitors gave rise to a distinctive genre of Persian literature. This was known as *malfuza*t which also contained didactic- poetry, anecdotes and pithy sayings. For more information about *malfuzat,* see S.A.A. Rizvi, *History of Sufism,* op. cit., pp. 3–8, 11–12.

27. Abdu'l Haqq, *Akhbar,* op. cit., p. 280.
28. Ibid., p. 280. *Sultanu'l-Masliaikh* means 'king of the saints'. *Mashaikh* is the plural form of Shaikh (saint).
29. Hamid Qalandar, *Khayr,* op. cit., pp. 227–8. Also see Abdu'l Haqq, op. cit., p. 281.
30.

بہم عشق طلب کنے و بہم جان خواہی
ہر در طلبی ولی میسر نشود

Abdu'l Haqq, op. cit., p. 280.
31. Ibid., p. 281.
32. Hamid Qalandar, *Khayr,* op. cit., p. 138.
33.

نان بر رویش داد و خود بعبادت مشغول شد

Ibid., p. 138.
34. Ibid..
35. Literally an *ibnu'l-waqt* means 'a time server' or 'a sycophant'. See Dr F. Steingass, *A Comprehensive Persian-English Dictionary,* 2nd Indian edn., New Delhi, 1981, p. 10.
But according to Sufi thought, an *ibnu'l-waqt* is one who understands the real value of human life through a constant awareness of its transience. See Hamid Qalandar, op. cit., p. 138.
36. Hamid Qalandar, op. cit., p. 138.
37. *Bangiya Sahitya Parishad Patrika,* 1323 Bengali year, cited in Girindra Nath Das, *Bangla Pir Sahityer Katha* (written in Bengali), Calcutta, 1976, p. 328. The page number of the *Bangiya Sahitya Parishad Patrika* was not mentioned by G.N. Das.
38. Abdu'l Gafur Siddiqi, *Balandar Pir Huzrat Gorachand Razi,* (written in Bengali), cited in G.N. Das, op. cit., p. 328. The page number of A.G. Siddiqi's book, *Balandar Pir Huzrat Gorachand Razi,* was not mentioned by G.N. Das.
39. *Kushdaha Patrika* (in Bengali), 1318 *Asvin* (Bengali year and month), p. III, cited in G.N. Das, op. cit., p. 330.
40. G.N. Das, op. cit., p. 328.
41. Also known as *sebayets* in many parts of Bengal. Ibid., p. 329.
42. *Minnat* is a Persian word which literally means service offered to anyone. In this case it means service offered to Raushan Bibi (or in the name of Raushan Bibi who died several centuries ago) with the expectation of getting her favour.
However in Bengal, the common devotees pronounce the word *minnat* as *manat.* Ibid., p. 329.
43. G.N. Das, op. cit., p. 329.
44. Ibid., pp. 331–2.
45. Ibid., p. 333.
46. Ibid.

47. بی بی اولیا از صالحات وقت خود بود

See Abdu'l Haqq, op. cit., p. 283.
48. Ibid.
49. قبر او بیرون قلعہ علائی است

Ibid.
50. Ibid. The word 'himam' is the plural form of 'himmat', which means magnanimous or high-minded, see Steingass, *Persian-English Dictionary*, op. cit., pp. 1508, 1511.
51. Abdu'l-Haqq, op. cit., p. 283.
52. A. Schimmel, *Mystical Dimensions*, op. cit., p. 433.
53. K.R. Qanungo, *Dara Shukoh*, Calcutta, 1935, see chap. 5, section 1.
54. Ibid., chap. 5, section 1.
55. Tawakkul Beg Kulali, *Neskhah-i-Ahwal Shahi* (in Persian), Ms. Brit. Mus Or: 3203, cited in M. Smith, *Rabia*, op. cit., p. 155.
56. T. Beg, *Neskhah*. fols. 41a, 41b, cited in M. Smith, *Rabia*, op. cit., p. 155.
57. Ibid., fols. 42a, 42b, cited in Smith, op. cit., p. 156.
58. M. Smith, op. cit., p. 156.
59. T. Beg, *Neskhah*, fol. 43b, cited in Smith, op. cit., p. 156.
60. M. Smith, op. cit., p. 156.
61. اگر عورت را خلافت و سجادہ مشایخ دادن روا بودے من بی بی شریعہ میرا دم

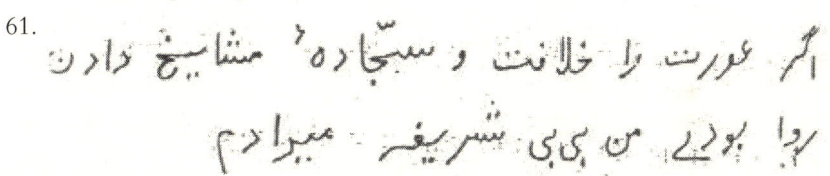

See Amir Khwurd, *Siyaru'l-Auliya* (in Persian), Delhi, 1302/1885, p. 191.
62. Amalendu De, 'Madhyayuger Prekshapate Bharatiya Renaissance,' in *India And Indology: Professor Sukumari Bhattacharji Felicitation Volume*, Bratindranath Mukherjee, ed., National Book Trust, Kolkata, 2009.
63. Krishna Sharma, *Bhakti and the Bhakti Movement: A New Perspective*, 2nd edn., New Delhi: Munshiram Manoharlal Pub. Pvt. Ltd., 2002, p. 178.
64. Amalendu De, *Theological Discourses in Indian History*. Presidential Address, 220th Annual General Meeting of the Asiatic Society, 2003–4, Kolkata. Also see Satish Chandra, *Historiography, Religion and State in Medieval India*, Har Anand Publication, New Delhi, 2nd repr., 2001, chaps. 8 and 9.
65. Ibid.
66. Thomas Patrick Hughes, *Dictionary of Islam*, Munshiram Manoharlal Pub. Pvt. Ltd., New Delhi, new edn., 1999, see *Wahdat-ul-Wajud*. Also, Satish Chandra, *Historiography*.
67. Satish Chandra, *Historiography*, p. 139.
68. Ibid., cited in p. 151.

69. De, '*Theological Discourses…*', p. 10.
70. Amalendu De, 'Nabachetanar Dui Agrapathik; Dara Shukoh Rammohun Roy', in *Rammohun Swaran* (in Bengali), Dilip Kr. Biswas, Pratul Chandra Gupta and others, eds., p. 294.
71. Muzaffar Alam, *The Languages of Political Islam in India,* Permanent Black, New Delhi, 2004.
73. *Majma–ul–Bahrain,* by Dara Shukoh, edited in the original Persian with English Translation, Notes and Variants by M. Mahfuz–ul–Haq, The Asiatic Society, Kolkata, 1st pub. 1929, repr., 1982, p. 5.
74. De, '*Theological Discourses…*', pp. 11–12.

CHAPTER THREE

Naturalization of the Nation and Nationalization of Nature: A Study of the Nationalist Literature of Bengal

ANURADHA ROY

T URNING TO NATURE as a source of personal inspiration and even collective identification is not new in history. But nationalism makes men perceive nature in a special way. The key concept with regard to national identity is authenticity. The process of authentication entails two sub-processes—historicizing the nation and naturalizing the nation; i.e. claiming continuity with a glorious historical past as well as creating a sense of naturalness of the nation. The idea is to establish an emotional link between a particular natural environment possessing certain sui generis qualities, and a national community, which in turn greatly helps the process of naturalizing the nation. This establishes that the nation exists primarily in the natural order, and that any social or legal bond comes later and derives from it. This, simultaneously, also reinforces the process of historicizing the nation; for nature is eternal, immemorial and perennial, and thus provides an authentic link between the past and the present (as well as the future). History and nature become symbiotically linked in this way and the nation is firmly established in both time and space.

From the middle of the nineteenth century, as the Bengali intelligentsia started imagining their nation, having borrowed the idea from the West, both the processes were manifest in their writings. While a number of scholars have probed the historicizing process in depth,[1] the naturalizing process remains neglected till now. The present study intends therefore, to address this lacuna, mainly on the basis of the literary representations of nature in the nationalist literature of nineteenth-century Bengal. Towards the end of the essay I will go beyond the nineteenth century and even make forays into the post-colonial years.

Nationalist Imagination Caught between History and Nature, i.e. between India and Bengal

People are emotionally attached to the land on which they have been living for generations. This emotion invariably becomes an important ingredient of nationalism and thus the land becomes a basic stimulus and referent of the nationalist literature.[2] The land and its features are bonds which an individual is born into, just like language, ethnicity or a historically forged cultural tradition. These can be likened to an individual's bond with his/her parents. Such bonds are extremely powerful, because one's relations with them are not based on self-interest and it is precisely for this reason that one can even lay down his life for their sake.

Ideally, nationalism blends the homeland sentiment with a pride in national history, which means a pride of lineage. In Bismarckian terminology 'Blut and Boden' (blood and soil) become mixed. But in the case of India—a land of many ethno-linguistic-religious-cultural groups as well of variegated natural features and landscapes—such a mixture was not easy to achieve. The blood and soil linkage becomes a possibility only for uni-homeland nations (one group of people and one homeland, with the former often lending its name to the latter), e.g. Deutschland, Ireland and the like. On the other hand, in a multicultural multi-homeland country like India, where no single ethno-linguistic criterion can be used for forging the nation, nature sometimes plays a crucial role as an organic principle. This is evident in how the Alpine landscape has acted as a homogenizing force cutting across linguistic and ethnic barriers in the case of Switzerland.[3] The vast subcontinent of India, however, is a land with many peoples with multiple ethnocultural attributes, who, in turn, are also diffused geographically—belonging to mountains, river valleys, deserts, coastal areas and so on. Thus the first question that piques our curiosity is: how then did our nationalist ancestors solve this problem?

The problem of multiple identities was solved by imagining all or at least most Indians as Hindu-Aryan. The religious-cum-cultural category Hindu was combined with the ethnic category Aryan to create this concept of a big and immemorially old 'we'. India was marked as the land of the Hindu-Aryans who had flourished gloriously in the past, but had fallen later. At the same time, however, India was defined largely in terms of nature as well.[4] Poem after poem sought to establish the Indian identity in terms of the majestic Himalayas and the Indian Ocean, as also the famous rivers like the Ganga (alternatively called Jahnavi or Bhagirathi), the Jamuna, the Narmada and the Kaveri. All these natural formations over the *longue duree* exercised an immense fascination upon the nationalist literary imagination which in turn, came to regard these as great cultural symbols of the great Indian nation. Sometimes instead of mentioning proper names, the poets celebrated common forests, woodlands, deserts, golden crops, singing birds or bumble bees as elements of Indian nature; the common motifs of the moon and the sun also featured prominently. Michael Madhusudan Datta had proudly said that he had been born in, 'The land where the sun rises on the top of the Great Mountains to lovingly kiss the forehead of the earth.' This poem entitled *Parichay* (Identity) lists various beautiful features of nature to define the land of the poet's birth.[5] Bhudev Mukhopadhyay's *Adhibharati* (a new deity imagined by him as the goddess India) was brilliantly colourful with her golden complexion, a green sari wrapped around her (evidently standing for the green fields full of crops) and the blue seas making obeisance at her feet.[6] This image of Mother India featured prominently in many more poems, where she was depicted as not only exquisitely beautiful, but also fabulously rich—bedecked with precious jewels as she was. The poets often hinted that it was her riches that had attracted foreign invaders again and again and thus caused utter misery to her and her sons.[7]

Nature in India was more often than not associated with Indian history, which, in the nationalist mind, was hardly distinguishable from mythology. The idea was that the glorious past of India cannot be traced in the slightest among the fallen Indians today, but it remains intact in nature. Nature hence assumed the role of a gratifying reminder of India's lost glory. The historical discourse was in a sense theological too: the writers seemed to be saying that there was a divine plan in nature which revealed itself through Indian history. It is a spiritualized-moralized-historicized nature that we find therefore in the nationalist literature of nineteenth-century Bengal. Not only the great Himalayas or the oceans, a sort of divinity seemed to pervade all aspects of nature in India. Riverbanks and woodlands, both generic and particular, were often associated with the ashramas of the Aryan sages, where the Vedic mantras had been heard for the first time along with the chirping of the birds. Panchabati was of course associated with Sita, the Kadmaba tree with Krishna playing on his flute.[8] Kamini Ray in her poem *Ashar Swapan* (a hopeful dream) wrote of hearing the banks of the rivers Janavi, Jamuna, Narmada, Godavari and Panchanad (the Five Rivers in the north-west) resonating with melodious hymns addressed to the gods.[9] Such famous rivers of India had, in any case, had strong religious association from very ancient times, and this helped the nationalist imagination. In Gobindachandra Ray's *Jamunalahari* (The Waves of the River Jamuna), the river babbles the story of her bygone days of glory.[10] In Rabindranath's *Hindu Melay Upahar* (A Gift to Hindu Mela), the sage Vyas, the composer of the epic *Mahabharata*, sits on his stone-seat on a peak of the sublime Himalayas, where his sweet music melts into the dazzling beauty of the full moon.[11] But the present situation causes despair to the teenage poet. He exclaims—let India become a desert and the Bhagirathi a firepit!

Thus nature caused both hope and anguish. Sometimes the poets would ask—the ever-young nature is infinitely rich; but what ends do her beauty and wealth serve? Kumudini Basu in her poem *Janmabhumi* (The Land of One's Birth) exclaims:

> The great world of nature is replenished constantly
> The birds sing as usual,
> Her body glitters with peerless beauty,
> Her golden crops are irresistible,
> Trees beautiful with leaves and flowers, yet her heart is like a crematorium
> Her sinful children are asleep by the fire there.[12]

Sometimes nature herself seems adversely affected by the decay in the human order. We often have such descriptions as—India's beauty is a mere dream, she is actually a crematorium where the funeral fire has been burning for 700 long years (i.e. since the time of Muslim invasion, marked by the Hindu-Aryan history as the time of India's loss of independence); or India is a vast treeless desert without any umbrage, or she is a desolate land engulfed in darkness, about to be destroyed by a devastating cyclone.[13]

One anonymous poet laments—'Oh Spring! Aren't you ever going to leave India alone?' The poem continues in this vein—spring appears beautiful on the bank of the Bhagirathi, with the south wind blowing joyously and the cuckoo singing; but this is a grief-stricken country, how can spring make it laugh? Rather let summer come and burn the entire land.[14] Yet another poet behind the veil of anonymity invites spring—India is plunged in darkness, the birds no longer sing; however, if you please come, the sun will rise and it will be a happy land.[15] The cuckoo, known as the friend of spring, frequently featured in its own right in the nationalist poems of the nineteenth century. Sometimes the bird is requested to sing and awaken the sleeping Indians,[16] while sometimes, the poet is so impatient with the cuckoo that he proceeds to say something like this—Let the bird die and the springtime take its leave; the love play of the king of seasons is required no more, we need to wage a terrible war now.[17] In both these instances and more, the springtime and the cuckoo were not so much real components of India's nature as they were metaphors. Similarly, we also find a metaphoric monsoon in a poem of Rajkrishna Ray:

> Nature! How can you have the heart to shower the slaves with rain?
> Rather hit them with your thunderbolt
> And let India, the land of slaves, be destroyed.[18]

So elements of nature were both real physical components of India as well as symbolic. When the poet felt hopelessly sad, when it seemed to him/her that his countrymen were utterly insensitive and did not care in the least for the motherland, he/she had to rivet faith on nature, resort to nature for sympathy and encouragement. And when the poets gave nature a metaphoric significance, it turned the human aspect of the nation (at least in the present) quite insignificant.[19] We also cannot help feeling that appropriating nature in their own terms was vitally urgent for the colonial intelligentsia, for colonial servitude is inaugurated by the loss of the locality to the outsider. Thus one of the first tasks of the culture of colonial resistance is to reclaim the land in the terms of the colonized, to establish a profound, plenary and proprietary claim on it and to restore the geographical identity of the nation. Loyalty to the British masters was an essential component of nationalism in those days. But the nationalists also felt an agony of subjection. The poems featuring nature helped the nationalists turn their face away from foreign rule. Nature was a site where they could assert their sovereignty in the face of the British masters (another site being their inner domain of culture, as famously pointed out by Partha Chatterjee).[20]

It has hopefully become clear by now that the nature of India was either associated with the history of the land or made of some indefinite elements not specifically related to India (desert, forest, moon, sun, etc.) or that it was purely symbolic. This nature was a forced imagination, perhaps helped by reading or some kind of second-hand experience. It was sublime and sensational, but not intimately lived and experienced in one's everyday life. This nature appeared strange and often untamed, converging with the divine and the infinite; but curiously shorn of any human association except in terms of the ancient Aryans. It inspired awe and reverence, but not a sense of intimacy. Those days not many Bengali poets were familiar with the Himalayas, or the oceans bordering the subcontinent on three sides, or all the great rivers like the Jahnavi, the Narmada and the Godavari. At least not all of these features of the land were within the personal experiences or memories of all of the nationalists. The Ganges was the only river that tended to bind Bengal with a large part of India beyond it. So the nature of India seemed somewhat distant and not quite adequate in authenticating the nation.

However, this inadequacy was compensated for by the nature of Bengal. The nationalists imagined two parallel nations at the same time—India and Bengal. Their Bengali nation was founded primarily on the basis of the Bengali language, but nature was its other important parameter (in fact, even their language was considered such a strong primary bond that it often appeared to the nationalists as almost an element of nature). In contrast to the nature of India, the nature of Bengal was obviously felt as very real and intimately known: in their relationship with it, the nationalists showed a more informed care for the familiar local and the everyday present. It was also more domesticated and human, to which they felt a strong rootedness and indebtedness. This nature was not sensational, but sentimental. In fact, the homeland sentiment of Bengali nationalists was centred on the nature of Bengal and not that of India. The landscapes, flora and fauna of Bengal evoked deep love in their hearts and they really doted on these. On the whole, it was like the children's love for their mother, a sentiment that does not depend on the greatness of the object of love. Or rather, the object seems great because one is intimately close to it/her.

We generally acknowledge today that all nations are imagined communities (courtesy of Benedict Anderson's seminal book), but the degree of imagination varies from case to case. A comparison between the Indian nation and the Bengali nation, as the nineteenth-century Bengali nationalists saw it, will bear this out clearly. It is true that the nature of Bengal was imaginary to some extent, but it was much less imaginary than in the case of India. Moreover, the eulogistic descriptions of the former were usually more popular than those of the latter. Numerous examples can be cited—from Bankimchandra's *Sujalang, Suphalang, Malayajashitalang* (Well-watered, well-fruited and cooled by the south wind), a mother figure whom Bankim obstinately kept as Mother Bengal and refused to turn into Mother India despite the request of his poet-friend Nabinchandra Sen,[21] to Satyendranath Datta's 'In which country are trees and creepers greener than those in the rest of the world?' followed by the inevitable answer—'That is our Bangladesh, our very own Bangla.'[22]

Of course, such portrayal of the nature of Bengal was largely selective. It engaged some select features of natural environment that the nationalists were interested in and hence celebrated. A cult-like enthusiasm was forged around the riparian and pastoral beauty of the plains of Bengal, neglecting its mountains and seas, with which they were not familiar or at least not intimate. The nationalists were mostly plainsmen. The plains of south Bengal was the birthplace of the majority of them and were hence associated with the memory of their childhood and youth. It was here that their family home was located and a web of human relationships existed. Later on, even if they went elsewhere in pursuit of higher education and career, they returned again and again to their village homes. In the absence of constant physical proximity, symbols began to replace actual experience. Some physical or natural features of the land could serve this function, for example, rivers, trees, ponds, paddy fields, mango groves, certain birds and animals. Thus was created an array of symbolic imageries, which were perceived again and again until they came to signify or represent the entire region. But these imageries were not like some unseen mountains or rivers or some indefinite forest or desert somewhere in India. Their significance lay in reinforcing the love for something more or less closely known. Added to these were the cycle of six seasons and some characteristics of the climate inextricably associated with the land. But it must be remembered that this was very different from the metaphorical spring of India and its metaphorical cuckoo. All in all this was the homeland, the *terra sacra* of the Bengali nationalists—a land of arcadian beauty, to which they wrote rhapsodic poems and sublime hymns. The tenderness with which the poets described the natural beauty of this place could not be applied to any other place on the earth.

The nationalist literature of nineteenth-century Bengal is replete with such examples. One remembers Michael Madhusudan Datta's earliest poems, which even though written in English, described places which were surely his native Bengal. One may also cite Madhusudan's Bengali sonnets such as 'The River Kapotaksha' (flowing along the poet's native village), 'The shrine of Siva under the Banyan Tree on the Riverside at Night', 'The Bird Bou-katha-kao', etc. They were all written by the nostalgic poet while living abroad.[23] For Madhusudan, going abroad at least meant leaving India. But for most Bengalis leaving even Bengal meant going to a foreign land. In Dinabandhu Mitra's *Prabasir Bilap* (Lamentations of one living abroad) the sweet homeland lovingly remembered was Bengal—in fact, the poet's own village and homestead.[24] The poet employed in the postal department, was most probably posted in Orissa at that time. The same sentiment was captured in Shitalakanta Chattopadhyay's poem *Deshparyatan* (Travelling countries). Though the Aryan monuments in Delhi, Agra and other places of north India amazed the poet, he remembered Bengal, the place of his birth, with special affection.[25]

The primarily historical India and the primarily natural Bengal were overlapping and interchangeable in the collective mind of the Bengali intelligentsia, though one would often seek ascendancy over the other. This inevitably led to some confusion between history and nature. History was sometimes imbued with misinterpreted nature-related imageries. The famous song *Dhanadhanyapushpabhara amader ei basundhara* (Filled with wealth, paddy and flowers is this earth of ours) in Dwijendralal Ray's play *Shahjahan*[26] was sung in praise of Mewar in Rajasthan, set as it was in the historical background of the struggle of the Rajputs against the Mughals. However, the reference to paddy in the very first line, even though applied to the entire earth and not to Mewar, makes the reader a bit suspicious. The full-fledged description of the nature of Mewar comes only in the second stanza, which starts by mentioning some unspecific 'charming rivers' and 'smoke-coloured hills', and Mewar indeed has hills and a few rivers. But the next line 'Where does the green field merge with the horizon in this way?' makes the reader all the more suspicious. After all, if it is a hilly land, green fields cannot be seen merging with the sky. And then in the final line of this stanza the poet completely (though perhaps inadvertently) gives himself away—'In whose country does the wind play in the paddy-field making such waves', a scene quite unthinkable in Mewar and rather typical of the Bengal countryside.

From Passive Nature to a Dynamic and Creative Force

The land and nature were not just a passive source of identity for the nationalists. Having been emotionally and ideologically charged, passive nature became an active creative force in the cultural corpus of nineteenth-century Bengal. To be such a force, nature had to be manipulated and imagined as exceptionally beautiful, a provider of prosperity and dispenser of affection for the nation. For this, of course, it had to be idealized with a lot of ethical and aesthetic excess.

One fascinating aspect of this was nationalization of nature in the image of the mother—both Mother India and Mother Bengal, the latter figuring more frequently in their literature and evoking a more intimate feeling. Mother India was usually a dignified and sorrowful woman lamenting her fate, while Mother Bengal was more often than not made up of natural elements. It is also to be noted that Mother India was always addressed with the pronoun 'tumi', while Mother Bengal was almost always addressed with 'tui', which denotes a profounder intimacy. This imagination of the land as mother made it seem vivid and adorable, generated a feeling of deep devotion and also helped the nationalists look upon all countrymen as brothers, which was very important for the sentiment of nationalism, for a nation is supposed to be a close-knit community. No bond in the world perhaps involves a deeper emotion than that between a mother and her child. It is admittedly the strongest primary bond in the world.

To describe the beauty of the motherland the poets just described its rivers, trees, birds, etc., trying to anthropomorphize them a little and moulding them in the image of a beautiful woman. Alongside describing the mother's beauty they also brought forth images that emphasized her love and care for her children. Rabindranath's poem *Sharat* (The Autumn)[27] was an excellent description of this mother, who was none other than Mother Bengal:

> Oh! What a lovely appearance you have before my eyes
> Today, in the autumn morn!
> Oh! Mother Bengal, your lush green body
> Is dazzling in unblemished beauty
> The rivers are overflowing
> The paddy-fields are more than full
> The *doyel* twitters and the *koyel* sings
> In the gathering held in your magnificent garden
> And amid all this you stand, my mother
> In this autumn morn.

In the last stanza of the poem, natural beauties turn into ornaments of the mother, thus personifying the land once again:

> On her neck dangles a garland of *shephali* blossoms
> Its fragrance filling the earth.
> The end of her *sari* is woven with waterless clouds
> As white as pure butter.
> Donning a glittering crown of sunbeam.
> She is sweetly gracious in green and gold.
> With anklets set with flowers around her feet
> There stands my mother.
> In light and dew, in flowers and crops
> All the world smiles.

In the rest of the poem this beautiful Mother Bengal is the mother of a big household, whose children are coming home from far and near for the autumn vacation, and who is busy making all arrangements for them, looking after their logistics above all. This ritual, of autumnal homecoming to the loving mother, was a very real experience for many Bengalis those days. The picture of the ripe autumnal harvest in the countryside of course facilitates this portrayal of a prosperous motherland. The poet calls:

> Come, come, come,
> Come ye all.
> Mother has opened the door of her storeroom.
> Food is in abundance—
> 'Who is crying of hunger?' she is asking.
> Come one and all.

To the nationalists, their homeland was both beautiful and bountiful. Needless to say, like the beauty of the land, its plenitude too was nothing but an idealized description. The economic reality of Bengal consisted of poverty and famines. But it is precisely what is absent in reality that has to be ideally constituted. Sometimes it is history that provides the raw material for such reconstitution, sometimes it is nature. The poets seemed to assert—We may be degraded today, but our motherland is glorious. Even at present, even though we are degraded, our motherland is prosperous. As Rabindranath said in another poem:

> You are giving unto us all you have, mother—
> Your golden crop and the water of your river Jahnavi.
> But what will these people give you in return?
> Nothing, simply nothing.
> They will only tell a lot of abominable lies.

Thus nature seemed to compensate for many human deficiencies.[28]

This image of motherland was sometimes juxtaposed with some goddesses of the Hindu pantheon (Durga or Kali or Lakshmi). But the concept of motherland more often than not had a secular overtone. Her image had little to do with any objectified idol representing a Hindu deity. It is true that the image of Mother India, even though made up of natural elements, often evoked an ancient Hindu-Aryan millennium, but Mother Bengal seemed just an anthropomorphized natural beauty, akin to a loving and giving human mother. Even in Bankimchandra's *Bande Mataram*, severely criticized later for equating the country with the goddess Durga, the latter comes in only in the second stanza. In the first stanza, which has always been much more popular, we just find a mother resplendent in natural beauty and wealth. She combines her natural beauty and prosperity (described as well-watered, well-fruited and so on) with a sweet smile, honeyed words and gifts of bliss and benediction.

In the twentieth century, the cult of motherland came to be widely regarded as part of the idolatrous practice of worshipping various mother goddesses in the Hindu religious tradition. Muslims in particular started resenting the practice of worshipping the motherland, finding it incompatible with Islam, and stopped conforming to it. However, in the nineteenth century and even in the early twentieth century they had not hesitated to address the land as mother—and of course, it had been a mother figure made of natural beauties and motherly attributes.[29]

Nature-Culture Dichotomy as Village-City Dichotomy in the Nationalist Mind

In the process of harnessing nature in the service of national sentiment, the nationalists romanticized the village as a space full of simplicity and purity, tranquility and security, which for them was the country at the micro-level. This imagined village was a rhetoric of lost authenticity and their true spiritual home—and they pitted it against the city, which they considered artificial and hated for despoiling nature and being alien to folk spirit. This also involved the romantic stereotype of the rural folk, particularly the peasant mystique—a celebration of peasants as nature's own people.[30] Aestheticizing nature and valorizing the rural folk for their diligence, frugality, honesty, simplicity, etc., went hand in hand. This was the nationalists' way of subscribing to the nature-culture dichotomy. Culture here is to be understood not in the sense of 'high culture', but whatever urban. Great Britain was perceived as an essentially urban civilization (though the British themselves perceived their nation as basically rural[31] and the citification of India was largely attributed to the British masters. So the dream-world of the nationalists here had to be largely rural.

This rural romance was a flagrant case of aesthetic and ideological imposition over the real. The nationalists' village with its rustic simplicity and bucolic delight was too unproblematic—simplified, sanitized and sublime. They made it almost mythic in time and space, ignoring all its negative elements and emptying it of all critical contents, such as references to poverty, unsanitary conditions and also squalid social reality. But of course, 'willing suspension of disbelief' is a typical characteristic of nationalist fantasies.

The following lines of Rabindranath's poem *Dui Bigha Jami* constitute an excellent example of this romantic attitude to the countryside:[32]

> I salute you Bengal, my beautiful mother,
> The soothing breeze on the banks of the Ganga comforts me.
> The open fields—the forehead of the sky—kiss the dust of your feet.
> Little abodes of peace are your villages
> Nestling in Dark and intimate shadows.

Here is another example: again a song composed by Rabindranath, put in the mouth of peasants in one of his plays, conforming to the nationalist notion of the happy peasant:[33]

> Happily do we grow crops
> Spending the whole day in the field
> In the sun and in the rain
> With the bamboo leaf making murmurs
> And the wind filled with the fragrance of cultivated soil.
> The music of the green life
> Becomes manifest in lines and colours.
> And the young poet dances along merrily.
> The joyous ears of the corn
> Make the entire earth laugh
> In the golden sun of *Aghran* as well as in the light full moon.

Rural romance became a staple of Bengali nationalist literature by the early twentiety century. However, whether the nationalists' attitude to the village was associated with a sensibility for the real rural environment and environmental balance or for the sufferings and struggle of the real peasantry is a question that would require some critical analysis. The fact is that this rural romance was basically an urban phenomenon. Dipesh Chakrabarty is more or less right in thus tracing its history:

Quintessentially a product of cities (mainly Calcutta), a picture of the ideal Bengali village had been developing since the 1880s, when a host of nationalists writers such as Bankimchandra Chatterjee and, later, Rabindranath Tagore drew on new perceptions of the countryside to create, for and behalf of the urban middle-classes, a powerfully nostalgic and pastoral image of the generic Bengali village.[34]

The nationalists were mostly residents of Calcutta or mofussil towns. Even if born in villages, they migrated to urban areas later, and never thought of settling in the countryside permanently. As Chakrabarty has also shown, their rural romance was a matter of accommodating the village and a putative folk culture in the rhythm of urban life, in which the village was mainly a place for holidaying. Here is an interesting test for the validity of this claim of the basic urbanism of rural romance, which will corroborate Chakrabarty. Language was an important criterion of the Bengali nationhood and so was the nature of Bengal; yet the language the nationalists standardized and upheld for their cultural nationalism was not the speech of nature, but of culture—not the speech of the Bengali peasant, but the refined language of the Calcutta elite.

Of course, we cannot deny some intimacy with and some concern for villages in the hearts of some of the nationalists from the nineteenth century. Harinath Majumdar's journal *Grambartaprakashika* testifies to this, associated as it was with his day-to-day work of rural uplift.[35] Rabindranath extensively toured his zamindari in East Bengal (today Bangladesh) from the 1890s and acquired first-hand knowledge of rural Bengal there. He discovered the real, the ordinary and the everyday nation in the rural surroundings of his zamindari estate, which went a long way towards demystifying the Hindu-Aryan nation in his mind. On the whole, the nationalists' love for the village got associated with a sort of real feeling from the turn of the century (although acquired from a certain distance) with the nationalist elite paying attention to the folk tradition and adopting folk forms for their own artistic creations. Again, the most famous example is Rabindranath. Many of his celebrated swadeshi songs composed on the occasion of the anti-Partition agitation were set to folk tunes. Revival of folk crafts and exploration of folklore became important items on the nationalist agenda. From about this time, the discovery of the folk roots of the nation seemed no less important to the nationalists than doting on its classicized heritage.

Also, as the nationalists became more and more familiar with rural Bengal, they could not remain blind to the evils of rural life. There came a time when instead of romanticizing the village, its natural beauty and the simplicity of rural folk, the nationalists looked at it with a realistically critical eye. The village was no longer idyllic to them, but suddenly full of caste politics, patriarchal oppression, jealousy, rivalry and fraudulence among its people, also marked by environmental imbalances, scarcity of drinking water, ponds as the breeding ground of malaria, poor health, and so on. All this became particularly glaring after the emotional excitement of the Swadeshi Movement had subsided. Sarat Chandra Chattopadhyay's novels like *Pallisamaj* (1916) are famous examples of the realistic nationalist attitude to the village. Rabindranath himself brought forth such images in his short stories written during his tour of East Bengal in the late nineteenth century.[36] Dipesh Chakrabarty claims that Rabindranath in particular and the nationalist writers in general developed a formalistic strategy for picturing the two entirely contradictory images of the same generic category that is the Bengal village. They made a division of labour between prose and poetry, employing the former for portraying a realistic image and the latter for a romantic one.[37] But we know that a role reversal was common too. There are many examples of poetry dealing with the mundane and harsh reality (as well as poetic prose) so far as the literary description of rural Bengal is concerned. We may cite as example the following parody of Rabindranath's *Sarat*, which was penned by Jatindraprasad Bhattacharya sometime in the 1920s:

> Oh! What a gloomy appearance you have before my eyes
> Today, in this autumn morn!
> Your dark and dirty body is full of pits and pools.
> People are down with fever
> And morbid enlargement of spleen.
> Jackals howl merrily in broad daylight
> In your precious village,
> In one corner of which you are crying helplessly
> In this autumn morn.[38]

Another work that may be cited in this context is Sabitriprasanna Chattopadhyay's *Byarthabodhan*, which, like Rabindranath's *Sarat*, is set in the background of the autumnal festival of Durga Puja. In sharp contrast to the latter, however, it announces the failed invocation of the goddess, because of the sorry state of the countryside:

> The roads of Bengal are full of weeds
> In the house of Chandi jackals are making terrible noise in the daytime.
> All the granaries of Bengal are lying with sadly empty chests
> Wind passes through them in a haphazard manner shaking their bones.
> The epidemic demon is dancing merrily at every home
> Famine is breathing poison upon the village of Bengal.
> O Mahamaya, a great calamity has returned to Bengal this Aswin
> Who will arrange for your festival on the bank of Bengal's dead river?[39]

The plight of the village generated not only criticism, but also a deep pathos, which, just like romantic attraction, lends itself easily to poetry.

Perhaps romanticism and realism should not be treated as binary opposites in this connection. Turning away from the reality was not a prerequisite to the efflorescence of romantic emotion regarding the village. In fact, the awareness of the sufferings of the countryside generated a deep love for it, which was conducive to romanticism. 'Sonar Bangla' turning into a 'shmashan'(creamatorium) provided the structural framework of the Bengali nationalist thinking for a long time to come. The foreign rulers were held mainly responsible for this, but not to the exclusion of some strident self-criticism. A popular poem of Jatindramohan Bagchi (*Oi je gnati jachchhe dekha airi kheter dhare*)[40] shows no illusion about the 'beauty and health' of the poet's native village and yet concludes on a note of romantic sentimentality:

> Whether or not it has beauty or health,
> My heart leaps with joy when I approach this village.
> Here I have all the peace and happiness in the world
> Father's affection, Mother's petting and the smile of my beloved
> That is why my birthplace is greater than heaven,
> It has stolen my entire heart.

We have seen that in the case of India, nature had often compensated for the deficiency of human beings. Now, in the case of Bengal, human sentiments seemed to be compensating for the deficiency of nature.

We must also remember that the negative and prosaic image of the countryside was not only reflected in the writings of the socially engaged nationalist writers, but the latter also acted upon this new perception, as evident in the rural reconstruction programme of Rabindranath from the early twentieth century and that of the Gandhian social workers since the 1920s. In fact, the 1920s saw efforts for rural upliftment in many pockets in Bengal, whatever their ideological and inspirational sources may have been. However, even this activism was not against rural romance. Gandhi's anti-modern social ideology perhaps made the nationalists even keener to postulate a pre-modern culture in harmony with nature and to evoke a simple communal lifestyle based on a rural idyll. Moreover, since the time of the First World War, the global modernity started intruding Indian life on an unprecedented scale. Rural romance was a weapon of cultural resistance against this intensified modernity with its promotion of rugged individualism, urbanization and so on. It provided the nationalists with the model of a harmonious human order in an increasingly alienating world.[41] Of course they realized that it was not a readymade model and they needed to fight against many odds to achieve this. Yet the 'is' and the 'ought' converged, in the sense that the 'ought' seemed to be somehow potentially present in the 'is'. So it was no paradox that alongside criticizing many aspects of rural life and trying to improve it, the nationalists continued to feel quite sentimental about the village. The nostalgic folksy and soft image of the village never quite died and helped mitigate all their realistic negative ideas about it. In fact, in the 1920s there rose a renewed romanticism for rural Bengal in the hearts of the nationalists, which was remarkably documented in Jibananda Das' *Rupasi Bangla*,[42] Jashimuddin's poems of pastoral romance[43] and many other works.[44]

Intellectual Sources of Nature-Worship by Nationalists

We will now try to understand how much of the nature-worship by the nationalists owed to the indigenous literary tradition and how much to Western Romanticism.

The religious attitude to the nature of India that we have noticed in the nationalist literature of the nineteenth century—particularly the providential nature of the great Himalayas, the seas and the big rivers—perhaps owed to a very ancient Indian literary source—the Vedas. It was the Vedic ecosophy based on a matricentric conception of the universe (the Vedic Aryans were patriarchal of course, but this trait perhaps derived from the pre-Aryan matriarchal tradition), acknowledging Mother Prakriti as the source of everything around and entailing a sense of all-encompassing unity.[45] Mother Prakriti perhaps became Mother India in the nationalist literature. A religious attitude to nature was also to be found in Christian theological discourse (as distinct from the newly developed scientific attitude to nature which involved seeing it as something to be studied through observations and experience). However, it seems that the Indian influence was much stronger in this case.

Even after the Vedas, Sanskrit literature continued to exhibit a fascination towards nature. The beautiful descriptions of nature in the Ramayana, the Mahabharata and the classical Sanskrit literature may be cited as evidence. However, according to Buddhadev Bose, while in the epics such descriptions are very lively enabling the reader to visualize the scenes before his mind's eyes, in the classical Sanskrit literature, they are mostly like well-decorated backdrops of theatre, to be seen but not to be participated in. Bose argues that the classical litterateurs were neither naïve (i.e. part of nature) nor sentimental (or romantic) in their relation to nature.[46] Their personal voices were rarely heard and lyricism was almost entirely absent in their eulogies of nature. This literature was prescribed by convention and mostly concentrated on linguistic acrobatics or display of rhetorical skill, catering to the need of an aristocratic readership. To them, style was more important than content.[47] However, even Bose concurs that in the hands of Kalidas, the most talented among them, descriptions of nature sometimes became meaningful. In Kalidasa's *Meghaduta* for example, the Yaksha separated from his wife for a year, sees sexually significant images in elements of nature—his libido, if not his love, permeates the vast natural world from Ramgiri to Alaka.[48] And despite Kalidas' sophistication and conventionalism, admits Bose, poetry is not totally banished from this masterpiece.

But Bose perhaps had a bee in his bonnet. In Kalidasa's works, mountains, forests and trees often seem to possess a conscious individuality. Moreover, as Rabindranath says, the attitude of the heroine of *Abhijnan Shakuntalam* to nature is surely naïve. Nature lies not outside Shakuntala, but permeates her character.[49] Many nineteenth century intellectuals like Rabindranath were influenced by the treatment of nature in classical Sanskrit literature. But they perhaps approached nature in a more romantic way, as they treated natural elements as sources of their own national identity. And of course, their personal identity was enmeshed in their collective national identity. Consequently they wrote many sentimental lyrics that sound like very private love-offerings to their motherland. For example, this simple but exquisitely beautiful song by Rabindranath, expressing his absorption in the physical richness of his land and an almost ethereal tenderness for it:

> I am gratified mother that I have been born in this country
> I am gratified by loving you.
> I don't know if you have riches like a queen
> But I do know that your shadows comfort my body.
> Don't know in which forest flowers are so ardently aromatic
> In which sky the moon smiles so sweetly.
> Your light soothed my eyes when I first opened them
> I shall shut these eyes for good, looking at that light.[50]

Of course, such exuberant lyricism cannot be found in the classical Sanskrit literature. This is the kind of sentiment that can make one lay down his/her life for the motherland—so much so that it is said that when the young militant nationalist Ullaskar Datta heard his death sentence pronounced by the judge in connection with the Alipore Bomb Case, he sang out this song then and there in that crowded courtroom, stunning everybody.[50]

This romanticism of the nineteenth-century Bengali nationalists was largely indebted to the Romantic literature of England. English Romanticism (and its Orientalist derivation) unmistakably fed their imagination and informed their style. This was seen in their treatment of Indian history (particularly the heroic struggle of the medieval Hindu chiefs against Muslim aggressors for political liberation) as well as their attitude to nature.[52] The influence could be seen in the poets' wide use of the Romantic trope of dreaming and waking up from a vision in their contemplation of the nature of India[53] and their intensely personal and idyllic descriptions of Bengal's countryside. But it was not just objective nature, the Romantic foregrounding of the 'natural' on the whole seemed to have a very special appeal for Bengali nationalists.[54] The love for the 'natural' was a correlate of the Romantic hankering for liberation from all artificial ties of authority and the Romantic melancholy on its non-achievement. The colonial intelligentsia suffered from a sense of melancholy due to their political subjugation and the stifling condition of their social life and hence the melancholic Romantics struck a chord in their heart. Their description of nature often showed a pensive mood.

But perhaps more important than the direct influence of the Romantic poets of the west, was the general urban perception of the village that involved new, often Western, ways of seeing the landscape, drawing upon varieties of European literature, art and even photograph. Dipesh Chakrabarty has raised this point, and to substantiate it, quoted from Rabindranath and Nirad C. Chaudhuri.[55] The former in his *Chhinnapatrabali*, a collection of letters written during his tour of East Bengal, deployed the notion of photograph to describe his enjoyment of the landscape—'Some people's minds are like the wet plate of a photograph; unless the photo is printed on paper right away, it is wasted. My mind is of that type. Whenever I see a (natural) scene, I think I must write it down carefully in a letter.' Nirad Chaudhuri in his *Autobiography* seemed quite aware of the recent origins of the practice of seeing the Bengal countryside beautiful and thus appreciated it himself in a very self-conscious way, comparing some scene with Constable's landscapes, feeling one with some other scene 'like Wordsworth's boy'.

There was an important genre in English literature preceding the nineteenth century Romanticism and in fact harking back to classical antecedents, that should also be mentioned in this connection. This was the genre of 'pastoral romance' which was written in remote and bucolic setting, invoking a contrast between the rustic simplicity of country life and the hectic and complex city, and entailing a nostalgia for the lost innocence and delight of rural life. The pastoral mode developed considerably in the unsettling era of the seventeenth century. The exact channel through which this influence came to Bengal needs to be investigated, but there was indeed an element of pastoral sensibility in the nineteenth-century Bengali poets.

In the eighteenth century there developed in English literature a strand of thought famously reflected in Oliver Goldsmith's celebrated poem 'The Deserted Village' demonstrating how human intervention caused degradation of life and environment in the traditional village. This perhaps influenced some of the Bengali nationalists in the twentieth century, helping to create an emotionally melancholic and yet practically realistic perspective on the village. Nature writings had existed in English literature in varied forms manifesting historically shifting human relationships with nature, even before the overwhelming Romantic interest in it emerged in the nineteenth century. And it is quite possible that some of these literary perspectives did influence the Bengalis.[56] Alongside there were a number of strands of Indian thought too that may have influenced them. But the emotion that was their major motivation in writing about nature was surely their nationalism.

Evolution of Nationalist Attitude to Nature over the Years

Nationalism is not something static. It keeps on redefining the national identity in the changing context of conditions and events. Consequently the symbolism attached to nature shifts too. As the air of romantic sentimentality regarding rural Bengal gave way to or rather got combined with a realistic perspective, some other changes in the nationalist discourse became noticeable in the course of the twentieth century. Some of the nationalists even started conforming to the theories of their colonial masters positing a causative link between climate, race and culture.

The encounter of the early British travellers and administrators with the Indian environment was an interesting occurrence,[57] one that had implications for the colonial medicine in particular. India was seen as an exotic space, where diseases although obeying the same universal law as in Europe, appeared to function in unfamiliar and extreme ways. The idea of tropicality was at work here. Jameson's book *The Influence of Tropical Climates, More Especially the Climate of India, on European Constitutions*, published in 1813, became quite popular. Medical topography paying attention to climate, season, etc. became influential; for example, J.R. Maritn's *Notes on the Medical Topography of Calcutta* (1837). All this helped fashion a new and censorious attitude to India. This was nowhere more so than in relation to Bengal, a land of famines and epidemics, though only decades earlier it had been seen as a land of abundance. Environmental determinism was evidents particularly in the understanding of malaria. The miasmic theory was invoked and it was believed that low-grass jungles, stagnant pools, heat and moisture of the climate generated a constant supply of malaria 'poison' in the province. And it was not just a medical discourse, but a medico-ethnographical one, contending that malaria, an emasculating disease, was rendering the Bengalis weak, sickly and 'effeminate'. The Bengalis' rice diet too was held partly responsible for this.

Gradually the nationalists also started explaining the physical and mental weakness of the Bengalis in terms of nature and particularly climate, drawing upon the colonial discourse to a great extent. They internalized the environmental determinism of the colonists, emphasizing the tropicality of Indian climate generating malaria and enforcing a rice diet in seeking to explain their physical and political weaknesses. The dual idea of 'frail heroes and virile history'[58] became an important component of the nationalist discourse. Very soon it became a communal discourse as well. The Bengali Hindus were considered to be a 'dying race', whereas the Muslims of east Bengal, where malaria was less prevalent, were found multiplying. This gradually became one of the issues behind mounting communal tension in

Bengal (though in the ensuing debate, factors other than malaria, such as diet and marriage customs, were also adduced to explain the vigour of the Muslims and their advantage over Hindus). In the twentieth century this fed into negative images of the Bengal countryside.

Another important development was that the cultural movement of the romantic recovery of the nation was combined with a political nationalism from the end of the nineteenth and the beginning of the twentieth century—and for political nationalism territorial boundaries are very important. A number of poems now invoked the Himalayas and the seas on the three sides as the natural boundaries of India. These natural formations had already been there as historically validated and divinely approved cultural symbols of India. But now they clearly served a political purpose, which also facilitated the forging of a pan-Indian nation instead of a narrow Hindu one.[59] Bengal too was now defined in terms of boundaries very often. For example, this celebrated poem by Satyendranath Datta priding in the achievements of the Bengalis, started by defining Bengal in terms of her natural boundaries:[60]

> She who holds flowers of orange in her left hand
> And a garland of Mahwa in the right
> And wears the crown of Mount Kanchenjungha on her head
> With its effulgence brightening up the entire world.
> Her lap full of golden paddy and her heart full of affection,
> The ocean singing her glory in hundreds of rolling waves—
> We Bengalis live in that desired land that is Bengal.

Here thus we find mention of Assam to the east of Bengal which is a land producing oranges, and Bihar to her west which is known for abundance of Mahwa trees. The mountains in the north and the ocean in the south are mentioned too.[61]

In the nationalist literature of the Western world, both mountains and seas are often associated with freedom. The freedom-loving nature of the Swiss people fighting feudalism under leaders like William Tell has often been attributed to the mountains dominating their landscape. The sense of affinity between seas and freedom is evident in the national anthem of Britain: 'rule Britannia, rule the waves/ Britons shall never never be slaves'. This is one of the reasons why the Britons considered their navy much more effective than armies of landlocked countries like Prussia. This particular meaning of mountains and oceans, however, mostly escaped the Bengali nationalist writers.[62]

After the First World War, in the face of the powerful intrusion by the forces of modernity in rural areas, many rural people could no longer sustain themselves there and started migrating in a large number. The traditional rural life crumbled. The kind of idyllic representations of the village that had been penned earlier seemed absolutely meaningless. Yet a romantic attachment to the village still remained, now expressed in yet newer modes as evident in Bibhutibhushan Bandyopadhyay, Tarasankar Bandyopadhyay and others. However, these authors merit separate studies.

The Post-colonial Period

The post-colonial period has witnessed a shift of emphasis from nature as a source of national identity to a primordialist association between man and nature, viewing people's attachment to their habitats and their adaptation to natural surroundings as a manifestation of basic socio-psychological needs. The background to this has been provided by:

1. Partition that uprooted many people from their natural environment in the name of nation-making.

The nostalgia for *Chhere Asa Gram* (The village left behind), the psychological crisis of displacement of the East Bengal refugees, was largely related to the dense conception of natural home founded in their lived experiences there—comprising multiple rivers and trees, abundance of fish and other food, etc.[63] Manas Ray, who grew up as a refugee boy in Kolkata, beautifully says: 'The big narrative of the big nation and of big emancipation, when they came, struck us head on. We lost our smallness, our "topophilia"— the visual pleasure and sensual delight, a fondness for our place simply because we are familiar with it and it was ours.'[64]

2. Intimate forms of community fostered in the countryside coming into acute conflict with the nation-state's large-scale projects of landscape-engineering (e.g. river-linking projects, dams, etc.) and also the global transnational interventions.

Such communities are now imagined as sites of great authenticity and antiquity. It is argued that each of them has a specific relationship to nature, to the ecology and landscape of the place and thus the community's right to the place is sought to be legitimized. We thus have varying agendas, aspirations and articulations as against the central government's claims that such projects would help national integration, contribute to national prosperity, and so on. Particularistic interests embedded in local communities and claiming identities located in the unbounded time of eternity and nature, invoke visions of other possibilities—possibilities of 'conflicting nationalisms'—a variety of assertions of nationhood, denying the centrist perspectives of the nation-state.[65]

From a slightly different perspective, today nature may no longer be perceived in terms of its national contours. In this age of environmental awareness drawing upon current theories of ecology, the catastrophic effects of human intervention in natural systems has become a deep concern for all rational human beings. Nationalism seems quite unimportant therefore, compared to the grave danger of environmental disaster that our planet faces today.

Notes

1. Among a number of such works I would like to cite two early ones: Ranajit Guha, *An Indian Historiography of India: A Nineteenth Cenury Agenda and Its Implications*, S.G. Deuskar Lectures on Indian History, published by K.P. Bagchi and Company for the Centre for Studies in Social Sciences, Calcutta, 1987; and Partha Chatterjee, 'Claims on the Past', in *Subaltern Studies*, vol. III (Essays in Honour of Ranajit Guha), ed. David Arnold and David Hardiman, OUP, Delhi, 1994. Also, *The Nation and its Fragments: Colonial and Postcolonial Histories*, Princeton University Press, 1993 (there is also a later edition published by OUP, Delhi, 1997). My own work *Nationalism as Poetic Discourse in Nineteenth Century Bengal*, Papyrus, Kolkata, 1993, deals with the nationalist view of history too.
2. See Leonard W. Doob, *Patriotism and Nationalism: Their Psychological Foundations*, Yale University Press, New Haven and London, 1964, the second chapter titled 'Ingredients', the section titled 'Land'.
3. Oliver Zimmer, 'Forging the Authentic Nation: Alpine Landscape and Swiss National Identity', in *Modern Roots: Studies of National Identity*, Alain Dieckhoff and Natividad Gutierrez, eds., Ashgate Publishing Limited, Hampshire, England, 2001.
4. Many examples could be found in my book *Swajatyabodher Gan o Kabita: Unabingsha Shatabdi* (compiled and edited) published by Paschim Banga Bangla Akademi, 2012. Here is one early example—Biharilal Chakrabarty's attempt to understand his country through 'Nisargasandarshan' (this is the name of a long poem meaning careful observation of Nature) written in 1870, available in *Granthabali* (*Swargiya Kabi Biharilal Chakrabarty Birachita*), Kolkata, 1320/1913. See the sections such as 'Chinta' (Thought) and 'Samudradarshan' (Viewing the Ocean).
5. Madhusudan Datta's 'Parichay' included in his *Chaturdashpadi Kabitabali* (1866), available in *Madhusudan Granthabali*, 1st vol., Basumati Sahitya Mandir, Kolkata, n.d.
6. In his book *Pushpanjali*, 1876.
7. A familiar example is Satyendranath Tagore's song 'Mile sabe Bharatsantan' (The children of India, having been united—), a part of which thus runs: 'Which mountain can match the Himalayas?/ A land full of fruits, fertile soil and rivers, as well as great virtues/ Also, a site of hundreds of quarries of precious gems'.

Another example is Madhusudan's 'Bharatbhumi'—'Who does not covet the gem on the hood of the serpent' (included in his *Chaturdashpadi Kabitabali*).
8. See Anandachandra Mitra's poem 'Ei ki Bharat' (Is this India?), included in an anthology of patriotic poems *Jatiya Uddipana* (The national enthusiasm) printed and published by Munshi Maulabaksh Printer in 1284 BS/1877. Also Kshirodprasad Bidyabinod's 'Janmabhumi' (The land of one's birth) (*Janmabhumi*, Bhadra, 1301/1894)—'Awake, Mother! Awake! Cries out the *Vedamantra*/ Sacrifices are made to the god of fire/ The sky breaks and a sea of nectar flows out.' And it is in this way that Mother incarnated in the dream of the ancient sages. Bijaychandra Majumdar's 'Brahmabarte' (*Bharati*, Bhadra, 1310/1903) also evokes the memory of the first chanting of the *Vedamantra* by the sages at a beautiful dawn on the bank of the river Saraswati, a place that is now a desert. An anonymous poet says in a poem included in *Bangalir Gan* (The songs of the Bengali) an anthology of songs edited by Durgadas Lahiri and published in 1905—'The Aryan glory is gone, / Gone the physical prowess/ Yet the same sun and moon, the same day and night/ India, utterly helpless, weeps silently.'
9. Kamini Ray, 'Ashar Swapan', included in her book of poems *Alo o Chhaya*, 1889.
10. Included in his book of poems *Geetikabita*, 1st part, 1288/1881.
11. Also Rabindranath's song 'Bharat re tor kalankita paramanurashi' (India, your sullied atoms) included in the anthology of songs *Jatiya Sangeet*, ed. Dwarakanath Gangopadhyay in 1878—'This sky touching the Himalayas reflects the history of the ancient Hindus'. His popular song 'Oi bhubanamanomohini' (Oh, you charmer of the entire world) written in 1303 Bengali year (1896/97) mentions 'The first Sama music in your hermitage' along with the Himalayas, Jahnavai-Jamuna, etc.
12. Kumudini Basu's verse book *Abha,* Comilla, 1312/1905. Another example—Dwijendralal Ray's song 'Keno Bhagirathi hasiye hasiye chaliya jao' (Why do you flow merrily, o Bhagirathi, even on viewing the plight of India?) included in his book of verses *Aryagatha*, 1st part, 1892. An anonymous poem 'Bharatbhumi' (*Bangadarshan*, Magh 1280/1874), where nature is described as beautiful and yet the poet feels sad—'The peacocks spread their colourful wings/ on noticing the fresh clouds/ And start dancing happily/ And yet the sea of sorrow surges up.'
13. See Nabinchandra Mukhopadhyay's long poem 'Aryasangeet' included in the anthology *Jatiya Uddipana*, op. cit. The projection of the nationalist melancholy on nature can be found in many other poems. In a couple of these, the defeat at Kurukshetra is juxtaposed with the lackluster or barren nature—'Geeti ke jeno gailo' (Who sang this song?') by an anonymous poet included in the anthology *Jatiya Uddipana*, op. cit. and a poem by Jogeshchandra Chowdhury, *Bharati*, Ashwin, 1311/1904. Kurukshtra is not only the site of the defeat of the Kauravas at the hands of the Pandavas in the *Mahabharata*, but also the site of the defeat of Prithwiraj, known as the last Hindu king of India, at the hands of the Muslim invaders. In the nationalist mind, the period of India's loss of independence began from this date.
14. 'Basanta, Bharat Ki Re Chharibi Na Aar?' written by an anonymous writer (mentioned as 'Shri Ha'), *Sadharani,* 30 Phalgun 1282/1876.

15. 'Bharati Bandana' by an anonymous writer, *Bharati*, Magh 1284/1878.
16. Ramlal Chakrabarty, 'Uddipan', *Jatiya Uddipana*, op. cit. Also remember the line 'Bharatshmashan karo purna puna kokilkujita kunje' (Please fill the crematorium that is India once again with bowers resonating with the song of the kokil) in Atulprasad Sen's famous song 'Utho go Bharatalakshmi', composed in the early 1890s.
17. Harimohan Mukhopadhyay, 'Kokil', *Jatuya Uddipana*, op. cit.
18. From Rajkrishna Ray's *Abasar Sarojini*, the first 2 parts were published in 1876 and 1879 respectively, available in his *Granthabali* published later. Another similar example, where rain stands for decline—Nabinchandra Sen's 'Bangalir Bishpan' (The drinking of poison by the Bengali) (*Bangadarshan*, Kartik, 1280/1273)—'A restless wind blows/ It rains heavily/ The wind hits the heart of the person separated from his lover/Where a fire burns ceaselessly.' In this poem Nabinchandra juxtaposes the heartache of the separated lover with the agony of the subjugated Bengali.
19. Some more examples—Anandachandra Mitra pledges to capture a bird of the forest and teach it songs in praise of India (in 'Bharat jashokirtan kariye katabo e char jiban' in the anthology of songs entitled Upendranath *Sangeetkosh*, ed. Mukhopadhyay, 1896). In a poem Nabinchandra Mukhopadhyay (using the pseudonym Bhubanmohini Devi) (*Sadharani*, 17 Jyastha, 1282/1875) asks the reader not to touch the rose, for it is a flower imported from abroad. In Sibnath Sastri's 'Utsarga' (included in his book of poems *Pushpamala*, originally published in 1875, 2nd edn., 1297/1880) and Rabindranath's song 'Ekbar tora "Ma" bolia dak' ('Cry out "Ma" but once') composed in 1885, the morning sun/dawn stands for hope. In Satyendranath Datta's long poem 'Sabita' (The sun) (first published as a booklet in 1900, later included in his book of poems *Benu o Beena*, available in *Satyendra Kabyaguchchha*, Sahitya Samsad, 1984), the newly risen sun dispelling darkness symbolizes the wealth and glory of knowledge and consciousness. Similarly the setting sun often stood for the decline of India.
20. The only exception to this in the nineteenth-century Bengali literature to my knowledge was Hemchandra Bandyopadhyay's 'Bindhyagiri' (based on the popular mythological story of the Sage Agastya who before crossing the Bindhyas told the great mountain to lie low until he returned, and he never returned)(included in Hemchandra's book of poems *Kabitabali*, 2nd part, Bangiya Sahitya Parishad edn, ed. Sajanikanta Das, 1st edn., 1953; 2nd edn., 1964)—'Wake up, you great mountain—Agastya has returned; English rule dazzles the mid-day sky of India'. This poem welcomes British rule for bringing about a regeneration of India.
21. Bankimchandra's celebrated and controversial song, first published in the journal *Bangadarshan* as part of his novel *Ananda Math* in Chaitra, 1287 BS (1881). We come to know about the request of Nabinchandra Sen from the latter's autobiography *Amar Jiban*, *Nabinchandra Rachanabali*, ed. Sajanikanta Das, Bangiya Sahitya Parishad.
22. The poem titled 'Kon Deshey' written in Asadh, 1300 BS and later included in the poet's anthology *Benu o Beena*, published in 1906.
    Another example—Kaliprasanna Kabyabisharad's 'How beautiful are the flowers of my Bengal/ Tell me flowers of which foreign land can be compared

with them'. This song was included in *Swadesh Sangeet*, an anthology comp. Jogendranath Sharma. Though the book was published during the Swadeshi Movement in the first decade of the twentieth century, some of the poems seem to have been written earlier and the above one was probably one of them.

23. All included in his *Chaturdashpadi Kabitabali*, op. cit. Let me cite another sonnet from the same book. This one is entitled 'To a Bird in Spring'. The poet was in France at the time of writing it. In that predominantly cold country, there was no springtime, no cuckoo; yet the cooing of some bird evoked the mood of spring and intensely reminded the poet of his homeland—'You are not the cuckoo, famous in India,/ The messenger of Spring, whose cooing/makes millions of flowers blossom in the beautiful bower!/ Yet the way you are singing,/ You great singer, you enthrall my heart!—This country is a land of merciless and death-like *Hemanta* (the season immediately preceding winter), very wicked and painful for the mankind./—However, oh bird, you herald spring, the king of seasons, in a charming manner.' This spring is evidently related to Bengal, the poet's familiar homeland, and not to India, though it is India that is mentioned in the poem.
24. From his *Dwadash Kabita* (1872). Included in *Dinabandhu Rachanabali*, Sahitya Samsad, Kolkata, 2nd edn., November, 1981.
25. Included in an anthology entitled *Jatiya Uddiana*, op. cit. Sometimes, however, even the nature of Bengal carried the memory of Aryan glory. An anonymous poet's 'Bangabhumi Janani Amar' (Bengal, my mother), *Aryadarshan*, Ashwin 1288/1881—'The Ganga and the Brahmaputra, two streams of good fortune/ Incessantly babbles sweet songs/ Evoking the old memory of the Aryans/ Rivers provide divinity to the land they flow through/ Hundreds of such rivers flow through Bengal.'
26. The play *Shahjahan* was published in 1909. For Dwijendralal's writings see *Dwijendra Rachanabali*, vols. I and II, Sahitya Samsad, Kolkata.
27. This poem is included in Rabindranath's book of poems *Kalpana*, 1307 BS (1900). Dipesh Chakrabarty in his essay 'Nation and Imagination' included in *Provincializing Europe: Postcolonial Thought and Historical Difference*, Princeton University Press, New Jersey, 2000, has used this poem as translated in Edward Thompson's book on Rabindranath Tagore, where it thus runs—'Today, in the autumn dawn/ Did I see your lovely form/ O my mother Bengal, your green limbs glowing in stainless beauty?' In this connection, Chakrabarty has said something interesting regarding the 'mode of seeing beyond' by the nationalists, questioning the analytical reach of the category 'imagination' used by Benedict Anderson. According to Chakrabarty, in such cases as in the above poem imagination was not a subject-centred, but a subjectless practice, merely indicative of a habit of speech. Otherwise how could a poet who was not idolatrous in his personal and doctrinal belief, use the idolatrous word *murati*? I have argued with Chakrabarty at some length in my book *Nationalism as Poetic Discourse*, op. cit., and here I would do it very briefly. I would not like to take away from the nationalists the originality and uniqueness of their imagination, particularly when it produces as inspiring an image of the

motherland as in the above poem by Rabindranath. In fact, each nationalist used different elements of nature and their configurations in his/her own way to fashion and refashion this image. Of course, I am talking of sensitive visionaries like Rabindranath and not of those who tried their hands at penning nationalist poetry in a kind of stock response. Also, because this mother worship was centred mostly on nature and was a sort of secular idolatry, even Brahmos and Muslims did not feel uneasy to conform to it.

28. The first line of the song is 'Keno cheye achho go ma mukhapaney' (Why are you looking at our faces, o mother?'). It was composed in 1293 BS (1886) and later included in *Geetabitan* (in the section titled 'Jatiya Sangeet'), Visva-Bharati.

29. Such poems about Mother Bengal multiplied during the Swadeshi Movement. A few examples:
Amritalal Basu, 'Bande Mataram' from *Amritalaler Granthabali*, the chapter titled 'Gan o Kabita':

> Who says my Bangla is a destitute?
> Where else will you find such fertile soil?
> Such lovely grass and crops?
> Such sweet fruits?
> Every field of Banga is shining golden.
> Garlands of beautiful flowers adorn my mother's body.
> Boats ply in rivers and canals.
> And on these boats rides Lakshmi Herself.
> Where else will you find granary after granary filled with paddy?
> And lotus smiling in the yards of ordinary houses?
> Where else do cattle graze in every field?
> And milk tastes like nectar?
> Where is the air so pure?
> Where else does the smiling moon dispel the
> darkness of night so effectively?
> Where else is the sunrise so beautiful?

Upendranath Charabarty, 'Mago, Tore baro Bhalobasi' from his book of poems *Banglar Gan*:

> Ma, I love you deeply.
> There is no other mother like you.
> You are our smiling mother.
> The border of your sari is woven with gold and jewels.
> Your home is full of food.
> Your rivers are full of nectar.
> There is no dearth of paddy to eat.
> Cows are always milking.
> Full moon floats in the blue sky.
> Ma, our sorrow beggars description
> There is no end to our regret

That despite having a mother like you
We are living like foreigners in our own land.

Karunanidhan Bandyopadhyay, 'Kolakuli' (The embrace) from his book of poems *Bangamangal*, 2nd edn.:

Mother wears conch-shell bangles made in Dhaka,
Our mother is a pet child of indulgent parents.
Enveloping her fancy tress are clouds in several layers
Floating above the trees and plants,
Gold gleams at the parting line of her hair.

Rabindranath's famous 'Rakhi Sangeet' ('Banglar mati Banglar jal') first published in *Bhandar*, Bhadra-Aswin, 1312 (1905)—

The soil of Bengal, the water of Bengal
The air of Bengal, the fruits of Bengal
May they be sacred, o God!
The hearts of Bengalis, the souls of Bengalis
All the brothers and sisters of Bengali homes
May they be united, o God.

Another famous song by Rabindranath 'Amar sonar Bangla', first published in *Nabaparyay Bangadarshan*, Kartik, 1312, set to a *baul* tune and sung a few days before the partition of Bengal at a huge public meeting at Town Hall (later made the national anthem of Bangladesh):

My golden Bengal, I love you
Your sky, your breezes ever play through the flute of my heart.
O Mother, the fragrance of your spring mango groves drives me wild
Ah me—
O Mother, what honeyed smiles
I have seen upon your fields of late autumn.

(Translation by Clinton Seely in his *A Poet Apart: A Literary Biography of the Bengali Poet Jibananada Das (1899–1954)*, Newark University of Delaware, 1990).

The idea of beauty and bounty of nature generated the popular concept of 'sonar Bangla' (Golden Bengal) and it was regretted again and again that the foreign power was ruining this Golden Bengal, e.g. 'Gelo re sonar Bangla rasatale', a song of Mymensingh Suhrid Samiti, quoted by Soumendra Gangopadhyay in his *Swadeshi Andolan o Bangla Sahitya*, 1960.

Now an example of a Muslim poet contributing to the Swadeshi Movement—Sheikh Fajlul Karim, 'O ma! Peetabase dhaka neela tanukhani', published in the journal *Nabyabharat*. As in Rabindranath's 'Sarat', here too nature has turned into the body and clothes of the motherland. It must be noted that, at least one Muslim poet, Kaji Najrul Islam, not only used features of nature to visualize his motherland, sometimes he even juxtaposed the image of Hindu goddesses like Durga or Kali with that of the motherland. And this he did during the 1920s and 1930s. Najrul was an exception in this respect at that time. By then (particularly in the wake of the Non-Cooperation Movement) the Muslims had mostly rejected the worship of the country as mother.

The above poems responding to the Swadeshi Movement and many more are available in *Swadhinata Sangramer Gan o Kabita* (comp. and ed. myself), Sahitya Akademi, 1999.

30. Nationalism often cultivates an 'ideology of the rural'. Tricia Cusack shows in an article titled 'A "Countryside Bright with Cosy Homesteads": Irish Nationalism and the Cottage Landscape' (*National Identities*, vol. 3, no. 3, 2001) how in the newly established Irish state the national identity was not only embodied in but maintained through cottage landscape imagery in literature and paintings. A repertoire of words and images carrying sentimental meaning were created to recall people to their rural heritage. The proliferation and dissemination of such words and images rather than their selection was stressed for providing a ready-made identity to common people and producing a homogenizing effect. A picturesque landscape inhabited by quaint people, close to the soil as well as to the past, feeling primitive emotions and enjoying primitive delights, representing pre-modern ways of life and even a sort of other-worldliness, became very popular in Ireland.

31. Samantha Humphreys in her essay 'Imagining Nature: Reconstructions of the English Countryside' in *Theorizing Culture: An Interdisciplinary Critique After Postmodernism,* ed. Barbara Adam and Stuart Allan, New York University Press, Washington Square, New York, 1995, considers 'the (mis)conceptions of Nature that we can detect in discourses and ideologies of the English countryside and, specifically, in articulations of the "rural myth"'. She shows how 'urbanized and industrialized England, even now, is *recreated as a rural nation*' [emphasis in original]. This rural myth claiming the 'truer' existence of country folk is a response to the crudities of the modern age manifest in industrialization and urbanization. The countryside is presented as 'a perfect past to the imperfect present and uncertain future'. Humphreys also shows that this myth is created essentially by and for people belonging to an urban society divorced from the land. Their ideas of rurality offer a readily acceptable vision of alternative England at the very time that the nation is, in practical terms, losing its rural identity. 'The very ideas of "the natural" may themselves be *un*natural' and yet they are very useful. Those with no personal memories or experiences of the countryside can simply 'borrow from the range of cultural (re)constructions presented to them, can share in the universal (and universally available) memories and experiences on offer.'

32. Tagore wrote 'Du Bigha Jami' around 1895 while travelling in East Bengal as a zamindar. Quoted by Dipesh Chakrabarty in 'Nation and Imagination', op. cit.

33. 'Amra chash kari anande' (Happily do we grow crops) was included in his play *Achalayatan* published in book form in 1318 BS (1911) after being serialized in the journal *Prabasi*. It is available in *Rabindra Rachanabali*, vol. 11, Visva-Bharati.

Another similar example—Sasankamohan Sen, 'Shailo Sangeet', *Bandhav*, agrahayan 1309. But Sen's poem is a bit different too, for here it is not a plains village, but a hilly one that is being celebrated. And this is surely an exception for the nationalist literature of those days—'My Motherland, o my mother/ Thy uneven lap strewn with pebbles/—the dawn comes, the cascade sings/ Unexpected fragrance of flowers emanates from the bower.' Here we have such lines as—'The peaceful and hardworking peasant and his wife,/ The heat and then the first shower of the monsoon—/ On seeing their sacred cottage, tears well up in my eyes.'

34. Dipesh Chakrabarty, 'Memories of Displacement: The Poetry and Prejudice of Dwelling', in *Habitations of Modernity: Essays in the Wake of Subaltern Studies*, Permanent Black, Delhi, 2002
35. The monthly *Grambartaprakashika* was published by Harinath Majumdar (popularly known as Kangal Harinath) from 1863. Later it became a fortnightly and then a weekly priced at one paisa. It protested against the oppression of the indigo planters, British bureaucrats as well as native zamindars. Ultimately it stopped publication due to financial reason and government repression. (From the entry 'Kangal Harinath', in *Samsad Bangali Charitabhidhan* (4th. revd edn.), vol. 1, Sahitya Samsad, Kolkata, 1998.
36. Compiled in *Galpaguchchha* published by Visva-Bharati.
37. Chakrabarty's 'Nation and Imagination', ibid.
38. Included in his book of poems *Hasi Halla* published sometime in the 1920s.
39. Included in his book of poems *Raktarekha*, 1924 and later in his *Kabyasanchay*. Earlier he had published another book of poems, the very name of which indicates its contents—*Pallibyatha* (The agony of the village), 1327. Hemendrakumar Ray's 'Smasanbasir Abedan'(The plea of someone residing in a cemetery), published in *Bijali*, 20 Aswin, 1330, was written in the same spirit. Several more examples can be cited.
40. Title of the poem is 'Janmabhumi (Pallichhabi)', published in *Bharati*, Ashadh, 1316.
41. In Bangiya Sahitya Parishat alone I have found about 30 journals concerned exclusively with rural reconstruction, published during the 1920s and some of them into the 1930s.
42. The poems of *Rupasi Bangla* were originally written during the 1920s and 1930s. But they were published posthumously in 1957.
43. Jasimuddin's most famous book of poems is *Naksi Kanthar Math*, published by Gurudas Chattopadhyay & Sons, Kolkata, 1st edn., 1336 BS (1929).
44. Apart from those already mentioned, there is Rangalal Ray's poem 'Pallibhavane' (Abar asinu phire/ Janani tomar kole'), *Prabasi*, Paush, 1313, for example. Chakrabarty says that a 'compromise between the two images of the Bengal village—the idyllic pastoral haunt of the nationalist imagination and the fallen social space calling for national reform—was reached in Bibhutibhushan Bandyopadhyay's famous novel *Pather Panchali*' ('Memories of Displacement', op. cit., p. 131).
45. S. Kappen, *Tradition Modernity Counterculture: An Asian Perspective*, Visthar, Bangalore, 1994, the chapter entitled 'Vedic Orientations for a Relevant Ecosophy'.

46. Schiller's celebrated categorization of human attitude to nature, used by Bose. See Buddhadev Basu, *Kalidaser Meghdoot* (translation and introduction by Basu), M.C. Sarkar and Sons Pvt. Ltd., first published, 1957, 7th edn., 2000.
47. Bose stresses the constructedness and artificiality of classical Sanskrit writings, which, according to him, became too evident in their stress on ornamentation (in Sanskrit *Rasa Shastra* and *Alamkar Shastra* were the same), use of typical imageries, analogies and so on. And they involved considerable repetitions too. Bose thus explains it—the classical writers were rich and honourable court poets patronized by the rulers. They enjoyed enough security and a lot of leisure. Hence perhaps their inclination towards sophistication and decorativeness.
48. Nationalists have sometimes attributed a sort of geographical nationalism to *Meghdutam* because of its description of the long stretch of landscape from Ramgiri to Alaka. Basu has also mentioned this.
49. The essay entitled 'Shakuntala' in *Prachin Sahitya*, available in *Rabindra Rachanabali*, vol. 5, Visva-Bharati, Kolkata, 1966.
50. 'Sarthak janam amar' was composed during the Swadeshi period. Included in *Geetabitan* as well as *Rabindra Rachanabali*, both published by Visva-Bharati.
51. For the incident see Sumit Sarkar, *The Swadeshi Movement in Bengal, 1905–1908*, PPH, Delhi, 1973.
52. Rosinka Chaudhuri in her *Gentlemen Poets in Colonial Bengal: Emergent Nationalism and Orientalist Project* (Seagull, Calcutta, 2002) shows the unmistakable influence of the English Romantic poets on the poets of nineteenth-century Bengal writing in English, despite the nationalist content of the latter's writings. The Romantic (and its derivative Orientalist) influence can be seen from Derozio and the circle around him to Michael Madhsudan Datta to the Dutt family of Calcutta. In *The Dutt Family Album*, some poems were self-consciously modelled on Romantic poetry, often with a particular poet in mind. Indian landscapes were sometimes described like English countryside. Chaudhury rightly says that eminent poets writing exclusively in Bengali also 'borrowed from some of the same sources the Dutts had used, as Sir Walter Scott and James Tod' (p. 151).
53. Numerous examples can be found in my forthcoming book (compiled and edited) *Swajatyabodher Gan o Kabita: Unabingsha Shatabdi*, to be published by Paschim Banga Bangla Akademi.
54. See Malini Bhattacharya and Anasuya Ghosh, eds., *Romanticism in Bengal 1881–1922: An Anthology of Articles from Bangla*, Papyrus, Kolkata, 2003. It appears from this book that till the 1880s the Romantic poets occupied a small space in the academic curriculum of Bengal, despite Richardson's anthology including some of them. People like Michael Madhusudan were influenced more by the epical style of the West than by Romanticism. But this model soon failed and the Romantic poets gained ground in the Bengali mind. The neglect of Romanticism was vigorously compensated from the 1880s onwards. An enormous intellectual excitement was generated in Bengal by the Romantic poets from the 1880s. This was precisely the time when the nationalist sentiment was intensifying too. Rabindranath was the foremost among the nationalist writers who welcomed Romanticism as a tool for liberation from all oppression. He wrote a number of poems from the 1880s to the 1920s using

Romanticism as an agent of freedom from the stifling situation. He extensively used the romantic trope of self-destruction as a means of renewal of life, vide his poems 'Duranta Asha', 'Jhulan', 'Ebar Phirao More'. In his 1922 article on Shelley, even at a time when anti-colonial movement had reached a critical point, he asserted the need for Indians to claim a common heritage with Shelley. Rabindranath seemed to say that the inequity enforced by the colonial situation made Shelley closer to the colonized rather than to the colonizer and he sought inspiration from Shelley on behalf of Indians to stand up in rebellion against the colonial masters.

However, as the above book also shows, the Bengali response to English Romanticism was not one of uncritical admiration. Apart from the reservations about the Romantics inherent in Victorian literary culture, which was very influential in the Bengali mind, indigenous conservatism too found much to condemn in Romanticism—its individualistic excesses, shameless defiance of all established norms, libertarianism, etc. It was branded as effeminate too (Keats, for example, was found very sensitive and delicate, and lacking in male strength) and the emergent nationalist consciousness in India attached a very special value to maleness. Critics also found Romanticism disturbing, because its sources were foreign and because it involved incursion of Western values. The nationalist consciousness was suspicious of Romanticism as a creed of hypersensitivity that might only have an enervating effect on the colonized. Being quite conservative in their social attitudes and very pro-British too, the Bengali nationalists did not always like the socio-political content of Romanticism. While they adored Rousseau and Shelley as 'children of nature', they had an objective nature in mind and not the broader philosophical dimension of the naturalness of the Romantics which had made the latter transgress and reject constructed social norms and assert the autonomy of the human self alone. But at least the Romantic fascination for objective nature, if not for nature as innate qualities of human beings, found it easy to inspire the Bengali mind. And this is important for our discussion.

55. Dipesh Chakrabarty, 'Memories of Displacement', op. cit.
56. See Bridget Keegan and James McKusick, eds., *Literature and Nature: Four Centuries of Nature Writing*, Prentice-Hall, New Jersey, 2001.
57. David Arnold has discussed this in detail in *New Cambridge History of India: Science, Technology and Medicine in Colonial India*, Cambridge, 2000.
58. Indira Chaudhuri, *The Frail Hero and Virile History: Gender and the Politics of Culture in Colonial Bengal*, Oxford University Press, New Delhi, 1998, paperback 2001.
59. As Dudley Stamp says, 'There are perhaps few parts of the world better marked off by nature as a region or a "realm" by itself than the Indian subcontinent', qtd. B.N. Mukherjee in *The Foreign Names of the Indian Subcontinent, Place Names Society of India*, Mysore, 1989, p. 1. This is indeed to the advantage of India as a politically bounded territorial nation. But nationalism in its earliest phase did not find this important enough, as this nationalism was then not so much interested in a territorial definition of the nation as much as it was preoccupied with forging a close-knit community based on a strong internal

principle traceable in history, and this it did by instituting the nation on a Hindu-Aryan foundation. Later, of course, in every school textbook of geography and history, India and Indianness came to be defined primarily in terms of the boundaries provided by the Himalayas in the north and the seas on the other three sides. The natural boundaries seemed particularly important for the independent nation-state of India.

60. The poem 'Amra Bangali' included in his book of poems *Kuhu o Keka* published in 1912. It is available in Dr. Alok Ray, ed., *Satyendra Kabyaguccha*, Sahitya Samsad, Kolkata, 1984.
61. But of course boundaries can be contested too. Questions like whether Chittagong belonged to Bengal or Arakan, i.e. whether Alaol was a Bengali poet or not, often intrigued Bengali intellectuals. A question of a similar nature in relation to India was whether Afghanistan belonged to India.
62. Though William Tell is said to have inspired Subhas Chandra Bose, who quoted him sometimes.
63. Dakshinaranjan Basu, comp. and ed., *Chhere Asa Gram* (The village left behind), Jugantar, Calcutta, 1975. Earlier these writings had been serialized in the newspaper *Jugantar*. Dipesh Chakrabarty's essay 'Memories of Displacement' mentioned above is basically a critique of this book.
64. Manas Ray, 'Growing up as a Refugee Boy in a Colony', in *Refugees in West Bengal: Institutional Processes and Contested Memoirs*, Pradip Bose, ed., Calcutta, 2000.
65. See Gunnel Cederlof and K. Sivaramakrishnan, eds., *Ecological Nationalisms: Nature, Livelihoods and Identities in South Asia,* Permanent Black, Delhi, 2005.

CHAPTER FOUR

The Radical Rabindranath: 'The Red Oleanders (*Rakta Karabi*)' and Dreams of a New World

CHHANDA CHATTERJEE

Tagore's drama *Rakta Karabi* (The Red Oleanders) which was written in 1923 after having gone through nine different drafts,[1] seemed for many to carry a message of revolution. Tagore had significantly opted for the 'crimson tint'[2]—not the gardenia, tuberose or white jasmine—but only the red oleanders, for 'in that red there is not only beauty, but also the fascination of fear'.[3] Years later Tagore confided to his colleague and close associate Kshitimohan Sen[4] the reason for this preference. In the course of his engagement with the many revisions of this drama in his Santiniketan home 'Uttarayan', he suddenly chanced upon a red flower obdurately trying to assert its proud existence through a heap of discarded building materials. This chance encounter immediately settled the dilemma about nomenclature in Tagore's mind and he made the *Rakta Karabi* the predominant symbol of his protest against capitalism and its handmaiden, imperialism, as also the concentration of wealth, mechanization and the dehumanization of labour. *Rakta Karabi* is thus regarded as Tagore's endorsement of the beginning of a new era, ushered by the proletarian revolution in Russia, when the downtrodden would no longer continue to submit meekly to their fate. Like the workers in the 'city of the Jinn (Yaksha Town)' they would also break into the prison and unfurl the flag of rebellion.

Tagore's critique of Western imperialism, however, was not a new thing; it began to appear in his writings long before the close of the nineteenth century. As early as 1881 he could perceive the evil effects of Britain's forcible export of opium to China to pay for the tea and silk that was much in demand in the European markets, subsequently he published an article called 'Death Traffic in China' by way of a review of an English translation of a German book.[5] The turn of the century saw a poetic despair at 'the naked passion of self-love of Nations, in its drunken delirium of greed',[6] manifested in the atrocities connected with the suppression of the Boxer Rebellion in China and the Boer War of 1898 that provoked the sonnets 64, 65 and 66 in *Naivedya* (1902).[7] Tagore's initial enthusiasm for nationalist resistance to Lord Curzon's partition of Bengal in 1905 evaporated fast as news of the unfavourable response from the poor Muslim cultivators in his zamindari estates in East Bengal began to reach him. The latter reacted strongly against forcible boycott of cheap foreign mill-made cloths by city-dwelling anti-Partition agitators. Revulsion turned into horror at the violent turn Swadeshi began to assume. He wrote his *Path O Patheya* (Ways and Means) on 25 May 1908—a month after a terrorist assassination of several Europeans—ridiculing the psychology behind such misdirected heroism.[8] Such violent expressions of nationalism were found to be antithetic to the pluralistic traditions of India, or 'illegitimate' as Ashis Nandy has termed it.[9]

Faith in the strength of the spirit as against brute force found expression in his *Reminiscences* composed in 1912 (tr. Surendranath Tagore in 1917 from *Jibansmriti*), where he spoke of the greater force of 'indomitable mind and spirit' in modern times while physical flesh and size predominated in the antediluvian age which belonged to the dead past.[10] The same theme recurred in his later correspondence with C.F. Andrews and Amiya Chakravarty, where he tried to demonstrate the inefficacy of huge machines and fatal weapons on which Western nation-states had based their strength. He wrote to Andrews in a letter dated 19 December 1920 that creation had begun with huge animal specimens with huge tails. But such species later disappeared and man was created naked and small. Similarly 'ambitions, that rely solely upon the suggestion of their tail and armour are condemned to carry their own obstruction till they have to stop'.[11] These ideas recurred in his mind till his last days, and in a letter of 20 June 1940 to Amiya Chakravarty, he went back to the same analogy of huge animals with claws and armours, who had made their exit from the face of earth long ago. The menacing postures of world powers in their battle array reminded him of those prehistoric creatures, who failed to survive the test of time. Tagore, however, refused to believe that such brute force was to get the better of human civilization and he hoped to see the ultimate triumph of moral power.[12] In his Santiniketan lectures also, some of which had been collected and published by Andrews as *Thoughts from Rabindranath Tagore* in 1929, Tagore pointed out the error of trying to measure Power by its quantity or bulk. 'Arithmetic will never serve to make true that which is untrue' and whenever the harmony of the universe was disturbed, the result was sheer destruction like the toppling over of the Tower of Babel. The source of real power was 'peace which rests on truth and consists in curbing of greed, in the forgiveness of sympathy'.[13]

Writing of revolution in a colonized country was not an easy task. Tagore's early involvement in the anti-Partition agitation, his *Rakhibandhan Utsav* to rally the Hindus and the Muslims in a united struggle to oppose the measure had made the colonial police extremely uneasy. Even after his later disillusionment with Swadeshi and its violent expressions in sporadic terrorist attacks on Europeans, Tagore could not escape suspicion and surveillance. His withdrawal to Santiniketan to concentrate on his school did not allay the suspicion of authorities and J.H. Kerr, Secretary to the Government of Bengal, issued a circular on 22 July 1912 in the name of the Lieutenant Governor of Eastern Bengal and Assam forbidding all government servants from sending their wards to Tagore's school in Bolpur.[14] This was probably the reason for the scant reference to the unprecedented occurrence of 1917 in Russia in Tagore's writings. He could only make veiled references to the hopes and enthusiasm ignited in his mind by this watershed event. While the imperialist wars fought by European nations all over the world had no moral ideals to draw upon, Russia was seen by Tagore as 'giving expression to man's indomitable soul against prosperity built upon moral nihilism'.[15] Gnatyuk Danil'Chuk interpreted this as 'aesopean language'[16] to escape censor from colonial authorities. The little that Tagore wrote on the new experiment in Russia reflected his high hopes from this great leap forward in human history. The birth of this new ideology in Russia, which charted out an alternative path of development, was endowed with the same significance in the poet's mind as the birth of a new prophet: 'The world is waiting for the birth of the child, who believes more than he knows, who is to be the crowned King of the future, who will come amply supplied with provisions for his daring adventures in the moral world, for his explorations in the region of man's inner being.'[17]

The early years of the Soviet experiment were neither very smooth nor very successful. Yet whatever little information filtered into this country through colonial censors was enough to promise the ushering of a new age for Tagore: 'If she fails with the flag of true ideals in her hands, then her failure will fade, like the morning star, only to usher in the sunrise of a New Age.'[18]

In *Rakta Karabi* Tagore wanted to speak of a new dawn when the workers in the city of the Jinn (Yaksha Town) would respond to the magic of life embodied in the girl Nandini and try to break out of their prison cells. Nandini was constantly talking about her companion Ranjan, who stood for the promise of a new life and both of them were wedded together by the tinge of red of which the flower *Rakta Karabi* stood as a symbol. In his *Paschim Yatrir Diary* (Diary of the Westward Traveller) Tagore tried to explain the message contained in the *Rakta Karabi*. In Tagore's perception, men become mechanized and dehumanized when their efforts lose all contact with life, of which the woman is only a symbol. Such men can only oppress and be oppressed by the machine they had created. In the ghost town, where the tunnel-diggers were constantly digging out gold nuggets from the bosom of the earth, men had forgotten that the joy of life is more precious than wealth. They had lost all contact with the universe and had taken shelter behind iron wires. They had forgotten that fulfilment lay in love and not in the domination of the world. Into this prison Nandini entered like a whirlwind calling men back to life. The drama reached its climax when the inspiration from the woman woke up the men and made them break the prison walls to respond to this call of life.[19]

This Yaksha Town stood in Tagore's imagination for the materialism of the west and capitalist accumulation. Tagore had spoken against such pursuit of profit to the exclusion of morality, which had brought the world to the threshold of degeneration and destruction in his 'Construction vs. Creation' written in 1920: 'With the help of science the possibility of profit has suddenly become immoderate. The whole of human society throughout its length and breadth has felt the gravitational pull of a giant planet of greed with its concentric rings of innumerable satellites. It has carried to our society a distinct deviation from its moral orbit, its mental balance being upset and its aspirations brought down to the dust.'[20]

The proliferation of luxuries and increasing use of machines did not indicate progress in Tagore's perception. His definition of progress could not do without an all round development of the human personality. 'I believe in life only when it is progressive, and in progress only when it is in harmony with life', Tagore had said.[21] The Yaksha Town in the Red Oleanders had exhausted all its energies in retrieving the dead wealth of the underworld and lost all contact with life in the process. Tagore found it to be 'a city under eclipse. The Shadow Demon, who lives in the gold caves, has eaten into it. It is not the whole itself, neither does it allow anyone to remain whole'.[22]

The rigorous routine of this ghost town exhausted all the energies of its tunnel diggers, so much so, that they were huddled together in shanty towns with no thoughts for their comfort or social life. As one worker in the ghost town put it, 'We are closely fitted to their profits only—like husks to grains of corn—with nothing of us left over.'[23] They were wrenched from their homes and robbed of all the freedom and comfort that their homes offered, leading them to acknowledge poignantly, that 'The road to our home is closed for ever' the tunnel diggers knew, 'our homes don't yield them any profit'.[24] For the capitalist does not worry about the fullness of life for his labourers. For him the workers represent only the work they can put in. The workers' demands for the necessaries of life appear to be an unnecessary tax for the investor of capital; in their eyes the workers were no better than sacrificial lambs, fit only to be butchered: 'Our mad Bishu says to remain whole is useful only for the lamb itself; those who eat it prefer to leave out its horns and hooves and even object to its bleating when butchered.'[25]

When the workers are robbed of the soothing touch of nature, the warmth of sunshine and the pleasures of their hearth, they turn to the artificial amusement of alcohol. As Bishu, the madcap puts it: 'For me nature's own ration of spirits is stopped; so my inner nature craves for the wine of the market place. . . . No open sky no leisure for us; so we have distilled the essence of all the song and laughter, all the sunlight of the twelve hours' day into one draught of liquid fire.'[26]

There was no escape from this Yaksha Town that Tagore had painted, as the curious thing about the matter was that the workers themselves had lost the will to return. They were tied to the pull of the city 'like a caged bird to its cage, hankering for its drugged food'.[27]

Images of such a mechanized and therefore, dehumanized society springing up as a result of the selfish use of science by capitalistic states recur in many other writings of Tagore. In one of his essays of 1930, the 'Meeting of the East and the West' he tried to elaborate his views: 'The civilization of the West today has its law and order, but no personality. It has come to the perfection of a mechanical order but what is there to humanize it? It is the person who is in the heart of all beings. When you follow the atoms, you come to something which has no form, no colour. It is all abstraction; it is reduced to some mathematical formulae. But personality goes beyond the heart of these atoms.'[28]

This was the argument dramatized by the Professor in Red Oleanders in the form of a question to Nandini, the symbol of life: 'Can blocks of gold ever answer to the swinging rhythm of your arms in the same way as fields of corn?'[29]

The 'King' of this drama is always insulated from the world by iron wires, to indicate a divide between the ruler and the ruled. This was probably an oblique reference to the Crown representing the colonies beyond the seas. Tagore had already mentioned in a letter to W.W. Pearson of the evil effects of this isolation of the ruler from the ruled: 'They are fully aware that they do not know us and yet they do not care to know us. And in consequence, thorny hedges are springing up of unscrupulous intermediaries between the rulers and the ruled, giving rise to conditions which are not only miserable, but unspeakably vulgar.'[30]

The King's confession to Nandini of how bankrupt he had become inwardly beneath the menacing aspect of his mask of power ('The flaming thirst of this desert licks up one fertile field after another only to enlarge itself—it can never annex the life of the frailest of grasses'[31]) was merely a dramatic rendition of Tagore's impression of the western world during his visit to the United States: 'What makes me feel so sad, in this country, is the fact that people here do not know they are not happy. They are proud, like the sandy desert, which is proud of its glitter. This Sahara is mightily big.'[32]

The contradictions between the fiat of giant commercial organizations supported by selfish nation-states, trying to annex the weaker nations as their colonies, and the higher ideals of humanity had struck Tagore even earlier. 'The conflict between man and woman, between master and dependent, between neighbours has become uncontrollable,' he postulated, 'because the bonds of human relationship have snapped or become loose.'[33]

The gaps created by the absence of human warmth could not be filled by the marvels of science for, science, though impressive, was impersonal. As Tagore put it: 'The real truth is that science is not man's nature, it is mere knowledge and training. By knowing the laws of material universe you do not change your deeper humanity. You can borrow knowledge from others, but you cannot borrow temperament.'[34]

The higher end of science, according to Tagore, was the alleviation of human suffering. But science deviates from its true mission when it becomes an instrument of personal gain and attainment of selfish power. Acts which are considered to be criminal, if performed by an individual, would be glorified as 'patriotism and nationality' when perpetrated under the label of nationalism. It marked the relationship of the strong with the weak by 'repression and restriction' and had allowed 'the wholesale feeding of nation upon nation'[35] while the relationship of nations, who were on an equal footing, was marked by 'vengefulness and competition'.[36] Ashis Nandy has analysed the psychology of such insensitivity to the deprivation and exploitation of colonized nations as 'the mechanomorphic view of nature and society' which is achieved by the splitting of cognition and effect, termed by Sigmund Freud as 'isolation'.[37] The colonized were looked upon not as fellow human beings, but as things, and the question of their health, drinking water and hygiene could therefore be relegated to the background. In his *Letters From Russia* Tagore had drawn attention to this kind of psychology on the part of the colonizers in his own country,

To the greedy the humanity of the object of greed loses its reality; it becomes natural to minimise its demands. India has grown small in the estimation of those with whom her lot has been cast for a century and half. That is why the authorities have remained indifferent to her vital needs. They have never taken much interest in the food that is available to the people, in the water we have to drink; the abysmal lack of our educational facilities do not worry them. For, the important thing is that we are necessary for them; that we also have our necessities, is unimportant.[38]

In his 'Nation' in *Creative Unity* Tagore spoke of this struggle between 'the living spirit of the people and the methods of nation organising'. The immediate prospects of material benefit associated with the 'cult of the Nation' gain new converts for this doctrine among other peoples as well, giving rise to 'conflicts of interest and jealousy' and 'increasing pride in their own race and hatred of others'. Selfishness, being a necessity for the attainment of such goals, becomes a virtue.[39]

Ultimately a time would come when the creator himself would lose command of this Frankenstein. In 'Nationalism in the West' in fact, Tagore foresaw such a situation 'when it can stop no longer, for the competition grows keener, organization grows vaster, and selfishness attains supremacy. Trading upon the greed and fear of man, it occupies more and more space in society, and at last becomes its ruling force'.[40] The same fear was expressed by Tagore in his letter to Andrews in December 1920 when he spoke of those commanding material resources having become 'slaves of their own instruments'.[41] This had been the lament of the King in *Rakta Karabi* when he spoke of his own instrument defying him.

Tagore's familiarity with the trappings of Western materialism had revealed to him the hollowness of its mask of power. Thus in his address to Japan in 1916 he spoke of the path of suicide being followed by Western nations:

The lumbering structure of modern progress, riveted by the iron bolt of efficiency, which runs upon the wheels of ambition, cannot hold together for long. Collisions are certain to occur; for it has to travel upon organized lines, it is too heavy to choose its course freely; and once it is off the rails, its endless train of vehicles is dislocated. A day will come when it will fall in a heap of ruin and cause serious obstruction to the traffic of the world.[42]

The King of *Rakta Karabi* too had said that 'overgrown power crushes itself inwardly by its own weight'.[43]

Capitalism and its offshoot imperialism sometimes used the camouflage of religion to sustain its massive edifice of exploitation. In Red Oleanders Tagore introduced the character of the Gossain (the pastor) who had been entrusted with the work of quelling unrest among the workers. The conversation of the *Gossain* and the Governor revealed the close collusion between the priest, the soldiers and the bureaucrat for extracting the fruits of the labour of the workers. Some of Tagore's early poems also foreshadowed his awareness of this abuse of religion to serve the purpose of capitalism. Poem no. 112 in his collection 'Poems' published by Macmillan contained derisive references to the gathering 'in their prayer-halls in a pious garb' and how 'in their roaring mingles the music of their hymns'.[44]

The Gossain in the Red Oleanders referred to the workers as the 'Sacred Tortoise of our scripture, that held up the sinking earth on its back'. He could not help admitting that the entire production system sustaining the structure of capitalism and its alter ego, imperialism was supported by the labour of the workers. 'Because they meekly suppress themselves underneath their burden,' as he put it, 'the upper world can keep its head aloft'.[45] But Tagore had also hinted that the workers had been waking up to the call of the new age and the Gossain spoke of the transformation of the Sacred Tortoise into the new incarnation of the Wild Boar mentioned in the ancient scriptures, which knew how to attack the perpetrators of its miseries. This rejuvenation could only come through Ranjan, 'who can put a beating heart behind these dead ribs'.[46] Ranjan was the new message and Nandini, the secret of life, and together they could bring to life the workers in the Yaksha Town who had become nameless numbers. *Rakta Karabi* ends in the marriage of Ranjan and Nandini, when the message of revolution could unite with the flow of life, leaving a trail of red—the colour of blood, the colour of revolution and the colour of the Red Oleanders.

The language of the drama became a bold and open statement during Tagore's visit to Russia in 1930,

The important thing is that to-day suffering humanity has a nobler vision of itself on the world stage than before, for in the past they saw themselves in isolation, they were unaware of their real power and relying on Fate they endured everything. To-day even in their utter helplessness people conjure up the Kingdom of Heaven where oppression disappears and humiliation is no more. For this very reason oppressed humanity is in revolt everywhere.

... Inordinate power cannot thrive against utter helplessness: had not the mighty been intoxicated with their own power, what they would fear most is the exaggeration of inequality, because all disharmony is opposed to the law of the universe.[47]

Tagore had been aware of the Russian proposals for the cessation of war at Brest-Litovsk and her subsequent interest in disarmament of the world. Haunted by memories of the First World War and alarmed by the rumblings of yet another such war, he wanted to mobilize the power of the proletariat all over the world against the war mongering of the capitalist world. 'The time is come for us,' he declared, 'to proclaim that there is no salvation for man if the power of the weak is not awakened at once.'[48]

The dawn of the new age would not allow the intellectual 'to burrow day and night in a mass of yellow pages'[49] and the Professor of the Red Oleanders would also be dragged out of his life of an insect in a hole. In his person Tagore had tried to create a caricature of the colonial system of education, which 'kills initiative and ability for work'. The purpose of such education was to turn out clerks for the East India Company's mercantile establishment in India. Such people had not much practical knowledge beyond their books and had no sympathy for the toiling classes. In fact no one in India gave much thought to organizing the masses or undertaking any constructive work for their benefit. The cooperative movement in India could not go beyond advancing loans to the cultivators and collecting interests from them. The Indian National Congress was merely a group of educated men of such genre, who remained 'tied to the pen' and could not think of any better outlets than 'plaintive outbursts' in political platforms and newspaper articles. 'It never occurs to us clearly that it is possible to do anything for those,' Tagore spelt out categorically, 'whom we cannot see in the darkness.'[50]

In the Red Oleanders Tagore made both the King and the Professor come out of their enclosures to respond to the call of life when the workers broke the prison walls. The dream that Tagore had dramatized in 1923 appeared as a reality in the Soviet system of spreading education among the masses. This had been made possible, as the aim of this education was to spread consciousness among the masses. Even peasants from the underdeveloped and desert areas of Turkomenistan were brought under its pale. They were thus able to get rid of their religious superstitions which had accounted for the frequent outbreak of riots between the Christians and the Jews during the Tsarist regime. Only a proper education in India, Tagore felt, would be able to tackle the evil of communalism and Hindu-Muslim ill-feelings prevalent at the time in India. The colonial regime in India wanted to keep the subjects divided so as to be able to perpetuate their mastery over them. But the outlook in Soviet Russia was different, Tagore argued, as there was not this 'barrier of greed'.[51]

In a speech delivered at the *Dom Soyuzov* on 24 September 1930 Tagore laid down clearly that the primary need of the country was to develop a proper system of education, which was the prerequisite of the ultimate programme of nation-building. 'My mission in life is education', Tagore told the *Dom Soyuzov*, 'and I believe that all the human problems will find their fundamental solution in education. And outside my own vocation as a poet I have accepted this responsibility to educate my people as much as lies in my power to do.'[52] Instead of remaining lost in the world of poetry and imagination, the intellectual could play a much more active role among the masses by trying to rouse consciousness in them and teaching them to break out of the prison walls of torture and exploitation. 'Our poverty, pestilence, the communal fights and industrial backwardness, in fact all that makes our life perilous,' Tagore emphasized, 'are owing to the meagreness of education.'[53]

Taking perhaps a cue from the Professor of the Red Oleanders Tagore too 'emerged from the loneliness of a literary worker, entered into society and began to help my compatriots'.[54] The people in India lived on the verge of famine and did not know how to get out of the situation because of their loss of faith and confidence 'in their own humanity'.[55]

Prolonged exploitation by colonial masters had undermined the courage of the peasants and they had lost the will to seek a way out of their distress which could have been expected of a strong and organized race of men. As a predominantly agricultural country like the Soviet Union in the 1930s when Tagore had visited that country, India too needed the knowledge of 'up to date methods of producing crops in order to meet the increasing demands of life'.[56] Craftsmen needed to be educated in the use of machines as 'the skill and methods of production on which the livelihood of craftsmen depended in the past have become obsolete owing to the competition of machinery'.[57] Among Asian countries Japan was quick to perceive the changes that had come in with respect to the techniques of production, as also clever enough to master them to keep pace with the new age. But in India there was no effort to bring the country up to date with the innovations of the modern age as the colonial government was apathetic to the country's priorities and 'water on this side evaporates into rain-clouds to pour down on the land beyond the seas'. The primary interest of the government was in siphoning off the agricultural surplus of the country and carrying it to their own country for investing it in the improvement of the metropolitan country. Thus, while the colonizing country was able to take advantage of the latest discoveries of science in their own country, the colonized country was starved of the necessary capital for investment in infrastructural and industrial development. This is precisely what had provoked Rabindranath to make such a comment.[58]

It appeared to Rabindranath that 'under modern civilization the human personality seems to exist in a kind of cage, cut off from the rest of society'.[59] Tagore saw the school as an 'indivisible part of life itself', believing that whatever lessons young minds learn, they should essentially be drawn from the usual rhythm of life. Tagore's own childhood experience had informed him of the oppressive and unimaginative methods of education in the city. When the teachers in the city school 'failed utterly to understand the soul of a child', as Tagore put it, 'they punished us for their own sins'.[60]

Tagore believed in a system of inclusive education where the city does not turn its face away from the village. In an article of 1924 titled the 'City and the Village' he said that man was 'digging holes into the very foundations of his life' when he was neglecting the village.[61] The contradictions between the city and the village were like the contradictions between *Kuvera* and *Lakshmi,* the former symbolizing mindless accumulation, while the latter stood for even distribution.[62] Such an attitude also resulted in concentration of wealth which was antithetical to democracy. Under such a dispensation the rich and the wealthy often tended to influence public opinion by controlling the media and capturing the public organizations in order to satisfy their own personal ambitions.[63]

Tagore would have liked a steady exchange between the city and the village where the rich would take pleasure in devoting their wealth for the public good. He wrote in his *Letters From Russia,*

In the old days, at any rate in our country, pomp of wealth consisted mainly in philanthropy and other social services, while now it consists in personal enjoyment. It dazzles, but does not please: it causes envy but raises no praise. The main thing is that in those days the use of wealth did not depend on the wish of the donor alone; it was subject to the strong pleasure of social will. Hence the benefactor had to make his gift humbly; the maxim *sraddhya deyam,* 'give reverently' held good.[64]

Tagore would have liked to go back to the ideals of social life which ensured a constant traffic between the rich and the poor instead of their aggressive confrontation as two mutually hostile classes. Instead of having recourse to revolutions and turning the world upside down, he would prefer a harmonious existence where each section of society would be able to look to the other for mutual sustenance. This was the kind of ideal put forward by him in his 'Wealth and Welfare',

In former days, in India, public opinion levied heavy taxes upon wealth and most of the public works of the country were voluntarily supported by the rich. Water supply, medical help, education and amusement were naturally maintained by men of property through a spontaneous adjustment of mutual obligation. This was made possible because the limits set to the individual right of self-indulgence were narrow, and the surplus wealth easily followed the channel of social responsibility. In such a society, property was the pillar that supported its civilisation and wealth gave opportunity to the fortunate for self-sacrifice.[65]

The Red Oleanders represented Tagore's protest against the use of men by men and 'the use of every variety of machinery to fortify themselves or their selfish ends against the dissolving power of beauty and love'. The King was divided from his people by 'the trust, the company, stocks and shares, investment machinery through which they can avoid all human connection'.[66] What Tagore essentially wanted, was the personality of man to assert itself through this 'gigantic system' like a fresh bunch of Red Oleanders.

Notes

1. Sankha Ghosh, *Rakta Karabi: Kayekti Tathya*, in *Urbashir Hashi,* Papyrus, 3rd edn., 2003, pp. 146–98; Tagore himself in a letter to Amiya Chakravarty dated

11 October 1923 mentioned drafting and redrafting the drama *Nandini,* as it was originally known, before finally putting it on the stage. Letter No. 26 in Rabindranath Tagore, *Chithipatra,* Visva-Bharati, 1st pub. BS 1381, repr. 1417, vol. 11, pp. 36–7.
2. Rabindranath Tagore, *The Red Oleanders* in Sisir Kumar Das, ed., *The English Works of Rabindranath Tagore,* vol. II, Sahitya Akademi, 1st pub. 1996, repr. 2008, p. 214.
3. Ibid.
4. Op. cit. Sankha Ghosh, *Rakta Karabi: Kayekti Tathya.*
5. Krishna Kripalani, *Tagore: A Life,* NBT, 1967, p. 47; Krishna Dutta and Andrew Robinson, *Rabindranath Tagore: The Myriad Minded Man,* Bloomsbury, 1995, p. 81.
6. A combined translation of the three poems is available in the EWRT, vol. II, p. 466.
7. Abu Sayeed Ayyub, *Tagore's Quest,* Papyrus, 1980, p. 47.
8. Op. cit. Dutta and Robinson, *Rabindranath Tagore,* pp. 151–2; A comprehensive translation of the article, 'Ways and Means' published in the Basumati of 6 and 13 June 1908 is available in Atish Dasgupta and Madhurima Sen, eds., *A Tribute to Rabindranath Tagore: Glimpses from Archival Records,* Directorate of State Archives, 2011, pp. 12–23.
9. Ashis Nandy, *Illegitimacy of Nationalism: Rabindranath Tagore and the Politics of Self,* OUP, 1998.
10. Rabindranath Tagore, *Reminiscences,* Macmillan & Co. Ltd., London, 1917.
11. Tagore to Andrews, New York, 19 December 1920 in *Letters to a Friend* in Sisir Kumar Das, ed., *The English Works of Rabindranath Tagore,* vol. III, 1st pub. 1996, repr. 2008, p. 272.
12. Rabindranath to Amiya Chakravarty, 20 June 1940, Letter No. 129 in *Chithipatra,* op. cit., pp. 331–3.
13. *Thoughts from Rabindranath Tagore,* item nos. 11-13, pp. 31–2 and item no. 52 in p. 43 in EWRT, vol. III.
14. D.O. Circular no. 126 T.–G. Dated Dacca, 22 July 1912, Education, General Department, in Political Dept., file no. 88/1912 in Atish Dasgupta and Madhurima Sen, eds., *Glimpses,* p. 257; Rathindranath Tagore, *On the Edges of Time,* Orient Longman, 1958, p. 177.
15. 'At the Cross Roads', written in 1918 in EWRT, vol. III, pp. 380–4.
16. A.P. Gnatyuk Danil'Chuk, *Tagore, India and Soviet Union: A Dream Fulfilled,* Translated from Russian by Harish C. Gupta, Firma KLM, 1986, p. 197.
17. Op. cit., 'At the Cross Roads'.
18. Ibid.
19. *Paschim Yatrir Diary* in *Rabindra Rachanabali,* Cheap edition published on the occasion of 125th anniversary, vol. X, p. 451.
20. 'Construction vs. Creation' in EWRT, vol. III, p. 404.
21. Qtd. by Krishna Kripalani, *Rabindranath Tagore: A Biography,* Visva-Bharati, 1980, p. 9.
22. *Red Oleanders* in EWRT, vol II, p. 213.
23. Ibid.

24. Ibid., p. 218.
25. Ibid.
26. Ibid.
27. Ibid.
28. 'Meeting of the East and the West' in EWRT, vol. III, pp. 631–4.
29. *Red Oleanders* in EWRT, vol. II, p. 214.
30. Tagore to W.W. Pearson, Calcutta, 6 March 1918 in *Letters to a Friend* in EWRT, vol. III, p. 253.
31. *Red Oleanders* in EWRT, vol. II, p. 217.
32. Tagore to Andrews, New York, 5 February 1921 in *Letters to a Friend* in EWRT, vol. III, p. 272.
33. 'An Oriental Culture and Japan's Mission' in EWRT, vol. III, pp. 604–10.
34. 'Nationalism in Japan' in *Nationalism* in EWRT, vol. II, pp. 436–52.
35. Ibid., p. 440.
36. 'The Meeting of the East and the West' in EWRT, vol. III, pp. 376–9.
37. Ashis Nandy, 'Science, Authoritarianism and Culture', in *Traditions, Tyranny, and Utopias: Essays in the Politics of Awareness,* OUP, 1987, pp. 95–126.
38. Rabindranath Tagore, *Letters from Russia,* Visva-Bharati, 1st pub. 1960, repr. 1984, tr. Sasadhar Sinha, p. 109.
39. 'The Nation' in *Creative Unity* in EWRT, vol. II, pp. 548–9.
40. 'Nationalism in the West' in EWRT, vol. II, p. 421.
41. Tagore to Andrews, 19 December 1920 in *Letters to a Friend* in EWRT, vol. III, p. 272.
42. 'Nationalism in Japan' in EWRT, vol. II, p. 451.
43. *Red Oleanders* in EWRT, vol. II, p. 217.
44. Poem No. 112 in 'Poems' in EWRT, vol. I, p. 387.
45. *Red Oleanders,* p. 223.
46. Ibid., p. 213.
47. Op. cit., *Letters From Russia,* pp. 12–13.
48. Ibid. Letter dated 25 September 1930, pp. 15, 25.
49. *Red Oleanders,* in EWRT, vol. II, p. 212.
50. *Letters From Russia,* pp. 22–4.
51. Ibid., p. 108.
52. Speech delivered by Rabindranarh Tagore at the *Dom Soyuzov,* 24 September 1930 in Microfilm material relating to Rabindranath Tagore, in English and Russian, in Private Papers Section, National Archives of India (henceforth NAI).
53. Ibid.
54. Ibid.
55. Ibid.
56. Ibid.
57. Rabindranath Tagore, *Letters From Russia,* pp. 99–100.
58. Ibid., p.105. Tagore here was echoing the drain theory of the nationalists which suggested that colonial masters were taking away all resources and not leaving any surplus for local use.
59. Speech of Tagore at the *Dom Soyuzov,* 24 September 1930, op. cit.

60. Ibid.
61. 'City and Village' in EWRT, vol. III, pp. 510–18.
62. Ibid. *Kuvera* is more like the mammon, tempting people to destruction. *Lakshmi* represents wealth along with peace.
63. Ibid.
64. *Letters From Russia,* p. 120.
65. 'Wealth and Welfare' in EWRT, vol. III, pp. 623–5.
66. Rabindranath Tagore, 'Red Oleanders: An Interpretation', in *The Visva-Bharati Quarterly,* November 1951–January 1952, pp. 210–11, qtd. Sankha Ghosh in his *Rakta Karabi: Kayekti Tathya* in *Urbashir Hashi,* Papyrus, 1st pub. 1981, repr. September 2003.

CHAPTER FIVE

Reading Tagore's *Letters from Russia* in the Twenty-first Century

SOBHANLAL DATTA GUPTA

U NLIKE NUMEROUS SOJOURNS in the West, Rabindranath visited Soviet Russia only once in 1930. During his stay, which extended for a period of just two weeks (11–25 September), he wrote fourteen letters to his friends and relatives, which were reflective of his impressions of post-revolutionary Russia. Three of them were dated Moscow, while the remaining letters were written after he left the Soviet territory and proceeded towards the United States. All these letters were compiled and published under the title *Russiar Chithi* (in Bengali) [*Letters from Russia*] in 1931 from Calcutta. The first English translation was done by Sasadhar Sinha and published from Visva-Bharati in 1960 (except the last letter, that is, letter no. 14). To outward appearances, in Tagore's enormous travelogue repertory which spanned almost all major countries of Asia and Europe, his single Russia visit seems to be of secondary importance.

In terms of duration and frequency, he visited England, the United States and Germany many times, the spells being, at times, moderately long. Yet his *Letters from Russia* deserves very special attention, in fact, a new reading today, for more than one reason. First, although his Russia visit took place in 1930, historical evidences indicate that he was desperately trying to establish contact with the Soviet authorities for almost a decade with the intention of visiting the country. What made him so much interested in Russia? Second, what was the Soviet perception of the Tagore visit? The question is important for the reason that it is now quite evident that a definite shift took place in the Soviet viewpoint from the early 1920s to the beginning of the 1930s, as the political situation in Russia witnessed significant changes. Third, what was the West's response to Tagore's visit to Russia? And finally, what was the Soviet response to *Letters from Russia*?

*For some of the information and materials used in this article I am grateful to Biswabandhu Bhattacharyya and Purabi Roy.

I

The events pertaining to Tagore's efforts towards establishing contacts with post-revolutionary Russia for almost a decade are quite significant. As early as 1918 in an article 'At the Crossroads', published in *Modern Review* he made the following assessment of the Russian Revolution which had taken place a few months earlier:

We know very little of the history of the present revolution in Russia, and with the scanty materials in our hands we cannot be certain if she, in her tribulations, is giving expression to man's indomitable soul against prosperity built upon moral nihilism. All that we can say is that the time to judge has not yet come,—especially as Real Politik is in such a sorry plight itself. No doubt if modern Russia did try to adjust herself to the orthodox tradition of Nation-worship, she would be in a more comfortable situation to-day, but this tremendousness of her struggle and hopelessness of her tangles do not, in themselves, prove that she has gone astray. It is not unlikely that, as a nation, she will fail; but if she fails with the flag of true ideals in her hands, then her failure will fade, like the morning star, only to usher in the sunrise of the New Age.[1]

What perhaps one can surmise from Tagore's reading of the October Revolution is that it is this 'flag of true ideals' which motivated him to undertake a visit of the Soviet state. Following the detailed information provided by the Soviet indologist A.P. Gnatyuk Danil'Chuk in his book *Tagore, India and the Soviet Union,*[2] more or less a sequence of events preceding his visit can be traced. On 17 June 1920 he met the famous Russan artist Nicholas Roerich in London through Suniti Kumar Chatterjee and expressed his keen desire to visit Russia. On 8 February 1921 in a letter written from the United States to C.F. Andrews, he noted his strong disapproval of the way the situation in Russia was being deliberately misrepresented in the West. He wrote: 'Everywhere there is an antipathy against Asia vented by a widespread campaign of calumny. Negroes are burnt alive, sometimes because they tried to exercise their right to vote, given to them by law. Germans are reviled. Conditions in Russia are deliberately misrepresented'.[3]

In 1924, during Tagore's visit to China, he met Lev Karakhan,[4] Soviet Ambassador in Beijing (1923–6), which was crucial in shaping his future visit to Russia. The information provided by Stephen Hay's study of the materials of this period[5] suggests that in this meeting Tagore expressed his strong desire to visit Russia, as he differentiated post-revolutionary Russia from the materialist West. In this connection he highlighted the relevance of Eastern spiritualism for Russia, although, interestingly, during his actual visit to the USSR in 1930 he refrained from making any reference to spiritualism. This is possibly explained by the fact that in China, in the course of his lecture programme he, indeed, referred to the spiritualist tradition of the Orient, which irked sections of the radical intelligentsia in China so much so that pamphlets were clandestinely distributed against his defence of spiritualism. Karakhan, a shrewd diplomat as he was, reciprocated Tagore in the following words:

From the political point of view my country is very willing to help and assist all the oppressed nations of the world, for in recent years my country has suffered greatly from Western material civilization and thus there is indeed a need for joint cooperation. From the intellectual point of view Tolstoy in the nineteenth century already rejected material civilization, so that his opinion is in actuality in accord with the essence of Eastern spiritual civilization.[6]

Furthermore, Kokusai (International), a Japanese news agency, in its dispatch from Beijing pointed out that the intentions of Tagore's visit to Russia were twofold: 'to study conditions there and to further among the Russian people the study of the civilization of India and the East'.[7] That this meeting with Karakhan was crucial for Tagore's Russia visit was evidenced by the next course of events. Immediately thereafter, following the formation of VOKS (All Union Society for Cultural Relations with Foreign Countries) in 1925, Tagore and C.V. Raman were invited to visit Russia but he could not go because of illness. In September 1926, while travelling in Europe, the poet met USSR Ambassador Alexander Arosyev in Stockholm and expressed his keen desire to visit the Soviet Union. On 27 September 1926 VOKS again sent an invitation to Tagore to visit Russia with programmes in Moscow, Leningrad, Baku and Tbilisi. The invitation was initiated by Anatoly Lunacharsky, Minister of Education and Culture and a top-ranking Soviet intellectual. Significantly, his programme in Russia was drawn up by Meyerhold and Stanislavsky, leading figures of Soviet intellectual life, and Orientalists like Oldenburg and Pavlovich. In 1927 Tagore and Jawaharlal Nehru were invited to Russia on the occasion of the tenth anniversary of the Russian Revolution, while on 27 August 1928, telegrams were sent to Gandhi and Tagore to visit Russia on the occasion of Tolstoy's birth centenary. But because of reasons of health Tagore could not undertake his journey on both the occasions. Finally, he could visit Russia in 1930, yet only for two weeks from 11 to 25 September.

II

The above account apparently creates the impression that Tagore's long cherished desire to visit post-revolutionary Russia was warmly reciprocated by the Soviet authorities. But if one takes into account the changing political scenario of the USSR after Lenin's death in 1924 and the ideological shifts that characterized the Communist Party of the Soviet Union thereafter, then a number of intriguing questions come up, which provide a different understanding of the Soviet perception of the Tagore visit in the sense that a subtle shift was evident in the Soviet attitude towards his journey to the USSR prior to his visit. To start with, although it is not clear whether Lenin harboured any specific viewpoint concerning Tagore this much information is available that his personal library contained the following writings of Tagore, namely, *Nationalism, Home and the World, Personality and Plays and Poems in Prose*.[8] Besides, between 1922 and 1927 thirty titles of Tagore had been translated in the Soviet Union which indicate that in 1930, when he visited Russia, he was already a known figure to the reading public in the USSR. This apparently popular image of Tagore, however, was not unanimously shared by sections of the intelligentsia attached to the Soviet Communist Party.

As Danilchu'k informs us, Orientalists like S. Veltman and his associates harboured a sharply negative attitude towards Tagore and Gandhi for their advocacy of spiritualism, in the fostering of which M.N. Roy, who in the 1920s was a key figure in the Communist International (Comintern) and thereby instrumental in shaping the understanding of the East in general and India in particular, played an important role.[9] Georg Lukács, in his criticism of Tagore's *Ghare Baire* (Home and the World) also replicated the same understanding in an article in *Rote Fahne* (Red Flag), the mouthpiece of KPD (Communist Party of Germany) in 1922, where he described it as 'a petty bourgeois yarn of the shoddiest kind'.[10] Recent findings indicate that when Tagore visited Hungary in 1926, he was criticized by a section of the Hungarian poets for his alleged 'pro-Western bias' towards the freedom struggle as against Gandhi's 'unfriendliness towards the West'.[11]

In fact, after 1928, following the Sixth Congress of Communist International (Comintern), it was resolved that the nationalist bourgeoisie in the colonial countries had ceased to be a progressive force and it had become counter-revolutionary, abetting imperialism. This was the outcome of the ultra-left and sectarian course adopted by the Soviet Communist Party and Comintern after 1928. In 1930, when Tagore undertook his visit to Russia, left-sectarianism, opposition to bourgeois nationalism in colonies like India had reached its peak. It is quite likely that this negative perception shaped the attitude of the Soviet authorities towards Tagore, which meant a shift away from the earlier relatively more positive view of the man and his outlook.

Another factor was the political turmoil that gripped the Soviet Communist Party after Lenin's death in 1924 and its impact on the culture and the arts. The struggle for power between Stalin and Trotsky ended in the expulsion of Trotsky in 1927 from the Party, followed by a centralization of party control in all spheres of life. As distinct from the relatively free and open atmosphere in Lenin's time, a tightening of Party control and surveillance now characterized the post-Lenin era. On 18 June 1925, in a resolution 'On Party Policy in the Sphere of Literature' adopted by the Politbureau (which was jointly drafted by Lunacharsky and Bukharin), it was stated:

With regard to proletarian writers, the Party must take the following position: while doing everything it can to foster their growth and supporting them in every way possible, the Party must use every means to prevent the manifestation of Communist conceit among them as a most ruinous phenomenon.... Communist criticism must drive out of its usage the tone of literary command.... While identifying unerringly the social and class content of literary trends, the Party as a whole can by no means limit itself to an attachment to any one tendency in *literary form*.... Therefore, the Party must speak out in favor of free competition among the various groups and trends in this sphere. Any other solution of the issue would be a bureaucratic pseudo solution. While in supporting proletarian and proletarian-peasant literature materially and morally, and while helping the fellow travelers, etc., the Party cannot grant a monopoly to any of the groups, even the most proletarian in its intellectual content. That would mean wrecking proletarian literature above all.[12] [emphasis original]

Presumably on 7 March 1927, Glavlit (Directorate of Literature—Central Censor Body) in a Directive 'On the activities of Glavlit' quite unambiguously stated the guidelines for the future in the sphere of literary and cultural activities:

...literature on problems of philosophy and sociology of a vividly idealist tendency and intended for a broad audience must not be allowed, permitting in limited print runs only, classical and scientific literature, if they cannot be replaced by textbooks and supplementary texts or serve for self-education, ... literature on natural science that is obviously not of a materialist tendency must not be allowed, ... economic literature of anti-Marxist content must not be allowed, ... of children's and young adult literature, allow publication only of literature that promotes a Communist upbringing, of religious literature, allow publication only of literature of a liturgical nature. These principles apply to all dogmas, sects, and tendencies.[13]

This being the orientation of the Soviet authorities when Rabindranath stepped into Russian territory in 1930, it is obvious that in their eyes he was a bourgeois poet professing idealist views, a non-proletarian figure and, therefore, a suspect. Therein perhaps lies the explanation of why no front-ranking Soviet intellectual like Lunacharsky, Stanislavsky or Meyerhold met Tagore, although many of them were earlier so greatly enthusiastic in planning his Soviet visit.

This possibly provides lead to another enigmatic question. Originally his Soviet trip was planned for one month. But, following the advice of the Russian doctors it was cut down to two weeks for reasons of health. But if health had been the factor, how is it that, on his return to Germany from Russia, he immediately undertook a long voyage to the USA.[14] In fact, most of the letters on Russia were written by Tagore when he was at sea. How then can this anomaly be explained? While advising Tagore to trim his original travel plan, was health the sole and the real consideration of the Soviet doctors?

III

This being the context, the question remains: how are we to read Tagore's *Letters from Russia*? First, it needs to be emphasized that although it appears to be a literary text, it is in essence a political one, where Tagore clearly takes sides, critiques what he disapproves and unambiguously states his choice. But the whole gamut of this understanding of Tagore cannot be found only in the fourteen letters on Russia which he sent out to his friends and relatives. One has to also take into consideration his talks with the peasants, children and persons and groups from different walks of life with whom he interacted in the course of his visit.[15] Besides, in a number of letters written by Tagore later to his contemporaries in an altogether different context, we come across his reflections on the Russia visit, which provide interesting leads to the reading of Tagore's text. It is this multilevel reading which could possibly bring out the hidden meaning of this work of Tagore.[16] His *Letters on Russia* are quite unique in the sense that he now shifts his emphasis from spiritualism, religion and theology, which characterized his thoughts on China, to humanism, as he critiques the materialist civilization of the West, its marker being the power of money under capitalism. In his letters he was deeply appreciative of the following aspects of life which the new Russia opened up before him. It is quite plausible that his description of the journey to Russia in letter no. 3 as a 'pilgrimage'[17] was based on this understanding. First, the emphasis on mass education and the programme of educating the masses undertaken by the Soviet government deeply inspired him. Second, the emphasis on child care and concern for the welfare of the child left on him a lasting impression. Third, the Soviet idea of uplifting the conditions of the peasantry as well as the quality of agricultural products through cooperatives was for him a challenging step forward, as reflected in letter no. 5 and his talks with the peasantry.[18] Fourth, what greatly moved him was the grand strategy adopted by the Soviet government to bring to the forefront all those who had remained backward for ages. In fact, he fully endorsed the idea of driving out the so-called educated middle class ('bhadralok', who in Tagore's letters figures sarcastically as 'bhaddar lok') virtually with a broomstick without being lured by money and wealth (letter nos. 2 and 4).[19] On 28 October 1930, in a letter written to Sudhindranath Datta, he wrote 'Very recently I have returned from Russia. There I have clearly seen how a country's path towards glory can be so perilous. Compared to the terrible sufferings its martyrs have gone through, police beatings are like showers of petals'.[20] On 31 October and 21 November in his letters to Rathindra Nath, his son, Tagore upheld Russia as the model which could be followed if priority were to be given to intelligence and initiative.[21] Russia, for Tagore, heralded the voice, the materialization of humanism, the ideal which was his own dream as well as his goal.[22]

Undoubtedly, Rabindranath was deeply impressed by the projects and the new experiments which were going on in Russia. Yet, he never allowed his understanding to be blinded by her achievements alone. What troubled him, what disturbed him, what made him deeply perturbed was the unilinearity of these programmes, as they did not recognize the notions of diversity and difference. That the denial of space to pluralism made a caricature of the meaning of freedom was the considered opinion of Tagore. As we will see later, this was exactly the criticism of Stalin's Russia, voiced by some of the top-ranking and, more importantly, Left intellectuals of Western Europe, who visited Russia in the 1920s and 1930s and who were otherwise ideologically inclined towards the Soviet Union, which Tagore certainly was not. In his very first letter where he distinguished Russia from all other countries which 'carried the infamous legacy of the oppressed having held the lampstands of human civilization on their heads for ages, the oil dripping down their bodies, and the light being received by those at the top',[23] he warned in its concluding part: 'I won't say that there is no defect in this system. Very serious defects are there. And for that reason one day they will face a crisis. In brief, it concerns their stereotyped education system . . . but stereotyped human beings would never last. If the learning system does not coalesce with the active mind, either one day the structure will explode or the mind will die out, human beings will be reduced to robots.'[24]

In letter no. 8, he highlighted the negative features of the Soviet system, that is, 'coercion', 'summary trial', the compulsion to act in compliance with the authorities—and compared them with the dark spots on the moon, while also stating at the same time that, after all, the moon is known by its light, not by its spots.[25] His letter no. 13 deserves special attention, particularly for the reason that in the Russian edition of Tagore's *Letters from Russia,* which was published in 1980, fifty years after his Russia visit, this letter was excluded. The reasons are not difficult to find. In this letter Tagore quite bluntly stated that the Soviet authorities had failed to understand the line of demarcation between the individual and the collective. In the name of giving priority to the collective, freedom of the individual was being suppressed rather brutally and that way 'they acted just like the fascists'.[26] Almost hinting at the phenomenon of what soon came to be described as Stalinism, Tagore wrote, 'Here it is dictatorship of an all-powerful individual. This kind of concentration of powers may, by chance, yield good results for some time, but not permanently.'[27] But, interestingly, he sought the way out of it within the Soviet system itself. By distinguishing fascism from Bolshevism, he now said: 'They have repressed the body but not the mind. Those who really want to do mischief they first kill the mind. But these people are enhancing the vitality of the mind and therein lies the way out.'[28] Tagore, it appears, was quite aware of the kind of censorship which was in force in regard to different schools of art and literature. A reference is to be found in an essay 'Shahityabichar' (Assessments of Literature) in 1940 where Tagore wrote: 'When I was in Moscow, my favorable opinion about Chekov suddenly drew rebuff, since, in Chekov's writings, because of fusion of multiple styles, allegedly a class deviation had taken place and so his plays were not staged.'[29]

That all these aspects disturbed and tormented Tagore very deeply was evident in an interview given to *Izvestia* on 25 September 1930, the day of his departure from Russia. After saying his words of appreciation in favour of the achievements of the Soviet system, he then concluded:

But I find here certain contradictions to the great mission which you have undertaken. Certain attitudes of mind are being cultivated which are contrary to your ideal.

I must ask you: Are you doing your ideal a service by arousing in the minds of those under your training, anger, class hatred and revengefulness against those not sharing your ideal, against those whom you consider to be your enemies? True, you have to fight against obstacles, you have to overcome ignorance and lack of sympathy, even persistently virulent antagonism. But your mission is not restricted to your own nation or own party, it is for the betterment of humanity according to your light. But does not humanity include those who do not agree with your aim? Just as you try to help peasants who have other ideas than yours about religion, economics, and social life, not by getting fatally angry with them, but by patiently teaching them and showing them where the evil lurks in secret, should you not have the same mission to those other people who have other ideals than your own? These you may consider to be mistaken ideals, but they have an historical origin and have become inevitable through a combination of circumstances. You may consider the men who hold them as misguided. But it should all the more be your mission to try to convert them by pity and love, realizing that they are as such a part of humanity as the peasants whom you serve.

If you dwell too much upon the evil elements in your opponents and assume that they are inherent in human nature meriting eternal damnation, you inspire an attitude of mind which with its content of hatred and revengefulness may some day react against your own ideal and destroy it. You are working in a great cause. Therefore, you must be great in your mind, great in your mercy, your understanding and your patience. I feel profound admiration for the greatness of the things you are trying to do, therefore I cannot help expecting for it a motive force of love and an environment of a charitable understanding.

There must be disagreement where minds are allowed to be free. It would not only be an uninteresting but a sterile world of mechanical regularity if all of our opinions were forcibly made alike. If you have a mission which includes all humanity, you must, for the sake of that living humanity, acknowledge the existence of differences of opinion. Opinions are constantly changed and rechanged only through the free circulation of intellectual forces and moral persuasion. Violence begets violence and blind stupidity. Freedom of mind is needed for the reception of truth; terror hopelessly kills it. The brute terror cannot subdue the brute. It is only the man who can do it.

Before leaving your country let me once again assure you that I am struck with admiration by all that you are doing to free those who once were in slavery, to raise up those who were lowly and oppressed, endeavoring to bring help to those who are utterly helpless all through the world, reminding them that the source of their salvation lies in a proper education and their power to combine their human resources. Therefore, for the sake of humanity I hope that you may never create a vicious force of violence which will go on weaving an interminable chain of violence and cruelty. Already you have inherited much of this legacy from the Tsarist regime. It is the worst legacy you possibly could have. You have tried to destroy many of the other evils of that regime. Why not try to destroy this one also? I have learnt much from you, how skilfully you evolve usefulness out of the helpfulness of the weak and ignorant. Your ideal is great and so I ask you for perfection in serving it, and a broad field of freedom for laying its permanent foundation.[30]

The English version of this long interview of Tagore was first published in *Manchester Guardian* on 14 October 1930, while, ironically, the reading public of Russia first came to know about it only in 1988 in the Gorbachev period. In 2011, on the occasion of Tagore's 150th birth anniversary in Moscow, Sergei Serebryanny, a noted Indologist, provided the explanation. This interview was not allowed to be published in *Izvestia*, he pointed out, on Stalin's personal orders, the reason being that he was irked by Tagore's critical comments on the Soviet system.[31] Interestingly, earlier, Tagore, in his conversation at the VOKS reception too, obliquely referred to this point. These were his words:

Don't you believe that much of what you do today has behind it the accumulated forces of active reaction against the oppressive regime of the past government? It is wonderful that this reaction should have been translated into higher forms of activity and not dissipated in mere retaliatory politics. You have of course, as I am sure you will freely admit, made grievous mistakes at the time of your first accession to power, but the sense of responsibility that this power brought along with it has quickly given you a full sense of reality, and you seem to lose no opportunity now of merging your racial individualities into a harmonious social existence.[32]

Tagore visited Russia in 1930, when Stalinism was consolidating itself. Between 1926 and 1936, the decade that witnessed the rise and victory of Stalinism, personalities such as Walter Benjamin, Jawaharlal Nehru, Romain Rolland and André Gide, to name a few, visited the Soviet Union and recorded their impressions. Unlike Tagore, all of them had quite pronounced Leftist inclinations and they had nothing to do with Tagore's visit of 1930. Yet, what is significant is the striking similarity between their impressions and those of Tagore. Walter Benjamin, the iconic figure of twentieth century German Marxism, wrote his *Moscow Diary* in course of his visit of Russia for two months, from December 1926 to January 1927. First, what irked Benjamin was the iconization of Lenin throughout the country, at times quite crudely.[33] Second, he noted that, while in the Soviet films it was quite impossible to provide any critique of the Soviet man, it was equally impossible to represent bourgeois life, just as representation of tragic love entanglements on film or stage was a taboo.[34] Third, 'To be a Communist in a state where the proletariat rules means completely giving up your private independence. You leave the responsibility for organizing your own life up to the Party, as it were.'[35] As already stated, both Nehru and Tagore were invited by VOKS to visit Russia in 1927 on the occasion of the tenth anniversary of the Russian Revolution. While Tagore could not go, Nehru's visit materialized. Interestingly, while Nehru, like Tagore, greatly admired the Soviet educational system, what troubled him was the severe victimization of the political opponents of the regime and the growing cult of Lenin.[36] Romain Rolland visited Moscow in June-July 1935 on the invitation of Maxim Gorky and left behind his impressions in *Voyage à Moscou (juin-juillet 1935)*, which was published from France only in 1992.[37] This travel account of Rolland is especially significant for it records his direct experience of conversing with Stalin. Three things are in order here. One: the growing personality cult centring around Stalin, which had replaced the Lenin cult, a phenomenon that had earlier drawn the attention of Benjamin and Nehru.[38] Two: justification of the punitive measures being taken against the enemies of socialism in the larger interest of the masses which were unavoidable, the state being a necessary evil.[39] Three: as regards freedom of the mind, he expressed his deep fear and cynicism about the kind of blind understanding of the common man that he had nothing to learn from the West, the Soviet Union being the repository of all knowledge and wisdom. This false conceit in the name of self-glorification, Rolland warned, would one day lead to turmoil, and this would happen without notice.[40] He further observed that in order to maintain this false image, what was necessary was the projection of a personality cult of the leaders, to generate an atmosphere of fear, suspicion and surveillance, that is, an 'atmosphere of war', so that this understanding would not be questioned by anyone.[41] André Gide, a towering figure of French intellectual life, visited the USSR in 1936 and stated the following: 'It too often happens that the friends of the Soviet Union refuse to see the bad side; so that, too often what is true about the USSR is said with enmity, and what is false with love.'[42] Gide, exactly like Tagore in 1930, was perturbed by the conformism, lack of critical thinking and the lurking threat of retribution that characterized the Soviet order. The striking similarities between Tagore's observations in 1930 and the impressions of Benjamin, Nehru, Gide and Rolland are, indeed, quite mind-boggling for an avid reader of these travel accounts today.

IV

Two closely interrelated questions are relevant in this context. First, what was the West's response to Tagore's visit? Second, what was the Soviet reaction to *Letters from Russia*? This, in fact, was Tagore's biggest irony. Just as Tagore's negative remarks irked the Soviet authorities, his positive comments angered the Western world. The publication of only the concluding section of the *Letters* in *Modern Review* led to the banning of its June 1934 issue in British India.[43] Again, according to the information provided by Sujit Mukherjee, as Tagore undertook his last visit to the United States (9 October—14 December 1930) after concluding his Russia visit, an article appeared in *Literary Digest* on 1 November 1930 which described him as a Soviet propagandist. Further, a month after Tagore left the United States, an organization of Russian immigrants, which called itself 'Circle of Russian Culture', wrote a letter to *New York Times* on 15 January 1931 in which Tagore was severely criticized for his 'evasive attitude toward the Communist grave-diggers of Russia' and for his 'strong and unjust support to a group of professional murderers'.[44] Krishna Dutta and Andrew Robinson also share this position when they describe his praise of the Soviet system as 'painfully misguided', since he felt obliged to defend the Russian experiment as a counterweight to Western propaganda against the Soviet Union and India's freedom struggle.[45]

As regards the Soviet reception of *Letters from Russia*, it is quite intriguing. The Russian version came out only in 1980 on the occasion of the 50th anniversary of Tagore's visit to Russia, but, as explained earlier, without letter no. 13. How is it that, while the English version was first published in India in 1960, it took the Soviet authorities twenty years to translate it?

It simply confirms that the Soviet authorities were not at all favourably disposed towards this particular work of Tagore.

V

Finally, a couple of unresolved questions stick out, demanding answers at appropriate levels. First, Tagore being a non-political personality, having no political affiliation, how is it that within a span of just two weeks, he read the Soviet system so accurately? Was he briefed by anyone? The only probable name that figures here is Sauymendra Nath Tagore, who was Tagore's nephew and who accompanied him, along with many others, on the tour. He was a man of distinct Marxist orientation, who had earlier been in Stalin's Russia. Second, in letter no. 2 dated 19 September, Tagore refers to his visit to a place outside Moscow, describing the huge building where he stayed, but not mentioning the person whose *dacha* (holiday home) it was. Later it is learnt from Russian sources[46] that it was the *dacha* of Lev Karakhan, whom he first met in Beijing in 1924, the man who was instrumental in initiating Soviet interest in Tagore's trip to the USSR. Some questions have remained unanswered till now. First: why doesn't Karakhan's name figure in Tagore's account? Second: Did any conversation take place between Karakhan and Tagore? Third: What was the KGB's assessment of Tagore? Undoubtedly, the KGB had its own file on Tagore; what role did this assessment play in the formation of the Soviet view of Tagore's visit to Stalin's Russia? Does the explanation of why no major figure of Soviet cultural and intellectual life (i.e. Gorky, Meyerhold, Lunacharsky Stanislavsky, most of whom were associated with the planning of Tagore's programme at the initial stage in the 1920s) meet Tagore lie here? These questions have remained unaddressed till now. Reading Tagore's *Letters from Russia* would remain incomplete in the twenty-first century until and unless these puzzling questions are resolved.

Notes

1. *The English Writings of Rabindranath Tagore*, Introduction by Mohit K. Ray, vol. 6, New Delhi: Atlantic Publishers, 2007, pp. 506–7.
2. A.P. Gnatyuk-Danil'Chuk, *Tagore, India and the Soviet Union*, Calcutta: Firma KLM, 1986.
3. *The English Writings of Rabindranath Tagore*, vol. 6, p. 363.
4. Karakhan was the Deputy Commissioner of Foreign Affairs, USSR in 1928–34 and a key functionary in the Communist International (Comintern), dealing with the Eastern countries. He perished in 1937 in the Moscow purges.

5. Stephen N. Hay, *Asian Ideas of East and West: Tagore and His Critics in Japan, China and India,* Bombay: Oxford University Press, 1970, pp. 173–4.
6. Cited in ibid., pp. 173–4.
7. Cited in ibid., p. 174.
8. Danil'Chuk, *Tagore, India and the Soviet Union,* pp. 167–8.
9. Ibid., pp. 156–62.
10. For the full text of this severely critical review of Tagore's novel, see George Lukács, *Essays and Reviews,* London: Merlin Press, 1983 under www.marxists.org/archive/lukacs/works/1922/tagore.htm, accessed on 30 March 2013.
11. See in this connection Imre Bangha, 'Rabindranath Tagore and Hungarian Politics', *Parabaas,* September 2008 under www.parabaas.com/rabindranath/articles/p Bangha.html, accessed on 30 March 2013.
12. Katerina Clark et al., eds., *Soviet Culture and Power: A History in Documents, 1917–1953,* New Haven and London: Yale University Press, 2007, document 21, pp. 43–4.
13. Ibid., document 59, p. 123.
14. Incidentally, this last visit of Tagore to the United States was of pretty long duration, namely, from 9 October to 14 December 1930. So the enigmatic question remains: how is it that after being advised to cut down his trip in Russia in September he could undertake such a long journey to the United States, and that too in the approaching winter?
15. See Appendix VI in Rabindranath Tagore, *Letters from Russia,* Calcutta: Viswa-Bharati, 1960.
16. For these methodological clues see the note in *Rabindra Rachanabali* (hereafter *RR*), West Bengal Government, 2001, vol. 16, pp. 1155–63.
17. *RR,* West Bengal Government, vol. 12, 1989, p. 380. In all citations from *Letters from Russia* the English translations are mine from the Bengali original.
18. *RR,* West Bengal Government, vol. 12, 1989, pp. 387–91. Also see Appendix VI in Tagore, *Letters from Russia,* pp. 176–87.
19. *RR,* West Bengal Government, vol. 12, 1989, pp. 378–80 and pp. 383–7.
20. *Chithipatro* [*Letters*], vol. 16, Kolkata: Viswa-Bharati, 1402, p. 35.
21. Ibid., vol. 2, Kolkata: Viswa-Bharati, 2012, pp. 201, 204.
22. See his letters to Pratima Devi dated 24 (?) October 1930 and 7 March 1935 and Amiya Chakrabarti dated 28 July, 1936, *Chithipatro* [*Letters*], vol. 16, Kolkata: Viswa-Bharati, 2003, p. 116 and *Chithipatro* [*Letters*], vol. 11, Kolkata: Viswa-Bharati, 1381, pp. 145–6, 196.
23. *RR,* West Bengal Government, 2001, vol. 12, 1989, p. 377.
24. Ibid., p. 378.
25. Ibid., p. 401.
26. Ibid., p. 413.
27. Ibid.
28. Ibid.
29. *RR,* West Bengal Government, vol. 10, 1989, p. 584.
30. *The English Writings of Rabindranath Tagore,* vol. 8, pp. 1282–4.
31. Reporting on a function organized on the occasion of Tagore's 150th birth anniversary celebrations in Moscow, PTI in its dispatch dated Moscow, 22 May

2011 under the heading 'Stalin had blocked out Rabindranath Tagore's criticism of the Communist system' referred to Serebryanny's disclosure.
32. Appendix VI in Tagore, *Letters from Russia*, pp. 162–3.
33. Walter Benjamin, *Moscow Diary*, Cambridge, Mass: Harvard University Press, 1986, p. 50.
34. Ibid., p. 55.
35. Ibid., p. 73.
36. Jawaharlal Nehru, *Soviet Russia: Some Random Sketches and Impressions*, Allahabad: Lala Ram Mohan Lal, 1928.
37. Yet to be translated in English, I have used the Bengali translation of this text of Rolland under the title Romain Rolland, *Moscowr Dinlipi*, Calcutta: Saraswat Library, 1996. The translation from original French was made by Abanti Sanyal.
38. Romain Rolland, *Moscowr Dinlipi*, Calcutta: Saraswat Library, 1996, p. 29.
39. Ibid., pp. 20–1.
40. Ibid., pp. 104–5.
41. Ibid., pp. 106–7.
42. André Gide, *Back from the USSR*, London: Martin Lecker and Warburg, 1937, p. 14.
43. See Note in *RR*, vol. 16, p. 1163.
44. For extensive discussion on this issue see Sujit Mukherjee, *Passage to America: The Reception of Rabindranath Tagore in the United States 1912–1941*, Calcutta: Bookland, 1964.
45. Krishna Dutta and Andrew Robinson, *Rabindranath Tagore: The Myriad-Minded Man*, London: Bloomsbury, 1995, p. 297.
46. Sailen Choudhury, ed., *'Tirthadarshaner' panchash bachhar* (Fifty years of the 'Pilgrimage'), Information Department of the Soviet Consulate in Calcutta: Kalantar Press, 1980, pp. 49–50.

CHAPTER SIX

The Evolution of Indian English Language and Literature: A Socio-Historical Survey

SOMDATTA MANDAL

> ...Why not let me speak in
> Any language I like? The language I speak
> Becomes mine, its distortions, its queernesses
> All mine, mine alone. It is half-English, half
> Indian, funny perhaps, but it is honest,
> It is as human as I am human, don't
> You see?...
> —KAMALA DAS, 'An Introduction'

Introduction

In the introduction to the book *The Vintage Book of Indian Writing* (1997) edited by Salman Rushdie and Elizabeth West and celebrating the fiftieth year of Indian independence, Rushdie went on to claim that 'this new, and still burgeoning, "Indo-Anglian" literature represents perhaps the most valuable contribution India has yet made to the world of books' and that 'the ironic proposition that India's best writing since independence may have been done in the language of the departed imperialists is simply too much for some folks to bear'. This was controversial, since the 'Indian writing' of the title was equated with 'Indian writing in English' and not the different *bhashas* in which Indian literature was written. Rushdie made his stance clearer and wrote further, '... the prose writing—both fiction and non-fiction—created in [the last fifty years] by Indian writers working in English, is proving to be a stronger and more important body of work than most of what has been produced in the 16 "official languages" of India, the so-called "vernacular languages", during the same time.'

On the other hand, Amit Chaudhuri in his edited book *The Picador Book of Modern Indian Literature* (2001) wondered, 'Can it be true that Indian writing, that endlessly rich, complex and problematic entity, is to be represented by a handful of writers who write in English, who live in England or America and whom one might have met at a party, most of whom have published no more than two novels, some of them only one?'

Chaudhuri, irascibly, begs to differ from Rushdie. How, he asks, would the 'West' react, if, in the event of some unanticipated bibliographic disaster, all of Britain's modern and ancient cultures disappeared from view, leaving the rest of the world to judge English literature on the basis of a few paltry contemporary novels? What if Julian Barnes, Angela Carter and Martin Amis, alone, were entrusted with the literary labour of bringing England out of an apparent age of obscurity? Refusing to indulge the false (and damaging) linguistic hierarchies so apparent in the Rushdie and West anthology, Chaudhuri in this volume draws our attention, anew, to the symbiotic development of vernacular and English literatures in modern India. If colonial education led directly to the rise of English in this country, it also provoked a concurrent efflorescence within the vernacular languages. So much so, that 'many of the greatest and most interesting writers in the vernacular languages were or are students or teachers of English literature.' These two different opinions, expressed not just by two critics, but by two established creative writers of Indian English literature, lead us into the basic problems of defining the genre itself.

This essay attempts to analyse the evolution of Indian English, both as a language and as literature and to show how the development of one actually influenced the other, as a result of which, they cannot be judged as separate monolithic constructs. Moreover, both the English language and literature as practiced in India cannot be evaluated without considering the socio-political background in which they were written. Glossing over a wide arena, this survey is divided into several sections. At the very beginning a lot of known historical facts are reiterated as this is necessary to understand how and why the English language actually arrived in India. The next section tries to show how Indian English has established itself as a language category of its own and cannot be equated with the original Queen's English. Scanning through the decades beginning from the eighteenth century to the present times, we shall then see how this language policy flourished in the literary context from those early times to the present day. Finally the analysis will hopefully be able to dispel the myth that Indian Writing in English is a new form of literary genre flourishing in India in post-colonial times like other variants of Asian Englishes.

Reiterating History

This section is selectively divided into four subgroups done chronologically to help us understand how Indian English arrived, flourished and established itself on the Indian soil. At the outset one must admit that it is not an all-inclusive survey—some historical events and authors have been discussed in detail whereas others have been totally omitted. This is not to belittle their influence or importance but has been done merely for the space constraint of this study.

From the Beginnings to 1857

It was during the seventeenth century that the East India Company, whose original aim was primarily commerce and not conquest, started trading in this subcontinent. Soon there was a pressing need for Indian clerks, translators and lower officials in administration, and knowledge of English came to be essential for these jobs. At the same time, with the rise of the Evangelist movement in Britain, the idea of spreading the word of Christ among the natives assumed vital importance for some Englishmen. India therefore attracted the Englishmen for two reasons, namely business and religion. In 1757 a British force under Robert Clive defeated the powerful ruler of Bengal, Siraj-ud-daula, thereby taking effective control of a large part of India. On the other hand, the English missionaries simultaneously began their efforts at educating the local people, and before the close of the eighteenth century, schools which taught English besides the vernaculars were already established in the South, in Bombay and in Bengal. It is a well known fact that linguistic colonialism soon and inevitably followed on the heels of the political acquisition of South Asia by the British in the mid-eighteenth century. In 1816, a gentleman from Calcutta named Baidyanath Mukhopadhyay pleaded with Edward Hyde-East, the Chief Justice of the Supreme Court of Bengal, stating that many leading Hindus were desirous to impart English education to their children; consequently by 20 January 1817 the Hindu College was founded in Calcutta. 1822 saw the establishment of the Anglo-Hindu School and in 1823, Rammohan Roy in his persuasive *Letter on Indian Education* to Lord Amherst, argued for imparting English education in India instead of Sanskrit.

What was the literary output during such times? Apart from Shaikh Din Muhammad's *Travels of Dean Mahomet* published in 1794 from Ireland, the first published composition in English of some length by an Indian was Cavelly Venkata Boriah's 'Account of the Jains' written in 1803 and published in *Asiatic Researches or Transactions of the Society instituted in Bengal for inquiring into the History and Antiquities, the Art, Science and Literature of Asia* (vol. IX; London, 1809). In 1817 appeared Raja Rammohan Roy's essay 'A Defence of Hindu Theism'. During this period a lot of prose writing on religious, social, historical and political subjects was also to be seen. This literary flowering proceeded at an amazing speed and by 1831 we already see the publication of the first Indian English play, *The Persecuted or Dramatic Scenes illustrative of the present state of Hindoo Society in Calcutta* written by Krishna Mohan Banerjee, a disciple of Henry Derozio. This was an attempt to present the conflict in the mind of a sensitive Bengali youth, between orthodoxy and the new ideas ushered in by Western education.

There are critics who tend to view Indian writing in English as a pan-Indian phenomenon born with the Bengal Renaissance of the nineteenth century since many of its first exponents like Raja Rammohun Roy, Henry Derozio, Radhakanta Deb, Toru Dutt, Rajnarain Dutt, Michael Madhusudan Datta, Kashiprosad Ghose, Sri Aurobindo and Vivekananda were products of that Renaissance. Interestingly, all of them were from the Bengal region. This first period of Indian English literature may be said to end in the 1850s, a few years before the Indian Revolt of 1857. By this time, most of the region now identified as South Asia, specifically the areas that now constitute the sovereign states of India, Pakistan, Bangladesh and Sri Lanka, had become part of the British Empire.

Here we have to mention two significant events that occurred in the year 1835. The first was the creation of English speaking bilinguals in India. Initially, British administrators debated amongst themselves whether they should impose English on the people of the Indian subcontinent or whether they should retain Persian and Sanskrit for legal and administrative purposes. This gave rise to a whole group of 'Orientalists' who favoured the retention of the 'native' languages for administrative work. But by 1835 the 'Anglicists'—the group in favour of the widespread use of English in offices—won the day since this was the year when Thomas Babington Macaulay, the English politician, historian, and writer, produced his famous Minutes on Law and Education as a member of the Supreme Council of India. According to Macaulay, introducing the English language to the subcontinent was essential:

... it is impossible for us, with our limited means to attempt to educate the body of the people. We must at present do our best to form a class who may be interpreters between us and the millions whom we govern,—a class of persons Indian in blood and colour, but English in tastes, in opinions, in morals and in intellect. To that class we may leave it to refine the vernacular dialects of the country, to enrich those dialects with terms of science borrowed from the Western nomenclature, and to render them by degrees fit vehicles for conveying knowledge to the great mass of the population.

This verdict was further ratified by Lord Bentinck, the governor-general of the period who declared that 'the great objects of British [rule in India] ought to be the promotion of European literature and science among the natives of India and all funds appropriated for the purpose of education would be best employed on English education alone,' implying thereby that the process of 'civilizing' India could only take place through the propagation of the English language. That very same year 1835 also saw the publication of the first fictional narrative in Indian English by Kylas Chunder Dutt, a student of the Hindoo College. Titled *A Journal of Forty-Eight Hours of the Year 1945*, it is a prose fantasy in which the author depicted a future rebellion against the British in which martyrs would die with rousing speeches of patriotism. This presentation uncannily foreshadowed not only Khudiram and his brigade's *swadeshi* acts of revolt but also the time of possible deliverance missing the actual date by only two years. The style of Dutt's narration reminds one of the long-drawn convoluted sentence structures of nineteenth century British/English prose, and it attempts to imitate the master's art. Thus it becomes clear that as an Indian, the history has been shaped as much by the institutions of this empire as by long tradition of struggle against them.

From 1857 to 1920

According to the literary critic M.K. Naik, 'Indian English literature really came of age after 1857, when India's rediscovery of her identity became a vigorous, all-absorbing quest and when she had learnt enough from the West to progress from imitation and assimilation to creation' (35). Naik therefore defines this period as 'Winds of Change'. Apart from the trio of Bengali intellectuals, Sir Aurobindo, Rabindranath Tagore and Swami Vivekananda who significantly contribute to this period, we witness Indianness for the first time flourishing in the literary arena. In 1964, Bankim Chandra Chattopadhyay published his English novel *Rajmohan's Wife* [serialized in a Calcutta weekly called *The Indian Field*], now considered as the first novel in English. Though borrowed heavily from the Gothic romance tradition of the British novel, for the first time in India, we meet a young landlord hero, obviously a beneficiary of the Permanent Settlement and educated in the colonizer's new system of education, who is always at odds with his family and society. Another significant year turns out to be 1874, as it saw Revd Lalbehari Day's *Govinda Samanta: The History of a Bengali Raiyot* emerging as the first realist fiction novel in India. It won a fifty pound reward offered by the zamindar of Uttarpara for the best novel to be written illustrating the 'Social and Domestic Life of the Rural Population and Working Classes of Bengal'. Govinda is the first underdog protagonist—a peasant oppressed equally by Hindu society, British government and natural calamities, and is not borrowed from the West.

The rest of the period also saw English being written in different narrative forms. In 1876, Toru Dutt's *A Sheaf Gleaned in the French Fields* was published. In 1910 Mahatma Gandhi translated his *Hind Swaraj* into English; 1913 brought the Nobel Prize for Rabindranath Tagore for his *Gitanjali*. During the 1920s, the rise of the *Swadeshi* or Nationalist movement brought some anti-English sentiment with it, even though the movement itself used English as its medium.

From 1920 to 1980

This period is the most productive for Indian English writers. Let us first cast a look at Dhan Gopal Mukherjee's works. Living in the United States, he wrote a lot of juvenile fiction like *Kari, the Elephant* (1922), *Hari, the Jungle-lad* (1926), and a novel called *My Brother's Face* (1924). Though not very well known, Mukherjee experimented with traditional Indian modes of storytelling such as 'emboxed narrative' (where one narrative opens within another, which are 'emboxed' in the main story, known as the 'frame story') and the mingling of prose and verse. India's past is brought to life through the many legends, folktales, and songs woven into the novel. He was also the first to introduce Sanskrit poetry into Indian English fiction; he generally uses translations but sometimes transliterates mantras when the sound demands it.

The three most well known novelists who straddle the entire twentieth century are of course Mulk Raj Anand, R.K. Narayan and Raja Rao. Often known as 'the triumvirate', all three were born in the first decade of the century, and each published his first novel in the 1930s. For Anand it was *Untouchable* (1935), for Narayan, *Swami and His Friends* (1935), and Raja Rao's first book was *Kanthapura* (1938). But the similarity ends there, for each wrote entirely different kinds of novels and also differed from the other in terms of their background, ideology and their use of the English language. Yet, interestingly, as Meenakshi Mukherjee rightly pointed out, the themes handled by them were 'pan-Indian; the caste system, the national movement, and later the partition of the country, the clash between tradition and modernity, faith and rationality and similar clichés of east-west encounter, disintegration of the joint family, exploitation of women—experiences that are familiar all across the country'(2). Anand wrote his first novel when he was living in England, Raja Rao while in France and Narayan never left India until he was in his fifties. Anand believed in socialism and wrote of the underprivileged and the exploited. His narrative mode was fundamentally based on traditional nineteenth century realism and he combined it with a vigorous style interjected with expletives and abuses in Hindi. Illustrating an important aspect of the Indian English novelist's struggle to get himself published, Anand recalled his dark days when he failed to find a publisher:

I must confess that I felt suicidal, until a young English poet, Oswald Blakeston, took the book to a small publisher called Wishart Books Ltd., and brought the assurance that they would publish it if E.M. Forster would write a preface to protect the book against being called 'dirty' because it dealt with dung.

Behind the bravado of the concluding part of the statement lurks the uneasy admission that *Untouchable* was accepted for publication because Forster wrote a preface for it. For Narayan the case was not much different. He too had to get a recommendation from Graham Greene before his long and illustrious career could begin. Creating a fictional world of Malgudi, he developed a unique narrative mode to present a galaxy of very ordinary men and women in mundane situations but from a point of view at once detached and comic. He kept his English as simple and transparent as possible and it was with him that the Indian fiction in English gained acceptance in the academia.

As for Raja Rao, he was initially a Gandhian but he later veered towards metaphysics and began foregrounding his Brahmin identity. Thus he experimented with his sentences making them sound sonorous like in Sanskrit. His *Kanthapura* is an attempt to convey fictionally the transformations wrought by Gandhi and the freedom struggle in the Indian consciousness even in remote and rural India—but it is also notable as an experiment with form and language. Rao claims that stylistically he had tried to convey the rhythms of Indian life in his own way. The celebrated and oft-quoted 'Foreword' of his book is now considered a manifesto in Indian Writing in English because it proposes very clearly a dual identity—different from English, yet not wholly Indian, both national and international, a hyphenated self. In his 'Introduction', Raja Rao also makes his readers aware of the fact that he is attempting his own version of a *sthala-purana*, that is to say, the 'legendary history' of a place popular in the Indian narrative tradition. As far as the language is concerned, he tries to find an answer to the problems faced by the Indian English novelist who feels compelled to tell a story 'in a language that is not one's own [in] the spirit that is one's own' (5).

With India gaining its independence in 1947, the perception of English as having an alien power base changed. The first exceptional Indian English novel that appeared in 1948 was G.V. Desani's *All About H. Hatterr*. A comic masterpiece and a linguistic experiment, it deals with the journey of a half-cast orphan through self-realization and hilarious adventures accompanied by his friend, philosopher and guide Banerrji, who is a quintessentially Anglophile babu. This ingenious mixture of the picaresque and the *bildungsroman* derives unique character from its inimitable style, a garrulous outpouring of Eurasian colloquial dialect with all its outrageous imperfections continuously digressing on almost everything on earth. The novel, revised again and again, practically went unnoticed until it was reissued with an introduction by Anthony Burgess in 1970. In several ways Desani was a writer born before the readers were ready for his kind of writing. In *Hatterr* he played with the English language, Indianizing it with comic abandon and whimsical self-mockery, and celebrated hybridity and dislocation long before Salman Rushdie made such things trendy.

While Desani spent his creative energy playing with the language, Sudhin N. Ghose, a contemporary of his, was doing just the reverse. Ghose's fictional tetralogy—*And Gazelles Leaping* (1949), *Cradles of the Clouds* (1951), *The Vermillion Boat* (1953) and *The Flame of the Forest* (1955) were experimental in nature, close to modes used in magic realism. In fact he was probably the only novelist during this time who tried seriously to make a synthesis between the inherited narrative tradition and the imported form of the nineteenth century novel. The Indian literary scenario became a lot more diverse during the fifties to the seventies decade. Nirad Chaudhuri's *Autobiography of an Unknown Indian* (1951), Kamala Markandaya's first novel *Nectar in a Sieve* (1954), Khushwant Singh's *Train to Pakistan* (1956), Anita Desai's first novel *Cry, the Peacock* (1963), Kamala Das' *Summer in Calcutta* (1965), the novels of Bhabani Bhattacharya, B. Rajan and several others are random examples showing how the genre flourished. 1975, the year Emergency was declared and fundamental rights of Indians were suspended by Indira Gandhi, saw the publication of Bharati Mukherjee's *Wife*, which spoke about new issues like expatriate problems and acculturation.

From 1981 to the present

The 1980s is a very important decade as it ushered in the reconfiguration of the ground realities in politics, economic technology and demography that had far-reaching consequences in the field of cultural production. The collapse of the Soviet Bloc led to the emergence of a unipolar world with the increasing hegemony of the United States (whose language was also English)—and globalization transformed the major part of the world into a single market whose commercial vehicle was English. Hence, English also became the preferred language in India. For convenience sake, most critics consider the year 1981, the year Salman Rushdie's *Midnight's Children* was published, as the watershed year dividing the old and the new schools of Indian English literature. It also triggered off the boom in Indian writing in English. The novel also marked a moment when the Nehruvian dream was about to be splintered in India. There is a nostalgic evocation of Nehru's unity-in-diversity ideal in the novel but Rushdie also critiques it by reminding the readers of all the multiple histories that were erased to write the grand narrative of the nation.

The last two decades of the twentieth century witnessed the emergence and widespread acceptance of a class of writers belonging to the anglicized upper middle class whose success stands in contrast to those peddling to the Western demand for enticing glimpses of Indian life injected with local flavour. Thematically their writing reflects very little of the Indian middle class ethos, unlike writing in regional languages which are firmly entrenched in ground realities of Indian social life. They do not profess the simple polarities that were present in the novelists of the earlier decades. Instead there is an implicit acceptance of hybridity as the necessary condition of post-colonial life. 'They are misappropriating the English language, creating and marketing imaginary homelands. Moreover, their jargon is tailored to the elite pseudo-culture in India,' expostulated critic Nilanjana S. Roy who called Indo-Anglian literature 'a Doon School—St. Stephens' conspiracy'(66). Thus it has to be accepted that the Indian Novel in English from this period onwards also seemed to become a product of a distinct culture as the writers were not only English speaking, but most of them were part of a pan-Indian urban community. Not only did Rushdie's masterpiece overwhelm literary circles in the West, its impact was also decisive in making *The New York Times* dub the young crop of Indian English novelists, viz., Amitav Ghosh, Vikram Seth, I. Allan Sealy, Upamanyu Chatterjee, Shashi Tharoor, Farrukh Dhondy, Rohinton Mistry and Firdaus Kanga as 'Rushdie's Children'.

Another significant aspect of Indian English writing during this period is that a lot of writing actually came from writers of the Indian diaspora. It was the beginning of many paths, opening up of new directions. Though the postmodern devaluation of conventional realism and valorization of exile may seem to suit the diasporic Indian novelists who lack the wherewithals demanded by the traditional form, in their best works, success depends on a very competent mingling of the individual, the family, and the nation in a complex and meaningful network which has been received very well, particularly in the West. Situated in a transnational, fluid state often with multiple identities, some of these contemporary Indian novelists like Vikram Seth, Amitav Ghosh, Gita Mehta, Rohinton Mistry, Anita Desai, Kiran Desai, Chitra Banerjee Divakaruni, Manil Suri, and many others hop, skip and jump continents at will. Their novels also represent sometimes the actual India or what Rushdie terms in his essay 'Imaginary Homelands' as 'Indias of the mind', i.e. an India that remains only in the bits and pieces of memory of the diasporic writer. Interestingly it is these diasporic Indian writers who have been keeping the flagship alive by winning maximum number of prizes and making the presence of Indian English fiction being felt globally. Speaking about 'The Diaspora in Indian Culture,' Amitav Ghosh states that India is, and has always been, a pervasive emotional and psychological presence for 'anybody anywhere who has even the most tenuous links' with it and 'the mother country simply does not have the cultural means to cut him off'(250).

Language: Then and Now

Indian English is a distinct variety of the English language. Many Indians claim that it is very similar to British English, but this opinion is based on a surface level examination of lexical similarities. Of course, one must keep in mind that not every linguistic item is used by every Indian English speaker and that a great deal of regional and educational differentiation exists. Even so, items can be identified which are indicative of Indian English speech and which are widely used. These operate on various phonological, morphological, lexical, and syntactic levels. It was during the Imperial period of the British Raj that British linguist, John Rupert Firth who had intensively researched the linguistic scene of the subcontinent and was Professor of English (1920–8) in Lahore, commented about Indian English that '[m]ost Indian English is kept going by the government, and though it has therefore, a certain local currency, it has no gold backing.' Firth rightly emphasized that 'to be linguistically solvent you must be able to exchange your terms somewhere and somehow for gold of intrinsic social value.' And now, as linguist and scholar Braj B. Kachru endorses, during the years that passed since Firth made this pragmatically insightful observation, not only has the face of the subcontinent altered—politically and otherwise—but all over Asia, linguistically speaking, the English language has become 'solvent', and has indeed turned into linguistic 'gold of social value'. It has become apparent that sticking to the purity of Queen's English is not always a solution. In spite of over a century of unending acrimonious debates on language issues, 'Asia has undoubtedly reached the Age of Asian Englishes' (xviii).

In his erudite article 'The Un-Makers of "Indian" English' Sudhakar Marathe focusing on 'English Teaching Enterprise in Fifty-year Old India', remembers the achievements in English of some sensitive and intelligent visionaries like Jawaharlal Nehru and Sri Aurobindo and at the same time takes stock of the situation at the opposite end of the historical as well as numerical scale. According to him the success threshold for the teaching of English is therefore *enabling*. How far has the English teaching enterprise succeeded in its task of *enabling* young Indians to exploit the English language fully and competently as and when required? This question definitely has a historical dimension, just as it has a social-justice dimension. That is to say, as the numbers of learners and teachers of English have grown astronomically during the past 50 years, so must the question confront the situation both numerically and demographically. Professor Marathe then gives us a good picture of the entire situation:

Before 1947 English was our colonial rulers' language, imposed on an extremely miniscule proportion of contemporary population of India. (That population has grown enormously now.) Some people had to learn it. Others wanted to learn it. Some saw personal advancement coming by means of it. Others plotted to use it by turning it against its own natives. Some saw it as a window on Europe (and on the rest of the world's approach to life and knowledge of it). Others still saw it as historically inevitable that English had to be learned by some if India were to make its way in the as-yet-imagined independence within a drastically modernizing world. In other words, English involved an extremely small number of people yet it did so terrifically significantly in political, economic, technological, cultural, even global terms. (283)

Now let us examine the evolution of Indian English ('Inglish') from *Raj Bhasha* to *Rashtra Bhasha*—from a language of British imperialism to one of free independent post-colonial Indian nation—in the post-colonial context. English was once perceived to be a colonial language, waiting to be discarded from a pluralistic Asian subcontinent in the 1940s. But—gradually, unexpectedly, and rather interestingly—what actually happened was that the language turned into a linguistic commodity with nativized ideological and functional reincarnations in the Indian context. Re-crafted at various linguistic, sociological and cultural levels and relocated in the subcontinent, English is now noted for its flexibility, vibrancy and inclusive nature. It is now adopted as an ethnically neutral language for wider communication. And in all societies of India, the English language still has strong association with higher education, internationalism, modernity and, at a personal level, job mobility and career development. These have ultimately contributed to a regional profile of English in India and to the gradual acculturation of Indian English on the one hand, and to the Englishization of regional languages of India on the other.

Indian English is a recognized dialect of English. If we trace its gradual evolution we notice that we have moved away from the farcical manner of babu-English as spoken by many nineteenth century Indians; to the early twentieth century in which Raja Rao (in 1937) talked of an Indian identity of English and propagated its use; to the late 1960s linguistic scene when social and political leaders like Atal Behari Vajpayee and Ram Manohar Lohia both articulated chants like 'Angrezi hatao' and 'Hindi lao'; to the 'chutneyfication' of the language as extolled by Salman Rushdie in the 1980s; to the support it received from the elite English-medium educated contemporary writers in the last two or three decades. For most of them, English is their first and often the only language for communication and creative writing.

With English the commonly spoken language in India, Indians are contributing their bit at enrichment. The effect of Indian English, more commonly known as 'Inglish' or 'Hinglish' as well as Indian words or Indianisms is being felt everywhere. For example, the latest edition of the *Oxford English Dictionary,* considered the world's favourite word store, is a reflection of this trend; the new collection of linguistic twisters (for Western people, that is) include words like 'bindaas', 'tamasha', 'mehndi', 'desi', 'lehnga', 'adda', 'langar', 'dicky', and 'kitty party'. Also, many words of daily use in English are of Indian origin. In an interview, Catherine Soanes, the editor of the *OED,* rejected criticism that misuse of English words was being legitimized. 'We are merely reflecting the language as it is today,' she said. 'Indian English is one of the growing areas of language, which is contributing to the language as a whole.'

According to *Collins English Dictionary,* English has also included commonly used words by Indians. Distinctly Hindi words that form the vocabulary of a large section of English speaking Indians have been incorporated—'aunti-ji', 'uncle-ji', 'freshie', 'filmi', 'gora', 'kutta', 'kutti', 'haramzada', 'yaar' to name a few. Like the *Oxford English Dictionary,* the editor of this dictionary has also officially acknowledged the role of 'Hinglish' in the evolution of English. 'The inclusion of Hinglish words in the dictionary marks an exciting development and a new phase of borrowing in English,' says editor in chief, Jeremy Butterfield. 'In the long run we can expect Hinglish to influence English in many fields, in the same way that Latin and French have over several centuries.'

Professor David Crystal, author of the *Cambridge Encyclopedia of the English Language* (2004) feels that 'Inglish' is the Indian's journey to 'conquer the world'. He predicts that Indian English will become the most widely spoken variant based on India's likely economic success in the twenty-first century and her sheer population size. 'If 100 million Indians pronounce an English word in a certain way,' he says, 'this is more than Britain's population—so its the only way to pronounce it.' Thus according to him, the language of the twenty-first century might well be 'Inglish' or at least English heavily influenced by India. The British linguist and writer David Graddol in *English Next* (2006) 'tries to look at what's been happening around us in the last four or five years and make sense of it'. Dealing with the transformation of English from 'a foreign language to a global one', English is according to him 'customized by all those who use it'. Graddol also states that India 'will play a major role in the development of global English' and argues that India and China will be responsible for the way English as a language will transform from one of literature to one of commerce and industry.

Discussion and explanation of the bilingual's creativity have resulted in a welcome shift from anecdotal research on 'mixing' and 'switching' of South

Asian languages with English. These two processes have now been studied within various socio-linguistic, stylistic, and psycho-linguistic approaches. Braj B. Kachru in his book *Asian Englishes: Beyond the Canon* (2005) speaks about the Asianness in Asian Englishes and their gradual, yet marked, distinctness which has developed over a long history in contexts of language and cultural contact. According to Kachru,

Asian Englishes are parting ways with the traditional canons of the Raj in the mantras they articulate while strengthening and expanding the link in the use of the English medium. . . . There is palpable excitement about what was earlier essentially a colonial linguistic weapon now turned to represent various dimensions of Asianness (xv).

Thus the Janus-like two faces of English—the *nativization* of English in South Asia and the *Englishization* of the languages of the region—are attracting increased attention. The scholar even detects 'linguistic schizophrenia' in the policies of the government, having both a 'visible' language policy and an 'invisible' one—where, despite the government's best efforts to impose Hindi as one and only national language, they cannot actually do away with English.

Here it would be interesting to review the connection between 'glocalization' and 'Inglish'. Statistics tells us that in India already 333 million people 'use' English to some degree—although only 5 per cent of the population can read or write it. Yet English is already having a significant impact on shaping the future English of industry, commerce and the Internet. Already the number of English speakers in Asia exceeds the number of mother-tongue English speakers and according to demographers, this number is likely to peak around 2 billion in India and China in the next decade. Also, as the use of English widens, it is becoming more localized with different cultures absorbing words and expressions from their own local languages to make an English of their own. This localization of English in India has produced 'Hinglish' or what should be called 'Inglish' because it is increasingly becoming pan-India's street language. So what is Inglish? According to Gurcharan Das (*Outlook India*, 3 May 2005), mixing English with our mother tongues has been going on for generations, but what is different this time around is that 'Inglish' has become both the aspirational language of the lower and middle middle-classes and the fashionable language of drawing rooms of the upper and upper-middle classes. Similar attempts in the past were considered downmarket, contemptuously put down by snob brown sahibs. This time 'Inglish' is the stylish language of Bollywood, of FM radio and of national advertising. Radio Mirchi, for example, has found overwhelming response to one tagline *Ladki ko mari line, girlfriend boli, I'm fine.*

Evaluating the current status of 'Inglish'/'Hinglish' we see that it has now become a two-way interaction, and our mass culture has taken English to the bazaar. Now very frequently English is interpolated with Hindi words in regular usage and this aspect of hybridity is very significant. Sometimes Hindi words are transcribed verbatim into English. Again there is the use of Hindi with interpolation of English words within a single sentence. For example, the advertisement 'Ye dil maange more' for Pepsi or 'Thanda matlab Coca Cola' convey the idea of glocalization much better than theoretical paradigms. So, Inglish is now our 'conquest of English' to use Rushdie's famous words. So far so good. But the obvious question that perplexes the average reader is why then Hinglish? We all know that Hindi as the national language of India, the 'Rashtra Bhasha', is still not accepted in the southern and some eastern states. Prevalent much more in the cowbelt (and with lots of political clout), it is regularly fed through the nationalized television channel Doordarshan and several other private 'Inglish' channels too. Like the inroads that SMS and emails have made in the globalized world, thus decimating chaste Queen's English, these advertisements usually cater to the burgeoning city-centred upwardly mobile Indians. Some items are directly related to characteristics of Indian languages. Indians will often ask, 'What is your good name?' which is a somewhat literal translation of 'Aapka shubh naam kya hai?' Shubh means auspicious or good, and it is basically used as a polite way of asking for someone's full name. An Indian English speaker says today morning (*aaj subha*) or yesterday night (*kal raat*) to mean this morning and last night.

David Graddol speaks of the importance of multilingualism and how the ability to speak more than one language has put other European nations at an advantage over the UK. To illustrate this phenomenon, I now focus on the use of 'Inglish' in contemporary media and advertisements. A random survey done on leading Indian journals and newspapers in English like *India Today, Outlook, The Statesman, The Telegraph,* and the in-flight magazines of Air India and Jet Airways shows that most of them are bilingual, deliberately using Hindi words with English syntax. So, the target readership is obviously the middle and upper-middle class English knowing Indians.

To conclude this section about the evolution of English as an 'Indian' language it must be mentioned that in our great 'linguistic melting pot country' we now speak 'Inglish' in all its local and regional variations with special emphasis on bilingualism, especially in the use of Hindi or regional syntax. Much of the rapid Hindi-ization (or regionalization) of English is thought to be the result of globalization, glocalization and British Asian interaction. However strange they may sound, the deliberate use of Hindi words attempts to bring in the linguistic unity of our language within culturally diverse groups, something that could not be implemented through legislation. It is true that the 'post-colonized' can never retrieve the pristine purity of their languages, as Simon During observes. English has acquired new structures and tonalities in India in the process of adapting it to native use. At a time when we have ceased to speak of Queen's English and speak instead of many Englishes, we need no longer be apologetic about Marathi/Gujarati/Bengali/Tamilian English that carry the tonalities and inflections of these mother tongues.

Thus however much the purists may argue, we cannot write off the presence of English in India over the past two centuries. If it was the language of colonial domination, it was also the language of anti-colonial resistance; our national leaders including Mahatma Gandhi and Jawaharlal Nehru had employed it in the service of the freedom struggle arousing the nation to fight the Empire. We may also remember that it was our own decision to retain English as a link language and a language of intellectual, emotional and imaginative articulation even after the British had left the country. Today India is the third largest English-using nation in the world; only the USA and UK have greater numbers of users of the language. It is used in India by close to 5 per cent of the population; some of the languages of the Eighth Schedule of the Constitution have far fewer than the 35 million users English has. English is also the state language of some of the Indian states in the north-east; it is our associate official language and the chief link language for not only international but even inter-regional communication. India has a large network of newspapers and journals in English besides several publishing houses that bring out books only in English. In fact India today is one of the three largest publishers of books in English. Salman Rushdie's Aurora Zogoiby (The Moor's Last Sigh) was not far wrong when she said, 'Only English brings us together.'

In the present age of globalization we find Indian English facing the same problem as other Englishes—language as a means of communication through texting, SMSs, is changing the language too fast. As it is, marketing gurus have already woken up to the fact that technological revolution which globalized English may in its new avatar displace it, now that software and digitalized intellectual property have crossed language barriers allowing new technical vocabulary to develop in languages other than English. It would become a new and different ballgame then.

Literature: Then and Now

Moving from language to literature, we must once again remember that Indian English literature began as an interesting by-product of an eventful encounter in the late eighteenth century between a vigorous and enterprising

Britain and a stagnant and chaotic India, and is more than 200 years old. It is literature written originally in English by authors Indian by birth, ancestry or nationality. It is no part of English literature, any more than American literature or Australian literature can be said to be a branch of British literature. It is legitimately a part of Indian literature, since 'its differentia is the expression in it of an Indian ethos' (Naik). Sahitya Akademi, the Indian National Academy of Literature has also accepted 'Indian English Literature' as the most suitable appellation for this body of writing. The term emphasizes two significant ideas: first, that this literature constitutes one of many streams that join the great ocean called Indian literature, which, though written in different languages, has an unmistakable unity; and secondly, that it is an inevitable product of the nativisation of the English language to express the Indian sensibility.

The constraints that Indian literature in English encounters, have best been articulated by one of its living practitioners, Shashi Deshpande in an article she wrote in *The Hindu*. One is, of course, its lack of a long tradition and the assurance that comes from it. There is hardly any archive, cultural register or community memory that it can fall back upon for drawing its images, archetypes and cultural symbols. It tries to make good at times by drawing on the larger 'Indian' mythology and epics or Greek, Roman or Persian traditions thus making it difficult to locate it specifically: this is particularly evident in Indian poetry in English as poetry depends, more than fiction does, on cultural memory to achieve its vertical semantic and associational dimension.

Before delving into the analysis of Indian English literature, it must be kept in mind that the definition of what constitutes this category is itself a matter of debate among critics and scholars. Firstly, we have to remember that this category of literature went through several nomenclatures like Indo-Anglian literature, Anglo-Indian Literature, Indo-English Literature, Indian English writing, before it was accepted as Indian Writing in English or simply Indian English Literature. Again, there is also the debate about whether a writer could be called an Indian English writer by just being a resident of the country or whether his passport defined him in the case he was a non-resident Indian or was a writer of the Indian diaspora. M.K. Naik, whose seminal work *A History of Indian English Literature* (1982) analyses in detail the different nomenclatures, emphatically states, Strictly speaking, Indian English literature may be defined as literature written *originally* in English by authors Indian by birth, ancestry or nationality. It is clear that neither 'Anglo-Indian Literature', nor literal translations by others (as distinguished from creative translations by the authors themselves) can legitimately form part of this literature (2).

Naik also categorically explains that the writings of British or Western authors like Kipling, Forster, Sir Edwin Arnold, John Masters, Paul Scott and many others concerning India obviously belongs to British literature. Similarly, translations from the Indian languages into English cannot also form part of Indian English literature, except when they are creative translations by the authors themselves. According to academic and critic Esha Dey, '[T]aken in its entirety, Indian Writing in English may not be perceived as a tree growing tall and sending deep roots into the soil, but it appears to have spread extensively like grass' (274).

Thus, it can be said that it is the sum of differences in attitudes, world views and responses that makes a novel 'Indian'. Here again the word 'Indian' needs to be used with caution since writers in English too belong to specific geographical regions or languages and this gives their works a local quality. For example, Mulk Raj Anand conveys a Punjabi flavour and is not very successful when he writes about regions other than his own; *Private Life of an Indian Prince* is an example. In R.K. Narayan's fiction one can easily perceive the presence of his region in the customs and manners he deals with; also, the language he employs has Tamil overtones. Raja Rao's *Kanthapura* shows conspicuous use of the nuances of Kannada; Bhabani Bhattacharya's fiction has something Bangla about it; Vikram Seth has Hindi beneath his English, and Arundhati Roy's novel *The God of Small Things* has the flavour of Malayalam. But as Meenakshi Mukherjee rightly notes, this regional dimension is missing in the 'public school English' of the novels of Shanta Rama Rau, Kamala Markandaya or Manohar Malgonkar who are not rooted in any specific Indian culture. This forces many writers to try exotic or Orientalist Indian themes or catchy phrases in order that their works look Indian on the surface. F.W. Bateson coined the word *Métèque* as a way of referring to writers for whom English was a second or third language, who don't respect (or don't know) 'the finer rules of English idiom and grammar'.

Take the case of Desani's novel again. The mad English—the deliberate use of among English—in *All About H. Hatterr* is a thoroughly self-conscious and finely controlled performance, as Burgess points out in the preface:

But it is the language that makes the book, a sort of creative chaos that grumbles at the restraining banks. It is what may be termed Whole Language, in which philosophical terms, the colloquialisms of Calcutta and London, Shakespearian archaisms, bazaar whinings, quack spiels, references to the Hindu pantheon, the jargon of Indian litigation, and shrill babu irritability seethe together. It is not pure English; it is, like the English of Shakespeare, Joyce and Kipling, gloriously impure.

Since *All About H. Hatterr* is a book more referred to as the first Indian English novel to play with the English language than actually read (one of the reasons being its unavailability in the Indian market), I fear that a slightly lengthy excerpt is necessary here to get a real taste of the artistic twists of language:

The name is H. Hatterr, and I am continuing . . .
Biologically, I am fifty-fifty of the species.
One of my parents was a European,

Christian-by-faith merchant merman (seaman). From which part of the Continent? Wish I could tell you. The other was an Oriental, a Malay Peninsula-resident lady, a steady non-voyaging, non-Christian human (no mermaid). From which part of the Peninsula? Couldn't tell you either. Barely a year after my baptism (in white, pure and holy), I was taken from Penang (Malay P.) to India (East). It was there that my old man kicked the bucket in a hurry. The via media? Chronic malaria and pneumonia-plus.

Whereupon, a local litigation for my possession ensued.

The odds were all in favour of the India-resident Dundee-born Scot, who was trading in jute.

He believed himself a good European, and a pious Kirk o' Scotland parishioner, whose right-divine Scotch blud mission it was to rescue the baptised mite me from any illiterate non-pi heathen influence. She didn't have a chance, my poor old ma, and the court gave him the possession award.

I don't know what happened to her. Maybe, she lives. Who cares?

Rejoicing at the just conclusion of the dictate of his conscience, and armed with the legal interpretation of the testament left by my post-mortem seaman parent, willing I be brought up Christian, and the court custody award, the jute factor had me adopted by an English Missionary Society, as one of their many Oriental and mixed-Oriental orphan-wards. And, thus it was that I became a sahib by adoption, the Christian lingo (English) being my second vernacular from the orphan-adoption age onwards.

The E.M. Society looked after me till the age of fourteen or thereabouts.

It was then that I found the constant childhood preoccupation with the whereabouts of my mother unbearable, the religious routine unsuited to my temperament, the evangelical stuff beyond my ken, and Rev. the Head (of the Society's school), M.A., D.Litt., D.D., also C.B.E., ex-Eton and Cantab. (Moths, Grates, and Home Civ), Protor par excellence, Feller of the Royal Geographical, Astronomical and Asiastic Societies (and a writer!), too much of a stimulus for my particular orphan constitution.

Desani's love of playing with the language, sometimes literally turning it into a conjurer's trick, is also evident in the Epigraph of the novel:

Indian middle-man (to author): Sir, if you do not identify your composition a novel, how then do we itemise it? Sir, the rank and file is entitled to know.

Author (to Indian middle-man): Sir, I identify it a gesture. Sir, the rank and file is entitled to know.

Indian middle-man (to author): Sir, there is no immediate demand for gestures. There is immediate demand for novels. Sir, we are literary agents, not free agents.

Author (to Indian middle-man): Sir, I identify it a novel. Sir, itemise it accordingly.

Commenting on *All About H. Hatterr,* Salman Rushdie maintains that Desani's work has 'showed how English could be bent and kneaded until it spoke in an authentically Indian voice . . .'. On the other hand, Amitav Ghosh believes that Desani was 'haunted by the incommensurability of what he wanted to say with the language he was saying it in. This is of course, an awareness that haunts many of us who write in English. But Desani was unique in that he alone had the courage to follow his perceptions to their natural conclusion—into the unreachable otherness of silence' (www.amitvghosh.com/essays/desani.html).

Many Indian writers in English experiment with diction, literally translating idioms, or with syntax, transforming the structure of the sentence. The literal translations can be seen mostly in Mulk Raj Anand. Look at some examples: 'Is this any talk?', 'Are you talking the true talk?', 'May I be your sacrifice.' There are Punjabi-Hindi expressions like 'counterfeit luck', swear words and abuses used by the peasants in Punjab as also proverbs like 'Your own calf's teeth seem golden' (*The Road,* 24); 'A goat in hand is better than a buffalo in the distance' (ibid., 22); 'The camels are being swept away, the ants say, they float' (*The Big Heart,* 206). Khushwant Singh too has a similar flavour to his English: 'Sardar Saheb, you are a big man and we are but small radishes from an unknown garden' (*I Shall not Hear the Nightingale Sing*). Bhabani Bhattacharya translates a Bengali saying: 'When an ant grows wings and starts flying in the air, it is not far from its doom' (*A Goddess Named Gold*). He also uses expressions like 'childling', 'wifeling', 'starveling', 'villagefuls of folk', 'joy-moments', 'picture-play' (for cinema). He also uses the Bengali idiom like the typical short sentences: 'Why speak? What use? Trees and rocks have a heart. Not man. Why speak?' (*So Many Hungers,* 76). Raja Rao also uses phrases like 'that-house people', 'next-house woman's kitchen', 'milk-infant', 'ten-eleven year old child', etc. Sometimes words in other languages are used directly as in Mulk Raj Anand: 'angrez-log', 'yar'; there are created verbs like 'burburred in his sleep', 'sisking with cold', 'thak-thakking at a cauldron'; at times the spellings indicate the speaker's illiteracy: 'yus' (yes), 'notus' (notice), 'Amrika' (America) or 'Girmany' (Germany).

Raja Rao uses Kannada figures of speech unobtrusively: 'Postman Subbayya, who had no fire in his stomach and was red with red and blue with blue' (*Kanthapura,* 154). 'You are a Bhatta and your voice is not a sparrow voice in your village and you should speak with your people and organize a Brahmin party. Otherwise, Brahminism is as good as kitchen ashes.' In *The Serpent and the Rope,* he tries changes in structure: 'He is so tender and fine-limbed, is my brother' (12). 'His Sona, one who is dead, was once tied to a tree and beaten' (149). Arundhati Roy in her *God of Small Things* uses Malayalam words directly, at times mixed with English words:

'Poda, pattee', 'Valare thanks', 'Thanks, ketto', 'Naley', 'Chacko Saar vannu', 'Veluthe! Ividay! Veluthe', 'mon', 'mol', 'kochamma', 'paravan', 'pulayan', she uses these Malayalam words in English script and does not care to give a glossary. Her descriptions invoke typical Ayemenem landscapes through their use of pepper vines, tapioca, etc. Sometimes she even uses innovative adjectives like 'a viable, dieable age,' or 'the orangedrink lemondrink man' or plays with words like *locus standi* as 'Locust-Stand-I' or creates new words like 'stopitted'.

In Salman Rushdie, as it has often been said, English is in dialogue with Indian languages, especially so in *Midnight's Children*. Upamanyu Chatterjee's *English, August* also at times uses a mixed language as in the expression 'hazar-fucked', a typical marriage of Urdu and American slang. Amitav Ghosh has used multilingualism most effectively in his *Sea of Poppies*, though the tendency is evident in his other works like *The Hungry Tide* and *The Glass Palace*. In *Sea of Poppies* he uses the tonal music of Bhojpuri, the language of its woman protagonist, very effectively and even brings in Bhojpuri folk songs; he also uses Hindustani in many forms, at times mixed with English, as in the slang used by the crew of the ship, Ibis. The experimentation with language becomes much more marked in the second volume of the trilogy, *River of Smoke*. Here babu-English, Bhojpuri, Kreole, pidgin English, Indian English, Cantonese, all rub shoulders as the story unfolds.

There is a self-conscious questioning of the boundaries of language in many of the works I referred to; often they bring languages into comic collision, testing the limits of communication between them. They celebrate India's linguistic diversity and take over the English language to meet the demands of the Indian context. In the process they also question the 'purity' of Indian culture and prove that it is a mixture, receiving influences from outside the subcontinent. English thus becomes a part of the polyphony and its colonial authority is relativised when it enters the complexity it describes. But English as a language has been associated with colonialism, modernity and the elite. The new writers are aware of this and hence refuse to privilege either tradition or modernity. The new writers after Rushdie are also more playful and confident; their abrogation of standard English is also seen as a sign of a certain cultural weightlessness, the deracinated insouciance of elite college boys, alienated from the natural community. It might also be interpreted by some critics to be an example of the Empire writing back.

Language and Literature: Interstices

At the time of the inauguration of Sahitya Akademi, Dr. Sarvapalli Radhakrishnan uttered a thoughtful observation: 'There are many languages in India but one literature.' This significant utterance should be recalled to avoid the controversy still raging—whether Indian English literature is indigenous or foreign and whether the native sensibility of the content and its expression in a 'foreign' language in terms of form are still two disparate entities. This may well serve as a guideline to critics evaluating all Indian literary output in English and in fact, debate continues in various forms even today. Indian critics of Indian writing in English like M.K. Naik, C.D. Narasimhaiah, Meenakshi Mukherjee, Makarand Paranjape, Shyamala Narayan, P.K. Rajan and Vinay Kirpal, besides scores of academics who have been contributing to anthologies, have tried to explore the field in varied and useful ways. While some of them have been more open in accepting the new genre and its experimentation with the English language, others like C.D. Narasimhaiah have been more critical and less enthusiastic. He reflects,

It is unfortunate that Rushdie for all his brilliance lent himself to be lumped up with them [Vikram Seth and Arundhati Roy] by what must have been pleased to call Rushdi-itis— his magic realism, a poor product of deteriorating British salesmanship, which proved to be disastrous. Simply put, it has come to this: Publishing firms and the media have taken over the functions of the teachers of English. Universities may as well retire all teachers of English and invite media-men to take over. And let them rule the roost. Far from brave claim of the Empire 'writing back' it continues to be dictated by the colonial cringe (15).

It is clear that neither the old Sanskrit poetics nor the new Western literary theories can adequately explain or interpret this genre of writing. Any meaningful criticism of this genre should necessarily take into account the multicultural milieu from which these writers emerge as they come from different regional cultures and linguistic backgrounds often woven into their texts.

As mentioned earlier, language has been one of the central issues in post-colonial fiction. After going through a phase of mimicry as found in the works of Raja Rao, it has led to 'chutneyfication' (coined by Salman Rushdie to explain the idea of the 'pickling effect' of language wherein a gratuitous mix of English, Hindi and Urdu words is found). This hybridity along with the chutneyfication of history has added a new dimension to the ongoing effort in theorizing the post-colonial discourse. In fact, on more than one occasion, such diction comforts the Western audience of Rushdie that after all Indians—or Asians in general—can only use a sort of pidgin English, or what used to be called Butler English. The focus has shifted from theory to textual politics in that as Jonathan White (1993: 209) claims: 'the novel [has become] an alternative way of doing history and politics'. The impetus for such a shift has come from Said's contention that imperialism is not perpetuated at gunpoint or by use of unbridled physical force only but by colonial textuality, for it produced the orient as colonizable. The Victorian novel and its bourgeois veneer represented the Standard English language as the most signifying colonizing code and its defining trope for cultural subjugation. With or without the Caliban paradigm it may be argued that breaking the English language and reproducing it as one's own is not only symptomatic of writing back but also is a way of chanelling the native energy for reproducing the hybrid language as a polyphonic reality.

According to K. Satchidanandan, the charge of 'elitism' against Indian writing in English is also hard to sustain as much of modern Indian writing in the languages too is considered 'obscure' and 'inaccessible' by some readers and critics. This is not in fact a question of the medium or class, but of the varying levels of sensibility. Some complain that the English writers cater only to the urban middle classes and hence deal only with the issues that concern them. Even if this was the case, we cannot neglect this 20 per cent of our population that has a major say in the affairs of the state. But this is not a true complaint either, as writers from Mulk Raj Anand, R.K. Narayan and G.V. Desani to Shashi Deshpande, Amitav Ghosh and Arundhati Roy have dealt with village life and the subaltern classes with great sympathy and understanding.

Many of the writers in the languages too deal with the problems of the middle class as they constitute the majority of Indian readership in either case and as it is an interestingly varied, struggling and mostly upwardly mobile class. Indian writers living in India, whatever the language they write in, live in the same milieu, undergo similar experiences, think and feel more or less in the same way and dream in the same way too. There is, no doubt, a difference in the writers who have spent most of their life abroad, a difference that is obvious in their concerns with issues like migration and their often outsiderish, exoticizing gaze that packages 'Indian' life for a largely foreign readership. Meenakshi Mukherjee in her *Twice-born Fiction* points to certain linguistic problems the Indian writers in English face: one, they have to write in English about people who do not normally speak or think in English; two, they have to write in an acquired language which is a situation very different from those of the American, Australian, Canadian or West Indian writer who can make use of living speech.

This leads us to the use of language and what creative purpose must have been meant to be achieved with the inclusion of Indian words in Indian English writing when they actually create a barrier in the understanding for the international reader. A few examples of this change in the use of language can be mentioned here. We all more or less agree with Rushdie's definition of how the English language in Indian Writing in English has been 'chutneyfied'. But one notices a major shift in the handling and use of words and phrases from the writers of the early decades of the twentieth century with those of the later and more contemporary ones. Earlier, with the aim of the comprehension of the Western reader in mind, we had Indian words being incorporated within the text, with italics and even a long glossary at the end of the text. For instance, Sudhin Ghose's novels even explained words like 'sindoor' as vermillion. This is what Ruchir Joshi defines as 'The Footnote School'. With Rushdie and even G.V. Desani, such glossary was done away with but the texts displayed several stylistic experiments—these were found in the use of Hindi and Urdu words, expressions, expletives, etc. ('O baba', 'Funtoosh'), bilingual echoic formations ('Writing-shiting') using vernacular idioms ('Who care two pice'), bilingual puns ('ladies and ladas'; 'Chand ka tukra'/Piece of the Moon; 'Padma'/dung flower), etc.

In contemporary diasporic as well as resident Indian writers, the use of vernacular words without references or explanations too has definitely become a new fad. Indian Writing in English has come a long way from the use of words with glossary at the end explaining their meanings; to use of words in italics without any glossary; to the present state when non-English words are no longer even italicized. Amit Chaudhuri's novels have several references to the alna, the unoon, the still eye of the pabda fish on the dining table, the lovely luchis for breakfast, etc. Sometimes it seems that the writers are doing this kind of exoticization with a sort of vengeance now—a kind of the empire writing back. In an interview given to me by Chitra Banerjee Divakaruni a few years ago, I had raised this point. Chitra disagreed about the exoticization element. According to her, when you create characters that are Indian, who think in the Indian way, why not express the Indian language too? Though she believes that it lends depth and authenticity to her Indian characters, this is not always the case; in fact they often tend to get stereotyped and quite predictable.

English writing in India also has a tendency to inflate itself and tends to exoticize, present or explain India and package it for a foreign audience as it happens mostly with the writers living outside the country. It does not have a close-knit community of readers as the language writing mostly has. This amorphous nature of the audience it addresses often leads to an ambivalence in English writing regarding what it can expect from the readers. This uncertainty of context is besides the ambiguity about its own historical positioning. One may well ask why there are no movements, like the Dalit movement for example, in English, except for *Touch* a recent novel by Meena Kandasamy. The more intelligent of the writers in English are aware of these issues and are, as we have seen, trying to find the means to overcome them. The Man Booker Prize winning Aravind Adiga's *The White Tiger* is another novel of critical dissent where he pits the darkness of the rural world of India's poor against the light of the new world of the rising upper middle class; here too he invents a language that is apparently light and full of fun, yet adequate to portray the horrors of Indian reality.

In recent times, one writer who has emerged as consciously including non-English words in his novels after doing serious research, is none other than Amitav Ghosh. These include not only Indian words (without glossary or italics) but also local words in other regions as per the situation and locale of his transnational novels. In *The Hungry Tide* (2005), Ghosh experiments with non-verbal communication between the Indian American research scientist Piya (who cannot speak Bangla, her mother tongue) and Fokir, the illiterate boatman in the remote region of the Sunderbans. Juxtaposed between these two extremes is Kanai, the official translator of languages who lives in Delhi but has come to the Sunderbans to meet his aunt Nilima. Kanai's inability to be an actual interpreter of languages in the real life context is something that Ghosh wants to highlight in the novel. Ghosh's serious interest in non-English words and their origins is further illustrated in the introduction of The Ibis Chrestomathy in *Sea of Poppies* (2008), the first volume of his trilogy. Basically, chrestomathy is a selection of passages from an author or authors used to help learn a language. In the novel Ghosh makes the character Neel become interested in The Ibis Chrestomathy thus:

Words! Neel was of the view that words, no less than people, are endowed with lives and destinies of their own. Why then were there no astrologers to calculate their kismat and pronounce upon their fate? The thought that he might be the one to take on this task probably came to him at about the time when he was first beginning to earn his livelihood as a linkister—that is to say during his years in southern China. From then on, for years afterwards, he made it his regular practice to jot down his divinations of the fate of certain words. The Chrestomathy then, is not so much a key to language as an astrological chart, crafted by a man who was obsessed with the destiny of words. Not all words were of equal interest of course and the Chrestomathy, let it be noted, deals only with a favoured few: it is devoted to a select number among the many migrants who have sailed from eastern waters towards the chilly shores of the English language. It is, in other words, a chart of the fortunes of a shipload of girmitiyas: this perhaps is why Neel named it after the Ibis.

But let there be no mistake: the Chrestomathy deals solely with words that have a claim to naturalization within the English language. Indeed the epiphany out of which it was born was Neel's discovery, in the late 1880s, that a complete and authoritative lexicon of the English language was under preparation: this was of course, the *Oxford English Dictionary* (or the *Oracle*, as it is invariably referred to in the Chrestomathy). Neel saw at once that the *Oracle* would provide him with an authoritative almanac against which to judge the accuracy of his predictions. Although he was already then an elderly man, his excitement was such that he immediately began to gather his papers together in preparation for the Oracle's publication. He was to be disappointed for decades would pass before the *Oxford English Dictionary* finally made its appearance: all he ever saw of it was a few facsicules. But the years of waiting were by no means wasted; Neel spent them in collating his notes with other glossaries, lexicons and word-lists. The story goes that in the last years of his life his reading consisted of nothing but dictionaries. When his eyesight began to fail, his grand- and great-grandchildren were made to perform this service for him (thus the family coinage 'to read the dicky', defined by Neel, as 'a gubbrowing of last resort').

On his deathbed, or so family legend has it, Neel told his children and grandchildren that so long as the knowledge of his words was kept alive within the family, it would tie them to their past and thus to each other. Inevitably, his warnings were ignored and his papers were locked away and forgotten; they were not to be retrieved till some 20 years later. The family was then in turmoil, with its many branches at odds with each other, and its collective affairs headed towards ruin. It was then that one of Neel's granddaughters (the grandmother of the present writer) remembered his words and dug out the old band-box that contained Neel's jottings. Coincidentally, that was the very year the *Oracle* was finally published—1928—and she was able to raise the money, by joint family subscription, to acquire the entire set. Thus began the process of disinterring Neel's horoscopes and checking them against the Oracle's pronouncements—and miraculously, no sooner did the work start than things began to turn around, so that the family was able to come through the worldwide Depression of the 1930s with its fortunes almost undiminished. After that never again was the *Chrestomathy* allowed to suffer prolonged neglect. By some strange miracle of heredity there was always, in every decade, at least one member of the family who had the time and the interest to serve as wordy-wallah, thus keeping alive this life-giving conversation with the founder of the line.

The *Chrestomathy* is a work that cannot, in principle, ever be considered finished. One reason for this is that new and previously unknown word-chits in Neel's hand have continued to turn up in places where he once resided—these unearthings have been regular enough, and frequent enough, to confound the idea of ever bringing the work to completion. But the Chrestomathy is also, in its very nature, a continuing dialogue, and the idea of bringing it to an end is one that evokes superstitious horror in all of Neel's descendants. Be it then clearly understood that it was not with any such intention that this compilation was assembled: it was rather the gradual decay of Neel's papers which gave birth to the proposal that the Chrestomathy (or what there was of it) be put into a form that might admit of wider circulation. It remains only to explain that since the Chrestomathy deals exclusively with the English language, Neel included, with very few exceptions, only such words as had already found a place in an English dictionary, lexicon or word-list. This is why its entries are almost always preceded either by the symbol of the Oracle (a+) or by the names of other glossaries, dictionaries or lexicons: these are, as it were, their credentials for admittance to the vessel of migration that was the Chrestomathy. However the power to grant full citizenship rested, in Neel's view, solely with the *Oracle* (thus his eagerness to scrutinize its rolls). Once a word had been admitted into the Oracle's cavern, it lost the names of its sponsors and was marked forever with its certificate of residence: the +. "After the *Oracle* has spoken the name of a word, the matter is settled: from then on the expression in question is no longer (or no longer only) Bengali, Arabic, Chinese, Hindi, Laskari or anything else—in its English incarnation, it is to be considered a new coinage, with a new persona and a renewed destiny.

The experiment with languages becomes even more pronounced in Ghosh's *River of Smoke*, the second volume of the Ibis Trilogy. Published in June 2011, the novel is full of non-italicized words from Kreol, Bhojpuri, Indian English, Hindusthani, Gujarati, Cantonese, and especially pidgin English as many of the characters land up in Canton, China. The careful reader has to negotiate with words and phrases like 'paltans of bonoys, belsers, bowjis, salas, sakubays and other inlaws'(3), chakkis, masalas, bhoots, rakshasa, tamasha, bandobast, the 'chutkis and chutkas', the 'laikas and laikis', the jaldi jaldi, granper, the bak-bak, jism, rooh, kya, cumshaws, bakshis, ishq, pyar, daftar, shaahbash, haraaming wives, budmashing, phataphat; the different names of workers like gentil-man, khidmatgars, daftardars, khansamas, chuprassies, peons, durwans, khazanadars, khalasis, and lascars (185); and the convoluted style of English spoken by several characters including the protagonist, Bahram Modi, the Parsi opium merchant from Bombay. But what is more interesting is the fact that Ghosh's own interest in the evolution of different hybrid languages is conveyed in detail to the readers at different points in the novel. The first detailed discussion takes place when Bahram and his Armenian friend Zadig go to meet Napoleon imprisoned in an island in the mid-Atlantic. The General asks them whether they had made any attempt to familiarize themselves with the Chinese language. They reply in the negative and this becomes a good opportunity for Ghosh to explain things in detail:

They answered in one voice: No, they said, they spoke no Chinese, because the common language of trade in southern China was a kind of patois—or, as some called it, 'pidgin', which meant merely 'business' and was thus well suited to describe a tongue which was used mainly to address matters of trade. Even though many Chinese spoke English with ease and fluency, they would not negotiate in it, believing that it put them at a disadvantage in relation to Europeans. In pidgin they reposed far greater trust, for the grammar was the same as that of Cantonese, while the words were mainly English, Portuguese and Hindusthani—and such being the case, everyone who spoke the jargon was at an equal disadvantage, which was considered a great benefit to all. It was, moreover, a simple tongue, not hard to master, and for those who did not know it, there existed a whole class of interpreters, known as linkisters, who could translate into it from both English and Chinese (171).

The interest in pidgin does not stop there. Neel, while working as a munshi of Bahram Modi in Canton, gets interested in the evolution of the Chinese language expressed through ideograms when he is sent by his employer to meet Compton who brings out a business paper called 'Ghost-People-Talk.'

Neel was greatly taken by the ingenuity of this: instead of using phonetic symbols, Compton had suggested the pronunciation of the English word by using a character that sounded similar when pronounced in the Cantonese dialect. For longer and more complicated words, he had joined together two or more one-syllable Cantonese words: thus 'today' became 'to-teay' and so on. (271)

Soon he comes up with a proposal for Compton to produce an English version of 'Devil-Talk' and like the *Ibis Chrestomathy* of the earlier volume, he decides to do a new one again:

Neel could already see the cover: it would feature a richly caparisoned mandarin. As for the title, that too had already come to him. He would call it: *The Celestial Chrestomathy, Comprising A Complete Guide To And Glossary Of The Language Of Commerce In Southern China*. (272)

This renewed interest in the way Indian English writers are using non-English words to augment the uniqueness of their craft now is actually the reverse of what their counterparts were doing in the nineteenth century, namely trying to ape and imitate the style of the British writers who wrote in chaste Queen's English. The process seems to have come to a full circle. According to Esha Dey,

The secret of the Indian writers' success lies in their creative use of English and complete mastery of medium, their ability to draw upon eclecticism going beyond Anglo-American stereotypes, their effective exploitation of post-modern aesthetic devices to bridge the unbridgeable gulf between land and language. The universe gained by Indian Writing in English coincides, indeed, forms part of the whole process of globalization which valorizes uprooting and migration, when exile has become a universal phenomenon. (274)

Indian English Tomorrow

In his article on 'The Autonomy of Indian Writing' Amit Chaudhuri states:

... Indian writing, in the last one hundred and fifty years, represents not so much a one-dimension struggle for, or embodiment of, power, as a many-sided cosmopolitanism. It isn't enough, today, to celebrate Indian writing's 'success', after having identified what its marks of success are (as if a whole tradition must only, and constantly, be thought of as an arriviste would be); one needs to engage with its long, subterranean history (as hard-earned as political freedom itself) of curiosity and openness. (4)

How Indians are using this in their literary output is clear from the sudden onrush of chick-lit flooding the Indian market. Every other day a new debut novel by an Indian author is making its way into the stands and unlike the more serious aspirants for the Man Booker or the Commonwealth Writer's Prize, these writers cater to the desi Indian English readers, particularly the younger generation. That is why Chetan Bhagat's *Five Point Someone* catapulted him into the limelight and earned him fame overnight. His next novel, *One Night@the Call Center* set in the world of the call centre at Gurgaon is also critical of the new lifestyle which is seen as a re-colonization of the city. Here again Bhagat uses colloquial English, the lingua franca of the urban middle class. The author is not concerned with literariness, but with the possibilities of identification. He freely mixes *Mahabharata* and James Bond, Western pop and Indian fables. Novels like Samit Basu's *The Simoquin Prophecies* and Rana Dasgupta's *Tokyo Cancelled* attain a new level of freedom by reflecting the new global space created by the market through their multiple locations. Their language reflects the new texture of life in India, a world where jazz and Bob Dylan are as popular as Bollywood film songs and ghazals. It is an openness that calls for interrogation as it traces the inner cartography of liberalized India that switches between cultures and is rooted nowhere. It also raises ethical questions like that of our behaviour toward immigrants and refugees. As regards globalization we also find a shift in the attitude of the writers. While Raja Rao's generation suffered from loneliness and a longing for roots, the modern Indian writer celebrates displacement. Take Bharati Mukherjee for example. She has made a name for herself in the literature of the New World and regards her writing as part of the American literary tradition. We can be certain that such confidence and exuberance would take various directions in future, some of which may be traced from the present trends. Also, for many Indian writers like Vikram Seth, labels of nationality or frontiers of political and geographical divisions will cease to exist.

This leads to the last question, but a very important one at that—do Indians appreciate their own English? Ultimately, I think they do. It has been said that Indians have made English into a native language with its own linguistic and cultural ecologies and socio-cultural contexts. Its special functions have engraved English into the cultural life of India, and it is very much a part of the experience of being Indian—even if one does not speak it. Many Indians feel that the use of English should be actively encouraged because of the many advantages it confers—the greatest of which is its universal character. The Indian writer and philosopher Raja Rao wrote,

Truth, said a great Indian sage, is not the monopoly of the Sanskrit language. Truth can use any language, and the more universal, the better it is. If metaphysics is India's primary contribution to world civilization, as we believe it is, then must she use the most universal language for her to be universal.... And as long as the English language is universal, it will always remain Indian.... It would then be correct to say as long as we are Indian—that is, not nationalists, but truly Indians of the Indian psyche—we shall have the English language with us and amongst us, and not as a guest or friend, but as one of our own, of our caste, our creed, our sect and our tradition. (quoted in Kachru 12)

Many others fear, perhaps legitimately, the loss of India's native languages. English has changed Indian languages in many ways—mostly through the incorporation of new words. However, the population of English speakers in India, though socially influential, is a small minority compared to the rest. Also, most of these individuals are conversant in at least one, if not two or three, other languages, and unless the situation necessitates English, they usually speak in their native language. Way back in 1968, Professor C.D. Narasimhaiah had defined Indian Writing in English as 'primarily part of the literature of India in the same way as the literatures written in various regional languages are or ought to be'. Esha Dey's point of view, expressed as late as 2006, sounds much more optimistic:

The future Indian writer may not be a Balzac or a Proust because we are no inhabitants of a monolithic ethos, nor have we participated in a uniform evolutionary process for centuries. India is a great mosaic of many motifs and patterns and its transition from various stages of civilization, primitive, ancient, medieval to the modern, going on simultaneously, offers great challenges to writers in English, particularly of fiction. We can be sure that Indian Writing in English has a bright future provided the status quo is maintained: the continuance of India as a union of states, the growth of English medium education as a means to cross territorial limits and the place of English at the leading edge of technology and scientific development. (278)

Though it is true that a lot of mediocrity often makes it difficult for us to segregate the grain from the chaff, it is also true that it is absolutely impossible to predict how Indian Writing in English will be defined just ten years from now.

References

Amit Chaudhuri, 'The Autonomy of Indian Writing', *Connecting,* April-May 2009, in *The Picador Book of Modern Indian Literature,* New York and London: Picador, 2001, pp. 2–4.

Esha Dey, 'The Future of Indian Writing in English', in *Indian Writing in English: Yesterday, Today and Tomorrow,* Pranati Dutta Gupta and Susmita Ray, eds., Kolkata: Vivekananda College, Thakurpukur, 2006 pp. 273–80.

G.V. Desani, *All About H. Hatterr,* Portland, OR, US: Aldor, 1948, repr. New York: Saturn Press, 1950; rev. edn., Farrar, Straus and Young, NY, USA, 1951; Further rev. edn. w/intro by Anthony Burgess, UK: The Bodley Head, 1970; revd. edn. with additional final chapter, USA: Lancer Books, 1972; repr. of this edition with further revisions, UK: Penguin/Hamish Hamilton, 1972.

Pranati Dutta Gupta and Susmita Ray, eds., *Indian Writing in English: Yesterday, Today and Tomorrow,* Kolkata: Vivekananda College, Thakurpukur, 2006.

Amitav Ghosh, 'The Diaspora in Indian Culture' in idem, *The Imam and the Indian,* Delhi: Permanent Black, 2002, pp. 243–50.

———, *Sea of Poppies,* Penguin/Hamish Hamilton, 2008.

———, *River of Smoke,* Penguin/Hamish Hamilton, 2011.

Braj B. Kachru, *Asian Englishes: Beyond the Canon,* New Delhi: Oxford University Press, 2005.

T.B. Macaulay, 'Minute by the Hon'ble T.B. Macaulay, dated the 2nd February 1835', http://www.mssu.edu/projectssouthasia/history/primarydocs/education/Macaulay001.htm

Sudhakar Marathe, 'The Un-Makers of "Indian" English: English Teaching Enterprise in Fifty-year Old India', in *Makers of Indian English Literature,* C.D. Narasimhaiah, ed., Delhi: Pencraft International, 2000, pp. 281–92.

Meenakshi Mukherjee, 'Indian Novels in English: Then and Now', in *Indian Writing in English: Yesterday, Today and Tomorrow,* Pranati Dutta Gupta and Susmita Ray, eds., Kolkata: Vivekananda College, Thakurpukur, 2006, pp. 1–8.

———, *The Twice-Born Fiction,* New Delhi: Heinemann, 1977.

M.K. Naik, *A History of Indian English Literature,* New Delhi: Sahitya Akademi, 1982.

C.D. Narasimhaiah, 'Making of Indian English: Some Reflections', in *Makers of Indian English Literature,* C.D. Narasimhaiah, ed., Delhi: Pencraft International, 2000, pp. 15–36.

Nilanjana S. Roy, 'Write Society: Indo-Anglican Literature as a Doon School—St. Stephens Conspiracy' *India Today,* 7 February 2000.

Salman Rushdie and Elizabeth West, eds., *The Vintage Book of Indian Writing 1947–1997,* London: Random House, 1997. Also published as *Mirrorwork: 50 Years of Indian Writing.*

K. Satchidanandan, 'Mother tongue, the other tongue.' *Seminar#* 600, August 2009.

CHAPTER SEVEN

'Tagore Syndrome': A Case Study of the West's Intercultural (Mis)readings

IGOR GRBIĆ

The Rise and Fall of a Poet

'[T]hese prose translations from Rabindranath Tagore have stirred my blood as nothing has for years. . . .'[1] This is William Butler Yeats in 1912, writing his famous Introduction to the English version of Rabindranath Tagore's *Gitanjali*, published the following year. We have here peeped into the second sentence of the Introduction. Yeats is so excited that he cannot postpone sharing it with his readers. He actually goes so far as to claim that 'Tagore's lyrics . . . display in their thought a world I have dreamed of all my life long. The work of a supreme culture . . . .' In 1935, however, Yeats begins a letter to his friend with the words 'Damn Tagore'.[2] What happened in those twenty-odd years to turn a qualified admirer into a detached denouncer? Actually, since Yeats' reaction was characteristic of the West, rather than an isolated instance, we had better ask what happened with the Western readers of Tagore?

Tagore was a writer of prodigious production. By the time he came out of his teens he had accumulated an opus that in itself would have been quite sufficient not to make the long 80 years of his life seem only modestly productive. He wrote in Bengali, his mother tongue, and enjoyed an extraordinary reputation among his countrymen, though not undivided. Indeed, not few were those objecting to the audacity of his style, all kinds of technical innovations and the unconventional treatment of only seemingly traditional motifs. In the West he was completely unknown.

All that dramatically changed at the poet's age of fifty-two. In 1912 Tagore presented a friend of his with a manuscript containing 103 poems in prose, translated to English by himself. The manuscript reached Yeats, who saw to its publication, prefaced with his introduction. The next year, the booklet, entitled *Gitanjali*, won him no less than the Nobel Prize, the first awarded to any non-Westerner.[3] The award rocketed him into heights that had not been seen before and have not been seen since. Amit Chaudhuri does not exaggerate when he observes that Tagore became 'the first global superstar or celebrity in literature'.[4] In the years to come he would be applauded, garlanded and adored wherever he went, including the Soviet Union and Fascist Italy. He made a dozen foreign tours, that took him to almost every continent. Among his enthusiasts were the most eminent men of letters such as André Gide and Boris Pasternak, both of whom translated him. In India, voices of dissension generally subsided and Tagore was by and large hailed as the national bard, pride of the country. It seemed as if the prophecy from Yeats' Introduction was becoming flesh and blood:

These verses will not lie in little well-printed books upon ladies' tables, who turn the pages with indolent hands that they may sigh over a life without meaning, which is yet all they can know of life, or be carried by students at the university to be laid aside when the work of life begins, but, as the generations pass, travellers will hum them on the highway and men rowing upon the rivers. Lovers, while they await one another, shall find, in murmuring them, this love of God a magic gulf wherein their own more bitter passion may bathe and renew its youth.

But then something went awry. To all appearances, the West was becoming tired of Tagore and Tagoreism. Among the disenchanted, once again, we find outstanding writers. Ezra Pound, to name one. In 1937 Graham Greene drew the line: 'As for Rabindranath Tagore, I cannot believe that anyone but Mr Yeats can still take his poems very seriously.'[5] We saw, however, that at that time Yeats had already *damned* Tagore. Nevertheless, his rejection was not total and he did include some of Tagore's early poems in *The Oxford Book of Modern Verse* that he prepared in 1936. During the uneasy years between the two world wars, and even after his glamour had started to wane in the West, Tagore preserved the aura of a spiritual authority, capable of transcending the current turmoils and battle cries. He died amidst these cries, in 1941. The post-war West seemed to have completely forgotten even that Tagore. In the mid-1960s, Anna Akhmatova, in her admiring and translating the Bengali minstrel, looked like a lonely bird still defying a flock that had flown away a long, long time ago. Eventually, in 2011, on the 150th anniversary of the poet's birth, *The Guardian*'s columnist Ian Jack could report that, much to his astonishment, he had opened the Oxford and the Penguin dictionaries of quotations only to find that, for Tagore, there was '[n]ot a single entry. They skipped from Tacitus to Hippolyte Taine as if there was nothing in Tagore's collected works (28 thick books, even with his 2,500 songs published separately) that ever had stuck in anyone's mind'.[6]

The Rise and Fall of a Poet's Public

Multiple are the reasons behind this shooting parabola. I shall here try to trace them, moving from the apparent to the less obvious. First of all, what has been stressed innumerable times has to be repeated once again: among those who have been able to read Tagore in the original it is a matter of common agreement that translations of his poetry, to any language, are only a very feeble echo of its original richness and sound. Bengali has been called the Italian of India and one of the most melodious Indo-European languages, occasionally even the most melodious. Moreover, contrary to Tagore's own and the bulk of subsequent translating practice, what we find as uneven poetic prose is, in Bengali, verse respecting rhythm, metre and rhyme that can be easily put to music (much of his poems are in fact songs and rely more on their formal features than on the content). Translating his own lines, Tagore must have felt the way he did when translating songs of Bengali *bauls* (wandering poet-singers), describing the job as presenting butterflies with their wings torn out. There are at least two reasons to Tagore's avoiding more formal translations of his own poems. Firstly, he never felt sufficiently confident of his English and had serious doubts even about his translations in prose. Second, he considered any attempt at saving the beauty of the original, a wild goose chase in the first place, the discrepancy between the original and any target language being, to his mind, unsurmountable. He even openly discouraged his aspiring translators from learning Bengali and resorting to the originals themselves and asked them to rather start from his own English translations. Fortunately, the aspiring translators have not always paid heed.

Tagore's translations of Tagore bring us to the next point. Numerous places in his letters and other writings, as well as personal accounts of people he was acquainted with, bear witness to the pains he took in order to produce a Tagore he considered was palatable to the average English reader. In other words, he deliberately and systematically worked to falsify his original poetic self, expunging or at least moderating everything he deemed 'too Indian', rephrasing or even adding what in fact had to serve as veiled footnotes, 'explaining the unexplainable'. Edward Thompson's *Rabindranath Tagore: Poet and Dramatist*, published in 1926, with the second, revised edition dating from 1948, offers quite a number of such missed translations, which more often than not succeed only in watering down the splendour and pregnancy of the original imagery. This tendency seems to have increased in the course of the years and we find Tagore constantly adapting and re-adapting the English versions of his plays even in his advanced age. It started, however, as early as his English debut; the *Gitanjali* he was awarded for is far from its Bengali version, but rather a patchwork made of selections from ten books of poetry (with at least one poem created as an amalgam of what was originally two poems). I suspect Thompson is right in taking it to be Tagore's finest translation. Whatever he subsequently translated for the Western readership will be heavily boiled down, rearranged and then served. Furthermore, even when it comes to his original works, Tagore was often enough rebuked for his repetitiveness; trying to conform to a safe pattern, his English translations reflect the tendency even more so. These facts undoubtedly figure as a major reason for the change in the Western perception, exemplified again by Yeats' weariness with the 'sentimental rubbish' of Tagore's later books and with his bad English (which, however, was probably just a misplaced rationalization of some other issues). Though never getting tired of rewriting his works, Tagore was at a different level well aware of the inadequate position he had found himself in. Here is a part of his letter to Thompson, dated 2 February 1921:

You know I began to pay court to your language when I was fifty. It was pretty late for me ever to hope to win her heart. Occasional gifts of favour do not delude me with false hopes. Not being a degree-holder of any of our universities I know my limitations—and I fear to rush into the field reserved for angels to tread. In my translations I timidly avoid all difficulties, which has the effect of making them smooth and thin. . . . When I began this career of falsifying my own coins I did it in play. Now I am becoming frightened of its enormity and am willing to make a confession of my misdeeds and withdraw into my original vocation as a mere Bengali poet. I hope it is not yet too late to make reparation.[7]

Just as in the case of Yeats, appealing to the problem of language does seem rather a way of beating about the bush.

Instead of pandering to what he perceived as the Western literary taste, Tagore would have done greater service to both East and West had he offered authentic literature of his own self and his background. Acclaimed as he was, he missed the historical opportunity to educate the West and joined, instead, in complacently fondling the prejudices existing in the Western mind. Still, the most responsible is the West itself, for it missed its own chance to be educated. The self-Westernized Tagore was not that Western, after all. For what one can gather today from the enthusiastic atmosphere prevalent at the time, even if a newly made devotee had been acquainted with the fact that singing and playing to one's own poems was not a Tagorean invention, but Indian tradition, he or she would have gladly sacrificed this knowledge to the coveted image of the saintly, white-bearded wise man from the East, the singular incarnation of all arts and insights. This figure landed in Europe at a moment most fragile and vulnerable for the continent, and the messianic effect subsequently produced had obviously least of all to do with literature. The post-war Europe badly needed Tagore's 'exotic' message of peace and love. No adequate translation would have corrected the distortions created in such an exalted state of mind. When the exaltation was over, it was over with Tagore.

Tagore himself was not unaware of the distorted reactions. In 1920, at the peak of his glory, he wrote to C.F. Andrews concerning some immoderate advocates of his: 'These people ... are like drunkards who are afraid of their lucid intervals.'[8] In another letter he is even more specific: 'People have taken to my work with such excessive enthusiasm that I cannot really accept it. My impression is that when a place from which nothing is expected somehow produces something, even an ordinary thing, people are amazed—that is the state of mind here.'[9] This is a very acute observation. If Tagore ever was guilty of condescending to the West, the West did the lion's share of the job, its eternal thirst for the exotic producing a Tagore very different from the Tagore that actually existed. For its own part, Bengal, afflicted with the colonial complex, readily mimicked the accolades imparted by the always better knowing ruler. The previous objections to Tagore's way of writing were by and large smoothed out and the poet became 'a fetish ... the holy mascot of Bengali provincial vanity'.[10] The problem with the exotic is that it has a shelf life. Once this expires, the exotic becomes just another platitude.

A good part of the blame for Tagore falling out of favour with the West certainly goes to those of its intellectual community who belittled the Indian dimension of his work and magnified the Western, in the desire to show that by praising Tagore the West actually praised itself. Very illustrative of such a stance is Luigi Luzzatti's Introduction to the Italian translation of Tagore's *The Crescent Moon*. He represents Tagore as a true Westernized Indian that did away with his native background and introduced a poetry hitherto unknown in India, highlighting the poet himself, singing about himself. Although Luzzatti draws on a great many of quotes from Tagore's poetry to prove his thesis, they do not exactly seem to corroborate his point. It is true that Indian classical literature avoids the first person singular, but this is certainly not true of popular, devotional and related poetry, where it is even common for the poet to openly mention his or her own name at the end of the poem. And this is precisely the kind of poetry that Tagore avowedly drew upon. His readings of English poetry and the influence it made on him were largely exaggerated, to the expense of his rootedness in native ground. Luzzatti should have gone back to the Introduction by Yeats, who saw the relationship between East and West in Tagore much more clearly. Instead, Luzzatti's own Introduction gets completely out of hand when, towards the end, it signals that 'Europe awarded India, that had given heed to its teachings'.[11] True, such criticism could also be heard among Tagore's countrymen back in India, as noticed by Thompson, but the latter, who was particularly familiar with the situation, advertently adds that 'such things were said by, at any rate, a minority of his own countrymen',[12] probably those who never came to terms with the poet's singular poetic vein, that expressed foremost his own idiosyncrasies, and only laterally any supposedly European ways. In other words, if Tagore at all sounded too little Indian, it was primarily because he was too much of an individual, re-articulating his own tradition in a fresh voice, and only very much secondarily because he was imitating European patterns.

'Tagore Syndrome': Echo and Pizza Effects

Admitting the alleged untranslatability of Bengali verse, admitting Tagore's own oversights in gaining his Western reputation and the relative flatness of much of his later writing, admitting the flaws in some of his Western interpreters, I would still argue that the main culprit for the poet's disappearance from the Western world is the latter's superficial curiosity and only slack readiness to open itself to the Other. Tagore's case has remained the gaudiest instance of a culture going from one extreme to the other in its appreciation of something belonging to a different culture. What began as excitation of the moment was doomed to soon exhaust itself once fresh fuel stopped coming and the interest not being genuine enough to enable any kind of deeper and sustained study. The episode ignominiously ended with Tagore even being accused of getting credit for the work of Yeats, who had supposedly 'rewritten' *Gitanjali*.[13] Tagore's diseased fate in the West became first and foremost a part of the anamnesis of the West itself. It was not his fall so much as the fall of his public.

This is the extreme version of the behavioural pattern we are repeatedly coming across, with Tagore only as a—or rather *the*—case in point. It typically manifests itself in a somewhat different way, with the West appropriating the Other by adapting it to its own point of view and sensibilities. Although I argued that this was not predominantly so in Tagore's case, the West still typically best acknowledges the Other when the latter is best representing qualities acquired from the West. I would call that the *echo effect*. In exemplifying it, let us stick to India. More than with Tagore, this indulging in its own reflection, its own echo, becomes visible in the four living Indian authors connected by the Booker Prize, which is generally considered the second best prize in literature at the global level. Salman Rushdie's *Midnight's Children* not only won its author the 1981 Booker, but also the 1993 Booker of Bookers, the only one awarded so far. In 1997 Arundhati Roy got hers for her debut novel *The God of Small Things*, with Kiran Desai's *The Inheritance of Loss* following suit in 2006.

Only two years later, it was awarded to Aravind Adiga's *The White Tiger*. It is certainly not my intention here to question any of these (though I do have a personal opinion about each). My present concern is rather to propose these cases as much likelier instances than Tagore's of the West paying homage to its own taste and/or caprice of the moment. *Midnight's Children*, and Rushdie in general, is hailed as a grand representative of magical realism, a mode of writing the West has come to love so much, being well-suited to its postmodern preference for undermining any stable concept of reality and creating pastiche. However, once the West outgrows its own fashion, it is my suspicion that Rushdie's dashing reputation will be among the first to suffer. *The God of Small Things* is very near to making linguistic exuberance its protagonist, which, coupled with a tragic, cross-religious love story in an exotic setting, sounds like a pretty safe formula for gaining the vote of a Western panel. I find Kiran Desai's example peculiarly interesting as it can be seen against that of her mother, Anita Desai, who, to my mind, sustainedly writes much more elaborate, penetrating, but, alas, also to a traditional prose to reach beyond the Booker shortlisting point of attraction (and no less than three times). Finally, *The White Tiger* contains at least two winning factors where Western prejudice is concerned: the always welcome semi-childlike perspective, and raw, unmitigated depiction of an exotic urban world. Once again, I am not arguing here that all or any of these writers won their awards *because of* the reasons I summarily sketched, but that these *are* worth considering as elements of an extraliterary pattern that keeps repeating itself in the Western appreciation of non-Western literatures.

If somebody might get the impression that the above remarks have put us off the track, let me clarify that, just as any syndrome, what I here propose to call 'Tagore syndrome' cannot be represented by one case only. Rather, it should be understood as a common denominator designating all kinds of variations within the given phenomenon. Tagore's simply happens to be the most celebrated and, at least in some respects, the most exemplary case. Let me rephrase the symptoms observed hitherto, in somewhat idealized lines, for the sake of clarity. The West loves when the non—West writes like the West. In Luzzatti's words, it loves when the non-West gives heed to its teachings. (Of course, much of the present examination could be generalized to encompass spheres outside writing itself, but this would require separate elaboration and a different kind of text). If the non-West does not write that way, the West loves it to be at least exotic, juicy, wild, anything that can tickle its curiosity, stimulate its constant excitability, momentarily quench its thirst for the new, as long as it remains unmenacingly different and safely distant. Consequently, such writing and such writers are particularly vulnerable to impermanence, a shooting star fading as soon as its novelty becomes as boring as that of the stars of yesterday. Myself coming from a country bordering on or even belonging to the recently war—torn Balkans, I had ample opportunity to witness instances of foreign book markets showing interest in Bosnian, Croatian or Montenegrin authors *because* they were coming from that most exotic part of Europe (the fact that geographically they *are* part of Europe only enhancing the exoticness), writing about first-hand experiences of something so exciting as ethnic war. (By the way, the same can be said about the cinematographies of the countries in question.)

The easiest and safest way to recognize Tagore syndrome is exactly the presence of such non-literary factors intervening in supposedly literary evaluation. Interestingly, though not surprisingly, Western judgements modify non-Western perceptions, due to the colonial complex now turned post-colonial. We have already observed the phenomenon in the changed reactions of Tagore's countrymen to his writing after the Nobel Prize. The effect has been noticed for some decades now and was labelled by Agehananda Bharati as *pizza effect*. Once looked down upon in its native country as a meal of the simple, pizza was made a hit by Italian immigrants in America and only then came back to Italy, now as a delicacy in its national cuisine and accepted worldwide. The same thing, adds Bharati, happened with yoga, become trendy in India after it had gained popularity in the West, or with Satyajit Ray, another Bengali, whose films became Indian pride only after Western critics had made him their darling.[14]

Final Remarks and a Tentative Conclusion

Arduous as it is, and for various reasons, constant care has to be taken to read literature simply for what it is. Though there are a number of factors that can and should be taken into account as contributing to our better appreciation, no extraliterary concern may claim to become the criterion of literary excellence. In this respect, contact with a different literary tradition or practice represents particularly slippery ground, there being so many distractions to tempt one into evaluating what should be simply appreciated. The road from impression to judgement is crowded with sirens and colourful blossoms the traveller may enjoy, but not follow.

Taking India as a representative of the non-West, exemplified primarily by Rabindranath Tagore, the present text has done nothing toward evaluating its or his literary quality. It has rather intended to clear some of the shrubbery and thus contribute to preparing the ground for a genuine start in unprejudiced literary examination. Tagore's solitary case turned into a syndrome, and everything should be done to eradicate it. It creates imbalances that severely undermine the chances of establishing authentic literary scholarship, not to mention the harm it does to realizing the lofty ideal of world literature and its study. Every time I revisit Tagore's case I seem less and less capable of spotting truly literary motives behind his past reputation in the West. The non-West, in its turn, is too easily conditioned by the West, and then eagerly sticks to the newly-created standards even after the West has abandoned them. So we find that the Western disenchantment with Tagore stirred up Indian enthusiasm for him, making Indians, and especially Bengalis, highly uncritical. As noticed by William Radice, Tagore's authoritative translator and interpreter, they 'have become fiercely protective towards him, and find it as difficult to face up to flaws and failings in him as parents do in a much-loved, vulnerable child'.[15] It would be instructive and highly advantageous to remember that what began as infatuation ended in fizzling out and creating the opposite kind of infatuation. Amidst such a literary scandal it becomes virtually impossible to discern Tagore's real literary worth (or to approach any nearer to that ideal goal).

Speaking for a while more through the emblematic case of Tagore, clearing up the ground has also to involve proper translation. This is actually the first specific step. In both his Preface and Introduction to Tagore's *Selected Short Stories*, Radice points out that adequate translations of his literature are a job yet to be done, a job in which Radice himself certainly has the lead. These would replace all kinds of Orientalized translations produced so far, or, only seemingly at the opposite pole, Tagore's imprudent concessions to the expectations of the West and his underrating of the latter's ability to widen its own perception. The readers' horizon of expectation is something that needs constant enhancing, when it comes both to producing a text and to its translation. And then, if Bengali verse really is that untranslatable, why are bilingual versions of Tagore's poetry rather rare exceptions than common practice, in an age when Westerners have long become used to read one another's poetry in precisely that manner? Why not attach also a recording of them being sung, the more so since that has been intended as their proper setting from the very start? Second, the West has been unjustly selective in its readings of Tagore, leaving his stories, essays and other genres of his many-sided creativity largely beyond its ken. On the other hand, his less literary and non-literary writings have unduly affected the way the West has been reading the purely literary ones. Radice takes up this subject in a separate article, stressing this filter of Tagore's ideas and ideals and the need to focus on the literary works themselves and on what and how they are saying as such.[16] Before these steps have been taken (and all of them, indeed), we are bound to keep half-consciously staggering along the vast expanse between the poles of condemnation and adoration.

At this point I hope it is needless to say that Tagore's has remained only the most dramatic instance of the perils inherent in both the (post)colonizer's patronizing of the (post)colonized and the latter's trying to please the former. One cannot possibly be too alert when it comes to maintaining intellectual hygiene, letting the Other speak for itself and trying to hear it with an ear untrammelled by one's own voice. In the present times, when colonialism has only become more sophisticated, one should be the more attentive about the insidiousness of seemingly innocuous trifles and catchwords. It is potentially offensive, and at a deeper level certainly detrimental, to speak of the greatest Indian poet Kalidasa as the Indian Shakespeare, particularly when the identification is one-way; we should cultivate ourselves into an amazed reaction at such rhetorics, just as we would react to hearing somebody call Shakespeare the English Kalidasa, a thing unimaginable only due to the ingrained partiality of the game. The game was very popular in Tagore's youth, too, when, even among Bengalis, the best way to honour a writer of their own was to insert him into a pervertedly domesticated copy of the English literary pantheon. So Tagore became the Bengali Shelley. Further, the inherent shortness of any informative article on Tagore or Kalidasa, such as those we found in encyclopedias, should normally make its author think twice before affording the spatial luxury of pointing out that the first was hailed by Yeats, while the second made Goethe sigh. Even when not deliberate, let alone malevolent, such description nevertheless subsists on the underlying assumption that it is actually this that recommends and guarantees the quality of those foreigners. If that chap Kalidasa was able to move grand Goethe—well then, he must be worth one's time! The 'collateral effect', however, is that in such practice non-Western authors are given the opportunity to fully exist only through their Western colleagues. They become the latter's avatars.

Rereading this text I find a thing or two that might look like exaggeration or unwarranted generalization. Of course, the matter *is* much more complicated and deserves further elaboration. Drawing the line, however, I do not feel the need to introduce any changes. I unreservedly believe in the far-reaching importance of the subject here sketched, as well as in the need to forgive the clarion its occasional shrillness, if it is trying to warn. I have attempted at making Tagore's case appear essential to a much wider phenomenon, since '[n]o reputation which was in reality so well founded ever suffered so greatly'.[17] It is essential to understand why that should not happen again.

Notes

1. W.B. Yeats, 'Introduction to *Geetanjali*', 1913, http://www.messagefrommasters.com/Mystic_Musings/Tagore/yeats.htm. accessed on 8 August 2011.

2. Quoted in A. Sen, *The Argumentative Indian: Writings on Indian History, Culture and Identity*, London: Penguin Books, 2005, p. 95.
3. Not infrequently one can read that it was the frist Nobel Prize given to a non-European, which is not true, Theodore Roosevelt having got it in 1906 for peace; it is a fact, however, that Tagore was the first non-European to be awarded the Nobel Prize in Literature.
4. A. Chaudhuri, 'Introduction', in *The Picador Book of Modern Indian Literature*, ed. A. Chaudhuri, London: Picador, 2001, p. xviii.
5. Quoted in Sen, *The Argumentative Indian*, p. 89.
6. I. Jack, 'Rabindranath Tagore was a global phenomenon, so why is he so neglected?', *The Guardian*, 7 May 2011, p. 39.
7. E. Thompson, *Rabindranath Tagore: Poet and Dramatist*, revd. edn., London: Oxford University Press, 1948, p. 264.
8. Quoted in Sen, *The Argumentative Indian*, p. 96.
9. R. Tagore, *Selected Letters of Rabindranath Tagore*, ed. and tr. K. Dutta and A. Robinson, Cambridge: Cambridge University Press, 1997, p. 90.
10. N. Chaudhuri, *Thy Hand Great Anarch! India 1921–1952*, London: Chatto & Windus, 1987, chap. 5.
11. L. Luzzatti, 'Introduzione', in R. Tagore, *La luna crescente*, tr. C. Zannoni-Chauvet, Lanciano: Dott. Gino Carabba Editore, 1920, p. xvi.
12. Thompson, *Rabindranath Tagore*, p. 316.
13. Sen, *The Argumentative Indian*, p. 96.
14. A. Bharati, *Hindu Views and Ways and the Hindu-Muslim Interface*, New Delhi: Munshiram Manoharlal Publishers, 1981, pp. 21–2. The term *pizza-effect* was first used by Bharati as early as 1970 (ibid).
15. W. Radice, 'Introduction', in R. Tagore, *Selected Short Stories*, revd. edn. and tr. W. Radice, London: Penguin Books, 1994, p. 26.
16. W. Radice, 'Sum ergo cogito: Tagore as a Thinker and Tagore as a Poet, and the Relationship between the Two', *Asian and African Studies*, vol. 14, no. 1, 2010, pp. 17–36.
17. Thompson, *Rabindranath Tagore*, p. 264.

References

A. Bharati, *Hindu Views and Ways and the Hindu-Muslim Interface*, New Delhi: Munshiram Manoharlal Publishers, 1981.

A. Chaudhuri, 'Introduction' in *The Picador Book of Modern Indian Literature*, ed. A. Chaudhuri, London: Picador, 2001, pp. xvii-xxxiv.

N. Chaudhuri, *Thy Hand Great Anarch! India 1921–1952*, London: Chatto & Windus, 1987.

I. Jack, 'Rabindranath Tagore was a global phenomenon, so why is he so neglected?', *The Guardian*, 7 May 2011, p. 39.

L. Luzzatti, 'Introduzione' in R. Tagore, *La luna crescente*, tr. C. Zannoni-Chauvet, Lanciano: Dott. Gino Carabba Editore, 1920, pp. i-xvi.

W. Radice, 'Introduction' in R. Tagore, *Selected Short Stories*, revd. edn. and tr. W. Radice, London: Penguin Books, 1994, pp. 1–28.

———, 'Preface' in R. Tagore, *Selected Short Stories*, revd. edn. and tr. W. Radice, London: Penguin Books, 1994, pp. vii-viii.

———, 'Sum ergo cogito: Tagore as a Thinker and Tagore as a Poet, and the Relationship between the Two', *Asian and African Studies*, vol. 14/1, 2010, pp. 17–36.

A. Sen, *The Argumentative Indian: Writings on Indian History, Culture and Identity*, London: Penguin Books, 2005.

R. Tagore, *Selected Letters of Rabindranath Tagore,* ed. and tr. K. Dutta and A. Robinson, Cambridge: Cambridge University Press, 1997.

E. Thompson, *Rabindranath Tagore: Poet and Dramatist*, revd. edn., London: Oxford University Press, 1948.

W.B. Yeats, 'Introduction to *Geetanjali*', http://www.messagefrommasters.com/Mystic_Musings/Tagore/yeats.htm. accessed on 8 August 2011.

CHAPTER EIGHT

The Politics and Poetics of Translating Indian Women's Fiction in English

SWATI GANGULY

Translation is usually understood as an activity of interlingual transference for the benefit of readers who do not have access to an original work in a particular language. It centres on the selection of the source language text and its transference in the target language. However, things are not as simple as they appear; translation activity involves a complex process of negotiation between cultures mediated through the market and the academia, both of which stake their claims on it, working sometimes in collusion and sometimes turning it into a terrain of contestations. Contemporary critics of literary institutions and translation studies have drawn attention to questions of what gets translated and for whom, the relation of power between the source and the target language, the role of publishing houses or the market in generating and disseminating the translated work and the methodology of translation.

In this essay I shall attempt to examine the role of each of these factors and argue that contemporary English translation of Indian women's writing, brings to the fore the tussle between mainstream notions of the canon and its alternative, traditional positions on translation and challenges posed to it by radical revisionings of translation theories, and the agency of the market and the academia. I shall attempt to 'problematize' the field of enquiry, examine the larger politics of culture that shapes its generation and reception—with special focus on women's fiction, and the fiction of Bengali women in particular. Let me begin by closely examining three volumes/ anthologies of English translations of writings from south Asia, brought out by mainstream publishing houses. It is my contention that all these anthologies practise, albeit without any deliberate intentionality, what may be regarded as the politics of omission and commission.

Framing Translations: The Politics of Omission and Commission

The Introduction to *The Penguin Book of Classic Urdu Stories* edited by M. Asaduddin may serve as an entry point into the discussion. Referring to the title of the anthology Asaduddin writes:

Classic has been used to indicate the enduring quality that is, literary works of a certain standard that have drawn generations of readers to them who found them satisfactory in terms of what they expect great literature to be, what may be called its aesthetics and in terms of engaging with issues and concerns that have both immediate and lasting appeal for the readers. The heritage of the Urdu short story is sufficiently rich to constitute such a tradition. My attempt here is to showcase the best samples of that tradition.[1]

Here in a nutshell we have the two main imperatives that determine a translation venture: one, that there exist certain kinds of works—'classics'— that need to be translated, and two that bringing them together and hence 'showcasing the best samples of that tradition' constitute the purpose of a translation anthology.

At this juncture, it is important to refer to the critical debate surrounding the formation of the literary canon—what is understood as classics—and the issue of value of artwork in aesthetic theory. Those who evoke and proselytize for the canon, and this includes famous philosophers like Immanuel Kant, influential literary critics like Mathew Arnold and T.S. Eliot to just name a few, see it as universal and timeless; they argue that classics possess what is regarded as the intrinsic literary/aesthetic merit. What is occluded from the view however, is the material, historical, institutional and ideological processes that form the canon or create notions of classics. Richard Ohmann, a leading contemporary critic in the field of literature, for example, challenges this view in 'The Shaping of a Canon: American Fiction, 1960–1975' by drawing attention to the role played by institutions such as publishing houses, advertising firms and book reviewing outlets, in the material production and distribution of literature. He argues that this complex set of institutional channels determines which books receive attention and are selected as potential entrants into the canon.[2] While the capitalist market is one of the major material factors in determining the canon, the institutions of traditional literary criticism in the academia also play a crucial role in the ideology of canon formation. This is done by fixing the aesthetic value of a work of art in terms of fulfilling certain parameters, which are in turn projected as timeless, eternal and enduring.

What implications do such naturalizing discourses of aesthetics and canon formation have for the woman writer? I want to turn to the selection of Urdu short stories once again. Of the sixteen writers included in the anthology only three are women—Ismat Chugtai, Qurratulain Hyder and Khalida Husain. Of these both Chugtai and Hyder are very well known whereas I, for example, had not even heard of, leave alone read Husain. According to the editor: '... while selecting the stories I was not guided by any consideration of the politics of representation or gender justice. The stories have been chosen solely and exclusively for their merit as good and compelling narratives.'[3]

In other words the editor says that the women included in this anthology are there because they fulfil the criterion of a timeless, enduring aesthetic value. The argument seems to be that the inclusion of greater number of women's writing could only be done through an act of gendered political correctness and would compromise this aesthetic value. What is never questioned is the politics that necessarily informs the process of canon formation, the idea of what constitutes aesthetic merit/value.

Another case in point of exclusion of women's fiction is the recent anthology of translation of Indian writing brought out by Penguin titled the *Best Loved Stories*. This anthology has just one short story by a woman writer—Krishna Sobti, who is no doubt a very important writer of Hindi literature. The editor/translators of this anthology have however, not even noted anything amiss. They simply assume that the category called 'best loved' is self evident and any exclusion of women writers is thus simply because they have failed to come up to the mark. The Penguin anthology is dictated by the demands of the market which is interested in selling what they regard as time tested works which have the stamp of approval of people's taste. It is clearly not interested in toppling the apple cart through a questioning or revising of the male centred canon and introducing women writers—though how they could have been so purblind to the presence of the significant number of women writing in *bhasha* literatures, is a matter of great wonder.

The unstated gender politics of canon formation, the exclusion of women writers from the mainstream is precisely the point of intervention of feminist critical theory and the emergence of the category called 'women's writing' in English literary studies and women's studies in the west and later in the Indian universities.

Feminist Theory, Gynocriticism and Women Writing in India

The entry of 'women's writing' as part of English literature syllabi was possible largely due to the intervention in the academia, of women's movements and feminist thinking in Europe and America. Many women students/researchers/academics began to feel deeply dissatisfied with mainstream literary studies and its methodology of criticism, which they felt 'alienated' the female reader. The feminist academics of the 70s and 80s had a revisionary imperative exposing the androcentric or male centred bias of the literary institution that continued to masquerade as universal and liberal. Directly linked with the latter issue was the devaluation of women's writing in academic 'phallic criticism'. It is important to understand the idea of 'phallic criticism'—a phrase used by feminist literary critics to refer to the sexual bias that underlies a significant section of male criticism of women's writing. In short, male critics tend to pass off as objective or neutral their judgements about women's writing—judgements which are hinged on their ideas of what constitutes the feminine. Broadly speaking, feminist criticism attempted to question both the representation of women in literature and the politics of women's exclusion/occlusion from the literary canon.

The emergence of 'gynocriticism' as scholarship that is 'concerned with woman as the producer of textual meaning, with the history, themes, genres and structures of literature by women'[4] is largely the contribution of American feminist scholars/literary historians who have tried to 're-member' the lost body of women's writing. There is, however, a strong debate within feminist academics/scholarship about the implications of treating 'women's writing' as a separate category with anxieties about whether this implies a further ghettoizing of an already marginalized field; the privileging of 'women's writing' as a more fruitful and invigorating field of feminist enquiry has made significant contributions to what Michel Foucault terms 'subjugated knowledges'.[5] Foucault speaks of traditional knowledge being created within the dominant systems of power; hence anything that exists outside this field of power is 'subjugated'. I use this Foucauldian phrase to emphasize how writing by women or dalits, for instance, constitutes subjugated knowledges.

In the context of India the first major attempt to consolidate a body of 'women's writing' resulted in the impressive anthology *Women Writing in India* by two feminist literary scholar-historians Susie Tharu and K. Lalitha.[6] Tharu and Lalitha, have made available in English translation Indian women's writing in their two volume magisterial *Women Writing in India*. This massive compendium of women's writing in the vernaculars from 600 BC to the present is an invaluable anthology for any scholar historian investigating the field of Indian women's writing.

This anthology is noteworthy for a number of reasons. It brings together an impressive number of 140 writers from eleven *bhasha* literatures through an extensive and meticulous research by scholars who 'searched through archives and spoke with writers and critics before they made the final selection'.[7] Each entry has a biographical headnote, making which was often a challenging task since there was often very little information on many of the authors of yesteryears that they had selected. The most important contribution, in my opinion, is the detailed Preface and Introduction of this anthology, charting out the assumptions, positions from which they worked, as well as the theoretical and critical paradigm used. The editors realized that it was important to evolve a strategy of reading 'against the grain of literary histories, taking special note of writers who were criticized or spoken about dismissively, and controversies that involved women'.[8]

A critical and crucial role has been played by feminist academics in establishing the visibility of the third world woman writer from *bhasha* literatures. Perhaps the most famous example is that of Mahasweta Devi who was translated into English in the early eighties by the prominent Marxist feminist deconstructionist academic Gayatri Chakrabarti Spivak. By the 1970s Mahasweta Devi was well known as a powerful writer among a circle of Bengali readers and also widely known through the translation of her works into other Indian languages. However, her canonical status in the curriculum of post-colonial studies and women's studies (both in the west and at home) was largely the effect of the prestige of her English language translator in the western academia. Needless to say Spivak is no ordinary translator; the author of the now canonical essay 'Can the Subaltern Speak', which is mandatory in any course on post-colonial/subaltern studies, Spivak's endorsement of Mahasweta as the most significant third world woman writer has no doubt played a crucial role in the inclusion of stories like 'Draupadi' or 'The Breast Giver' (Stanadayini) in courses either in women's writing or post-colonial literatures.

Indeed, it is interesting to note that in *Three Sides of Life: Short Stories by Bengali Women Writers*—an anthology published in 2007 by Oxford, three of Mahasweta Devi's stories have been included from English translations of her fiction brought out by Seagull, another prestigious publishing house. The implicit, unstated reason for including the already well known translations of Mahasweta's writing is that no anthology of Bengali women's fiction can be judged respectable without her presence. Yet, there is an absence of other significant 'second wave' women writers like Sabitri Roy, Sulekha Sanyal and Chabi Basu. Ironically, the Introduction to this volume clearly refers to how Bengali women negotiated the most important historical events of their own times in their fiction.

Yet, when it comes to making a selection, these writers get marginalized and silenced despite the claim put forth in this anthology, that 'Gender operates as the matrix of alterity and enables marginalized and subjugated female issues to be articulated within patriarchy'.[9] Perhaps, one might speculate that the reason for their absence is that they do not constitute the mainstream canon of women writers, which is dominated by the popular publishing houses and their market oriented policies. This anthology attests to the curious tug felt by prestigious publishing houses in accommodating the respectable alternative, avowedly feminist with the mainstream/popular woman writers, represented by the likes of Bani Basu and Suchitra Bhattacharya. It could thus be surmised that translations of women's writing from *bhasha* literatures is often determined by their visibility in the source language—ensured by mainstream and powerful publishing houses. However, in the global book market *bhasha* literatures have also to contend with Indian authors who write in English. Indeed, in the domain of what is now recognized as 'post-colonial literatures' it is these English language writers who represent India.

Third World Literatures and the Predicament of the Post-colonial non-English Writer

Indians who write in English are, to use Pico Iyer's evocative term, the 'new makers of World fiction'[10]. They are a generation of writers who truly reap the benefits of a globalized economy. Recipients not only of prestigious literary awards they often make headlines with whooping sums of advance that they have received from their publishers. These writers enjoy a power and prominence in the world literary market unimagined by those who wrote fiction in English in the 30s or 60s. Tracing the contours of this difference is outside the purview of this discussion and I only mention the global image of the English language writer from post-colonial nations because it has had serious consequences for the notion of post-colonial literary productions per se.

In his introduction to the *Vintage Book of Indian Writing (1947–1997)* which no doubt serves as an authoritative and representative volume of Indian writing to the Western metropolitan reader, Salman Rushdie champions the cause of 'English-language Indian writing' in a manner that would have made Thomas Babington Macaulay proud. Indian writing in English, states Rushdie:

is proving to be a *stronger and more important body of work than most of what has been produced in the 16 'official languages' of India, the so-called 'vernacular languages' during the same time;* and indeed this new and still burgeoning 'Indo-Anglian' literature represents perhaps the most valuable contribution India has yet made to the world of books.[11] [emphasis mine]

I quote Rushdie at length highlighting what Gayatri Spivak terms his 'sanctioned ignorance'[12] for several reasons. Rushdie's introduction, which proselytizes the cause of what he evocatively and perhaps with a degree of self-referentiality terms the 'bastard child of Empire, sired on India by the departing British'[13] is complicit in a neo-colonial/neo-Imperialist programme through a two-way process. First, by silencing, occluding the counter-discourses of *bhasha* literatures by designating them 'parochial', and second, by positing writing in English as the only form of 'national literature' bearing the stamp of a national consciousness which has placed India on the map of world literatures. In spite of its hundreds of years of sophisticated and evolved literary tradition *bhasha* literatures are now orphans in a global market that refuse to grant them legitimacy and recognition. The Empire it seems is writing back with a vengeance and in the process settling a score with its own sibling, the vernacular or *bhasha* literatures that had once regarded it as an imposter and foundling in the heyday of the Empire.

This renewed interest in and impetus for producing and disseminating writing in English has profound implications for the emergence of post-colonial literatures. The issue of English is not merely a question of language but a point of entry into the domain of what is now understood as 'Third World Literatures' read/interpreted through the lens of sophisticated post-colonial theories. Though a discussion of post-colonial theory is outside the purview of this discussion, suffice it to say that this theory is largely generated under the aegis of the Anglo-American academies and for the consumption of the West. Critics have noted this Western endorsement of a certain kind of cultural politics as the defining quality of the post-colonial. Arif Dirilk fixes the originary point of the post-colonial as the moment 'When the Third World intellectuals have arrived in the First World academe'.[14] This relatively small group of writers and thinkers—the third world intellectuals work in metropolitan academies in the West—formulate post-colonial theory in the register of English. This implies that not only is English the language of their theoretical formulations but also that they are dependent on the English literatures from erstwhile colonies to make their formulations.

It is therefore hardly surprising that the syllabi of post-colonial literatures in the academia both at home and in the West are dominated by Salman Rushdie and his ilk. I hasten to add that my polemics is not directed towards discrediting the achievement and the literary merit of Indian writing in English both in the colonial and the post-colonial period. Earlier, this used to be referred to as Anglo Indian writing an primarily referred to the poetry of Derozio, Sarojini Naidu and Toru Dutt. For those of us who grew up studying literature in the universities in the middle and late 80s (though it was never included as part of the syllabus) this meant the writings of Anita Desai, R.K. Narayan, V.S. Naipaul, Nissim Ezekiel, A.K. Ramanujam, Dom Mores, Kamala Das, and others. For our students, who fortunately or unfortunately, do a mandatory/optional course in Indian writing in English this implies writers apart apart from stalwarts like Naipul, Anita Desai, Mulk Raj Anand, R.K. Narayan, Salman Rushdie, Vikram Seth and Amitav Ghosh—the newer generation of writers like, Arundhati Roy, Jhumpa

Lahiri and a host of writers from the diaspora. Thus this is not to discredit the contribution of this formidable group of writers but merely to provide a necessary corrective to the rather ridiculous swagger of vanity expressed by the writer-critics like Rushdie who dominate the domain of 'third world literatures' and serve as the face of Indian 'national' literatures. Their power and pre-eminence in the world literary scene continue to produce a blinkered vision of Indian literatures—so much so that we have to resort to underlining the obvious; i.e. that the post-colonial nations like India also produce significant and powerful literatures in Indian regional languages or what is now known as *bhasha* literatures. The blinkered vision of post-colonial literatures it seems can only be corrected through dissemination of post-colonial *bhasha* literatures in English translation. Indeed one might say that it is the post-colonial predicament of the non-English writer—her/his identity as a postcolonial writer—is hinged on the critic/readers' accessibility to her/his works in English. Since English is the linguistic register of a globalized world, English language translations thus determine the visibility of the writer from multilingual ex-colonies to the West and at home.

The new breed of elite English medium educated monolingual readers could perhaps be made aware of the rich tradition of Indian literatures if it were available in English translation. But there is always a possibility that they might turn up their noses at the *desi* writers because of the strange stigma associated with reading translations, exacerbated no doubt by the notion that the aesthetic pleasures of an original are necessarily diminished in translation. The usual common sense attitude (endorsed continually through the book reviews in the popular English press) is that English translations can never approximate the literary and cultural merit of the original (its unique flavour as it were) and thus best to be shunned. Interestingly, this biased approach to translations seems to be restricted to English translations of *bhasha* literatures and does not seem to apply to European literatures (classical or modern) or to Latin American literatures for that matter. Hence the contemporary intellectual metropolitan reader takes delight in Gabriel Garcia Marquez, Jorge Luis Borjes, Umberto Eco, Jose Saramago and Orhan Pamuk seldom bothering to reflect on the fact that their works/fictions were originally written in Spanish, Portugese, Italian and not in English.

How is it that pleasure from these works is not in any way hampered because of translations in English? Perhaps this has to do with the prestige of the Western publishing houses which ensure a quality of translation which most readers feel cannot be matched with those produced in India. Nor is this view entirely unfounded. Translation activity in India still remains an amateur venture without a sustained theory and praxis of translation, a consensus regarding its methodology on the one hand and the short shrift given to the translator on the other. Most of us engaged in translations know that it is often an underpaid job with little acknowledgement involved. Very often even prestigious publishing houses do not feel the need to mention the name of the translator (especially if it is an anthology with a large number of entries), and the rights of the translation do not rest with the translator. Given this scenario, it needs little imagination to grasp that the odds against the *bhasha* literatures in terms of their finding a space within the domain of English translation, are immense.

It is only 'canonical' texts, each of which occupy a position of power and prestige within the critical oeuvre of its own languages, that usually gets selected for translation. Hence, Rabindranath Tagore is the most translated author of Bengali literature and Prem Chand that from Hindi. Such canonical status also ensures the inclusion of writers from *bhasha* literatures in the syllabi of third world literatures or post-colonial writings in the academia. Thus, the metropolitan English language reader from the West and home would be familiar with Tagore's *Ghare Baire* (The Home and the World) as with Prem Chand's *Godaan* and perhaps Ananthamurthy's *Samskara*. Outside the canon or the classics of modern *bhasha* literatures (and by that I mean literatures produced during and after the nineteenth century), fictions which have won awards like the Gyanpith or the Sahitya Academi stand a strong chance of being translated. Sometimes the prestige or popularilty of a film which has as its acknowledged source a work of literature is able to achieve the same zenit—Satyajit Ray's *Pather Panchali*, for example, generated an interest in Bibhutibhusan Bandopadhyay's novel, resulting hence in its translation. The point that I am trying to make is that given the vastness of the field of *bhasha* literatures only a miniscule portion of this is likely to get translated. These current trends in translation need to be historically contextualized.

Traditional/Modern Translation: The Role of English Language Publishing Houses

Post-colonial English translation needs to be conceived as a radical practice and be distinguished from the indigenous traditions that have existed in India over a long period. Meenakshi Mukherjee has observed that 'Translations have always been a vital part of Indian literary culture even when the word "translation" or any of its Indian language equivalents—*anuvad, tarjuma, bhasantar* or *vivartanam*—were not evoked to describe the activity'.[15] The important point to note is that such *anuvad, tarjuma* or *bhasantar* almost never drew attention to its own status as translations thus creating a notion of seamless narratives that are a part of an entire body of writing from a culture. However, what was evidently a virtue/plus point in the indigenous tradition can take on an entirely different political/ ideological connotation when translations occur in the powered relation that exist between languages such as a vernacular and English in a colonial and post-colonial context.

Mukherjee also points out that there was a healthy tradition of translation from one vernacular into another by which a reader of Kannada or Marathi could access literature in Bangla or Oriya without the mediation of English.[16] This form of continuous cultural exchange and interaction accounted for making India into a nation that is 'a translation area'[17]. However, this has lamentably declined over the years for the sheer lack of translators who are proficient in another Indian *bhasha* or vernacular apart from her/his mother tongue. As a case in point Mukherjee refers to the 1996 Kavery—Ganga project launched by Katha to produce direct translations among three languages—Bangla, Tamil and Kannada—whose major stumbling block was locating bilingual translators.[18] It is at this point that one has to look into the role played by the state supported Sahitya Akademis that were set up with the purpose of translating the representative or best works of regional/vernacular/bhasha literatures into English.

The Sahitya Akademis have no doubt contributed in a major way to foster cross-cultural exchange with the objective of linking literature. However, as Ritu Menon points out, in these non-commercial ventures the quality of translation and production values were secondary.[19] Both Meenakshi Mukherjee and Ritu Menon have traced the development in the 60s of private publishing houses, like Jaico, Hind Pocket Books, Sangam Books, Vikas, OUP and Bell Books that took up translation as viable commercial ventures. Some of these ventures unfortunately ceased publication or became sporadic in their attempts in the late 1980's, though OUP has continued to remain active in the field of translation. Their special interests in Tagore's writings which are meticulously edited and translated deserve special mention. Also to be noted is the role played by three independent publishing companies namely Kali for Women (1984), Penguin India (1985) and Katha (1988).[20] Of these Katha has consistently given a fillip to translation through their annual competitions that have encouraged young translators to engage in translation activities—otherwise a thankless and often ill-paid job in India.

Kali, deserves a special mention as a publishing house set up with the avowed aim of dealing exclusively with women's writing, creating a kind of revolution in feminist/women's studies in India. It paved the way for feminist scholars who have used translation as a tool of recovery and discovery of forgotten and neglected women writers from *bhasha* literatures.[21] This in turn has opened up new dimensions for research into women's contribution/role in history, politics and literature, in various disciplines in the universities and centers for culture studies.

However, in spite of the spate of translation activities that now mark the publishing enterprise there is little consensus among them about the theoretical underpinnings of such work. Thus it is difficult to trace the emergence of a theory and methodology of translation in/through these texts, which is indispensable for translation studies and/post-colonial studies in the academia. The presence or the lack of translation apparatus such as glossary, a detailed translator's note/preface along with an indication of the status of the original in its own culture/language is left to the discretion of the individual translator or publishing houses. However, such inconsistencies and neglect go a long way in perpetuating the short shrift that is given to translation in our culture. An awareness of the politics of translation cannot be treated as the special provenance of post-colonial culture critics who have shown how Orientalist translations in colonial India served as a tool of hegemonic control.[22] This is where academic institutions/universities can step in to work in tandem with publishing houses by taking up translation projects that, by using current/contemporary translation theory, can turn the practice into a radical cultural-political one.

Contemporary Theories of Translation: Challenging Fluency and Fidelity

Traditionally the two F's which have dominated translation practice, are fidelity or faithfulness to the source language text and its fluency in the target language. Their unstated presence however looms large in translation reviews in the popular print media. I shall choose to discuss the cultural and ideological implications of 'fluency' because publishing houses continue to prioritize this as a marker of good/readable translation above everything else. For the average/common reader this seems like a reasonable demand that a good translation is one that reads as if it were produced in the target language itself. However, its pernicious effect works both on the status of the translator as well as the translated text, whose ideological/cultural-political implications have been discussed extensively by Lawrence Venuti:

A fluent strategy aims to efface the translator's crucial intervention in the foreign language text: he or she actively rewrites it in a different language to circulate it in a different culture, but this very process results in a self-annihilation, ultimately contributing to the cultural marginality and economic exploitation which translators suffer today. At the same time, a fluent strategy effaces the linguistic and cultural difference of the foreign text: this gets rewritten in the transparent discourse dominating the target language culture....[23]

Venuti's analysis of the politics of 'fluency' and 'transparency' that end up in 'domesticating' a text and perpetuating the cultural hegemony/'imperialism' of the target language is a theoretical position that can be profitably used to understand the role of translation in the post-colonial context. It is crucial to continually remind ourselves that with the lure of a global market for translated post-colonial texts the temptations of fluency and transparency can be immense. But to do so would be to participate/collude in a cultural/linguistic imperialism that perpetuates the dominance/hegemony of Anglo-American cultures.

With poststructuralism and deconstruction radically revising the notion of *original* and questioning the status of authority/authorship, recent translation theory has destabilized the relationship of power between the original and the translated text. In this context it is important to consider the radical potentials of the term *uttarupaniveshbad* (Hindi/Bengali for post-colonialism). As Harish Trivedi has pointed out, the term contains within it the notion of an active dialogue (the Sanskrit prefix uttar means both 'after' as well an 'answer and opposition to') with colonialism and its legacies.[24]

Thus it is crucial to engage in a translation practice that is committed to maintaining the nuances and markers of cultural/linguistic difference of the source language text. This is possible by an insistence on the textual apparatus of translated works, which will, to use Venuti's term, 'foreignize' a text bringing home the point that is so crucial to post-colonial studies—that we are encountering a cultural 'other'—and not attempt to efface it or render it invisible. As practicing translators we have to be conscious of the dangers of domesticating the vernacular text and resist a form of fluency that would convey the impression that it were written in English.

The greatest stumbling block on the path of such radical practice is to run a risk of the critical common place of one's work being termed 'a bad translation' which invariably translates as that it does not read like an English text. The crucial point is that we need to revise and monitor the kinds of expectation that we bring to a post-colonial translated text, which through years of our experience as the colonized we have internalized as 'natural' and legitimate. Perhaps a more fruitful way would be to recognize that a translated work can neither occupy the position of an original in the target language nor can it wholly be an unchanged version of its originary source language. Rather it is a hybrid product that occupies a third space, a place of in-betweenness.[25]

I shall turn once again to *Women Writing in India* as a rare example of an anthology of Indian women's writing in English translation that addresses these issues in its translation praxis. What Tharu and Lalitha do not emphasize is the special relationship that women writers have to language especially to conventions of writing. This is not to take recourse to the notion of special women's language as done by traditional male critics who essentialize the relationship between women and language, and neither to make a case for the sophisticated notions of *ecriture feminine* posed by French feminist writers like Helene Cixous, Luce Irigary and Monique Witting.

The point I am making is that since women have had a longer tradition of access to oral forms, of story telling and to traditional or proverbial sayings within the culture it stands to reason that their writings will contain greater markers of such negotiation with the oral and popular cultures. English translation of Indian women's writing has to be particularly sensitive to such nuances, use of dialects, or colloquialisms, and standardize them to erase differences in favour of smooth marketable translations.

Notes

1. M. Asaduddin, Introduction, *The Penguin Book of Classic Urdu Stories*, New Delhi: Penguin/Viking, 2006, pp. xi-xii.
2. Richard Ohman, 'The Shaping of a Canon: U.S. Fiction 1960–1975', in *The Norton Anthology of Theory and Criticism,* Vincent B. Leitch, ed., New York and London: W.W. Norton & Company, 2010, pp. 880–7.
3. Ibid., p. pxxiii.
4. Elaine Showalter, 'Towards a Feminist Poetics' in *The New Feminist Criticism,* ed. Elaine Showalter, London: Virago, 1986, p. 128. This essay was originally published in *Women Writing and Writing about Women,* ed. Mary Jacobus, New York, 1979, pp. 22–43.
5. Michel Foucault, *Power/Knowledge: Selected Interviews & Other Writings 1972–1977,* ed. Colin Gordon, New York: Pantheon Books, 1980, pp. 81–2.
6. Susie Tharu and K. Laitha, eds., *Women Writing in India: 600 B.C. to the Present,* New Delhi: Oxford University Press, 1991.
7. Ibid., p. xx.
8. Ibid., p. xviii.
9. Tutun Mukherjee, Introduction to Saumitra Chakravarty, ed., *Three Sides of Life: Short Stories by Bengali Women Writers,* New Delhi: OUP, 2007, p. xxiv.
10. Pico Ayer, 'The Empire Writes Back', *Time,* 8 February 1993, pp. 46–56.
11. Salman Rushdie and Elizabeth West, eds., *The Vintage Book of Indian Writing, 1947–1997,* Vintage Books, 1997, p. x.
12. Gayatri C. Spivak, *A Critique of Postcolonial Reason: Toward a History of the Vanishing Present,* Calcutta: Seagull, 1999, p. 369 fn.
13. Salman Rushdie, p. xii.
14. Arif Dirlik, 'The Postcolonial Aura: Third World Criticism in the Age of Global Capitalism', *Critical Inquiry,* vol. 20, 1994, p. 328.
15. Meenakshi Mukherjee, *The Perishable Empire,* New Delhi: Oxford University Press, 2000, p. 187.
16. Ibid., p. 193.
17. Vanamala Viswanatha and Sherry Simon, 'Shifting grounds of exchange: B.M. Srikantiah and Kannada translation', in Harish Trivedi and Susan Bassnett, eds., *Postcolonial Translation Theory and Practice,* London and NY: Routledge, 1999, p. 163.
18. Mukherjee, p. 192.

19. See Ritu Menon, 'Publishing and Translation', in *Translation, Text and Theory: The Paradigm of India*, Rukmini Bhaya Nair, ed., New Delhi: Sage Publications, 2001, p. 123.
20. Ibid., pp. 123–5.
21. I have in mind of course the encyclopedic work, Susie Tharu and K. Lalitha, eds., *Women Writing in India,* New Delhi: Oxford University Press, 1991, not to mention a large number of autobiographies and memoirs that have been translated by feminists in the recent times.
22. See Tejaswini Niranjana, *Siting Translation*, Hyderabad: Orient Longman, 1992.
23. Lawrence Venuti, ed., *Rethinking Translation: Discourse, Subjectivity, Ideology*, London and NY: Routledge, 1992, pp. 4–5.
24. Harish Trivedi, 'India and Postcolonial Discourse', in *Critical Theory: Western and Indian,* Prafulla C. Kar, ed., New Delhi: Pencraft International, 1997, pp. 36–55.
25. See Homi Bhabha, *The Location of Culture*, London and NY: Routledge, 1994, pp. 38–9.

Editor and Contributors

CHHANDA CHATTERJEE is Professor and Director, Centre for Guru Nanak Dev Studies and Programme Coordinator, UGC SAP DRS II of the Department of History at Visva-Bharati, Santiniketan, West Bengal. Her earlier publications include *Ecology, the Sikh Legacy and the Raj Punjab, 1849-1887* (1997), *Ideology, the Rural Power Structure and Imperial Rule: Awadh and Punjab, 1858-1887* (1999), and *Rabindranath Tagore and the Sikh Gurus: A Search for an Indigenous Modernity* (2014).

AMIT DEY is a Professor of History, University of Calcutta. His publications include *The Image of the Prophet in Bengali Muslim Piety: 1850-1947* (2006) and *Sufism in India* (1996). He has jointly edited *Between Tradition and Modernity: Aspects of Islam in South Asia* (2011).

SWATI GANGULY is Associate Professor of English at the Department of English and Other Modern European Languages, Visva-Bharati, Santiniketan, West Bengal. She has translated and co-edited (with Sarmistha Duttagupta) *The Stream Within: Short Stories by Contemporary Bengali Women* (1999). She is also the co-editor of *Rabindranath Tagore and the Nation* (2011) and the Departmental journal *apperception: The Renaissance and Afterlife* (2013). She has been awarded the New India Foundation Fellowship to work on a book project, '"Saving Tagore's life's best treasure": A History of Visva-Bharati (1951-61)'. She writes fiction in Bengali.

IGOR GRBIĆ is Associate Professor of the theory and history of literature at the Juraj Dobrila University, Pula, Croatia. As a literary writer, he has authored several books of fiction, poetry and essays. He has translated a number of books. His writing and translation have won him numerous awards, both national and international.

SOBHANLAL DATTA GUPTA was associated with Presidency College, Burdwan University, Centre for Studies in Social Sciences, Kolkata and the University of Calcutta till his retirement in 2008 as Surendra Nath Banerjee Professor of Political Science at the University of Calcutta. His published works include *The State of Political Theory: Some Marxist Essays* (co-author, 1977), *Justice and the Political Order in India* (1978), and *Comintern and the Destiny of Communism in India: 1919-1943, Dialectics of Real and a Possible History* (2006, 2011). He has edited *PC Joshi, K. Damodaran, A Documented History* of the *Communist Movement in India. Select Materials from Archives on Contemporary History,* vol. I: 1917-1922, vol. II: 1923-1925 (2007), *Ryutin Platform (Stalin and the Crisis of Proletarian Dictatorship)* (2010), and *Marxism in Dark Times: Select Essays for the New Century* (2012).

SOMDATTA MANDAL is Professor of English and at present the Chairperson of the Department of English and Other Modern European Languages, Visva-Bharati, Santiniketan, West Bengal. She has written three academic books and edited and co-edited fifteen books and journals. She has also received a Sahitya Akademi award for translating short fiction.

ANURADHA ROY is Professor at the Department of History, Jadavpur University. She is the author of *Nationalism as Poetic Discourse in Nineteenth Century Bengal* (2003), a book on the novels written by women in nineteenth-century Bengal entitled *Dukkhini Sati Charit: Unish Shataker Bangali Meyeder Upanyas* (2011), and *Cultural Communism in Bengal, 1936-1952* (forthcoming). She has edited two authoritative collections of nationalist songs and poems for the Bangla Akademi and the Sahitya Akademi and has also compiled and edited select writings from the journal *Sangathan* launched just before Independence to coordinate Gandhian rural work in Bengal (2009).

GANAPATHY SUBBIAH is former Professor, Ancient Indian History, Culture and Archaeology at Visva-Bharati, Santiniketan, West Bengal. He is the author of *Roots of Tamil Religious Thought* (1991). He was President of Ancient History Section, Indian History Congress in 2005.

Index

Abul Fazl 5, 40
Adiga, Aravind 13, 131, 145
   White Tiger 13, 131, 145
administration 7, 10, 111
   colonial 7
Akbar, the Great Mughal 5–6, 28, 35, 39–40, 43
   liberal predilections 6
Akhmatova, Anna 13, 140
Al Beruni 5
   Chandayan 5, 39
   Chiragh-i-Delhi 5
Alka 7
Amir Khasrau 5
Amis, Martin 110
Anand, Mulk Raj 11, 114, 125, 127, 130, 157
   Untouchable 11, 114–15
Andrews, C.F. 82, 87, 96, 143
   Thoughts from Rabindranath Tagore 82
anthologies 2, 7, 13, 19–20, 23, 110, 129, 151–5, 159, 162
   West 110
Antuvan 21, 24
anuvad 159
appreciation 5, 9, 12, 38–9, 102, 144–6
   public 12
   Western 12, 145
aql 6, 41
Arab settlers 5
archaeological sources 17–18
   reliability of 17
Arnold, Sir Edwin 124
Arosyev, Alexander 97
aryans 7, 50–3, 55, 58, 63
   hermitage 7
authenticity 2, 49, 58, 68, 131
Azad, Maulana 6

Baba Farid 29–30, 32, 37
Bada'un 31
Balanda 33
Bangha, Imre 10
Bangladesh 54, 60, 112
Baraka 4
Barnes, Julian 110
Basirhat 4, 33
Basu, Chhabi 13
Basu, Kumudini 7, 52
   Janmabhumi 7, 52
belief 3, 10, 30, 33–4
   Sufi 30
Bengal 4, 6–7, 11, 33, 37, 42, 49–51, 53–62, 64–8, 82–3, 111–13, 143
Benjamin, Walter 104–5
   Moscow Diary 104
Bhakti movement 5
Bharati, Agehananda 13, 146
bhasantar 159
Bibi Auliya 4, 35, 37
Bibi Fatima Sam 4, 32–3
Bibi Jamal Khatun 4, 35
Bibi Sara 3, 29
Bibi Sharifa 4–5, 30, 37
Bibi Zulaykha 3, 30–1
Bible 6, 42
biographies 4, 28, 35
   Sufi 28
Boer War 82
Bolshevism 102
Britain 58, 67, 81, 110–11, 120, 124
Bukharin 99

Cankam age 21
capitalism 14, 81, 87–8, 100
capitalists 8
   foreign 8
Carter, Angela 110

Index

Castes 6, 8, 11, 60, 114, 137
  consciousness 8
Celva-k-kaṭunkō-v-āli-y-ātan 23–4
cēral 2, 19–22, 24
  family 19
  irumpoṟai 21
Cēralar 2, 19, 21, 23
Chakravarty, Amiya 82
Chattopadhyay, Bankim Chandra 7, 10, 113
  Anandamath 7
  Bande Mataram 7, 58
Chattopadhyay, Sabitri Prasanna 8
  Byarthabodhan 8, 61
Chattopadhyay, Sarat Chandra 8, 60
  Palli Samaj 8
Chaudhuri, Amit 12, 110, 131, 135, 140
  The Picador Book of Modern Indian Literature 110
Chekov, Anton 9, 102
children 7, 10–11, 30, 34, 52, 54, 56–7, 99–100, 111, 117, 133
  care of 10
Chimera 10
China 9, 12, 81–2, 96–7, 100, 120–1, 132, 134–5
Chishti silsilah 32
Chishti Order 4
Chōla 20
  inscriptions 20
Christianity 6, 10, 42–3
chronology 21–2
  sangam 21
cirupuṟam ena 24
city 7–8, 58, 65, 81–5, 90–1, 122, 136
coins 17, 24, 142
commentators 2
Communist International (Comintern) 98
communities 6, 14, 38, 54, 68
compilation 19, 133
consciousness 8, 11, 43, 89, 115, 157
  caste 8
conspiracy 9, 117
  against the Communist experiment
    in Russia 9
contentment 2, 19, 23
controversy 10–11, 129
  Orientalist-Anglicist 10
criticism 10, 12, 61–2, 98–9, 101, 120, 129, 143, 152–4
  literary 12, 152
critics 12–13, 110, 112, 116, 124, 128–30, 146, 151–2, 154, 157–8, 161–2
  Western 13, 146
cultural transformation 10
culture 5–6, 9, 14, 38–40, 42, 53, 58, 60, 62, 66, 97–8, 105, 117, 122, 125, 128, 139, 144, 151, 159–61, 163
  Indian 5, 40, 117, 125, 128
  Islamic 5
  local 5
  print 6

Dalmia, Vasudha 2
Danil'Chuk, A.P. Gnatyuk 8, 83, 96
Dara Shikoh, Mughal Prince 4
Dasgupta, Ashin 1
Das, Kamala 11, 116, 157
Datta, Satyendranath 54, 67
Datta, Sudhindranath 101
Desai, Anita 11, 116–17, 145, 157
Desai, Kiran 13, 117, 144–5
  The Inheritance of Loss 13, 144
Devi, Mahasweta 13, 155
  Stanadayini 13, 155
Dey, Amit 3, 5–6, 11, 14, 27, 42–3, 125, 135, 137
diversity 9, 39, 101, 116, 128
  notions of 9, 101
Dom Soyuzov 89
drama 81, 84–5, 88
Duraiswami Pillai, Vidvan Avvai Su. 2, 19
Dutta, Krishna 105
Dutta, Michael Madhusudan 7, 10, 51, 55, 112
  Parichay 7, 51
duzdi 29

Index

East Europe 13
East India Company 89, 111
echo effect 144
economy 8, 156
  village 8
education 8–9, 31, 54, 89–91, 97, 99–101, 103, 110–13, 119, 137
  system 9, 101
    stereotyped 9, 101
emotions 1, 50, 56, 61, 65
England 64, 95, 110, 114
Enlightenment 6, 14, 38
  European 6
epilogue 2, 20
Ettuttokai 2, 19, 23
exotic, the 13, 66, 125, 143, 145–6

fable 2, 18
Forster 115, 124
France 104, 114
Friday prayers 3
fundamentalism 6, 37, 41

Gandhi 10–11, 62, 97–8, 114–16, 123
Germany 10, 95, 98, 100, 127
Ghosh, Amitav 11–12, 117, 127–8, 130, 132, 157
Gide, André 13, 104–5, 140
Gitanjali 13, 114, 139, 141, 144
Glavlit 10, 99
Goethe 13, 148
Gorbachev 103
Gorky 104, 106
Gosains 8
Grambartaprakashika 60
Guha, Ranajit 1, 17–19
  History at the Limit of World-History 17–18
gynocriticism 154

Hama Ust 5, 39
Hasan, Amir 3, 29
  Fawa'id-u'l-Fu'ad 3, 29
Hay, Stephen 96
Hazrat Mian Mir 4
Hazrat Sayeda Zainab Khatun 4, 33

Hemistich 33
Himalayas 7, 50–1, 53, 63, 67
Hinduism 6, 38–9, 42–3
Hindu-Muslim 89
Hindus 5, 7, 11, 34, 39–40, 42–3, 50–2, 58, 64, 66–7, 83, 111–12, 114, 125
Hindu, The 124
historicality 1, 14, 17–19
historiography 1, 18–19
  academic 1
  failure of 19
  Indian 18
  literary 1
  modern 18
  objective 1
  pedantic 18
  poverty of 18
  rational 1
  scientific 1
history
  Indian 17, 51, 64
  prose of 18
hujra 4, 35
humanity 10, 35, 86, 88, 90, 102–3
humiliation 31, 88
hymns 7, 51, 55, 88

identity 7, 49–51, 53, 56, 64, 66, 68, 113, 115, 119, 158
  cultural 7
idolatrous imagery 7
idol worship 5, 7, 39
ijtihad 6, 41
ilm 6, 41
imagination 7, 50–1, 53–4, 56, 64, 84, 89, 159
imperialism 81, 87–8, 98, 119, 129, 161–2
India 1, 3, 5–8, 10–11, 17, 27–8, 31, 33, 35, 37–43, 50–6, 58, 62–3, 66–7, 82, 86, 89–91, 97–8, 105, 109–26, 128–31, 136–7, 140–1, 143–4, 146, 153–4, 156–61
  British rule in 10
  eclectic traditions 27, 37, 41

Hindu Aryan imagery of 7
  medieval 3, 27, 37
    Persian sources of 27
  modern 110
  pluralistic traditions of 82
  pre-colonial 1, 41–2
  Sufi movement of 28
Indian National Academy of Literature 124
Indian National Congress 89
inscriptions 2, 17, 20–3
  Ahmi 22
  Chola 20
  Damili 22
  Pugalur 21–3
  Pugalur Tamil-Brahmin 2, 21–3
  Tamil-Brāhmi 21–2
intellectuals 9–10, 14, 64, 101, 113, 157
  Communist 9–10
    Indian 10
  revolutionary 10
  Soviet 9
  Third World 14, 157
inter-faith debates 5
invaders 6, 51
  foreign 6, 51
irfan 6
Irumporai, Peruñcēral 21
Islam 3, 5–6, 14, 27–9, 33, 35, 38, 40–3, 58
  interest in Indian culture 5
Islamic
  opinion 14
  orthodoxy 3
  religious life 28
  thinking 6
Izvestia 9–10, 102–3

Jahan Ara or Fatima 4
  Munis-ul-Arwa 4
  Risala-i-Sahibiyya 4
Jalal-ud-din Rumi 3, 27
jamat khanas 5
Jambai 22
Jibansmriti 82

Joshi, Ruchir 12, 131

kafirs 5
Kalidasa 7, 13, 63, 148
  Meghadootam 7
  Shakuntala 7
kānam 24
Kapilar 21, 23–4
Karakhan, Lev, the Russian ambassador to China 9
Kashmir 5, 36, 39
Kerala 2, 19–20
  chronicle of 2
Kerr, J.H. 83
KGB 106
Khalifa 4, 30, 37
khanqas 5
Khwaja Mu'in-ud-din Chisti 4
Khwaja Qutbu'd-din Bakhtiyar Kaki 29
Kipling 124–5
knowledge 1, 5–6, 9, 18, 24, 36–8, 40–3, 60, 86, 89–90, 104, 111–12, 119, 133, 142, 154
  colonialist 18
  divine 6, 42
Kō ātan Cel-Irumporai 21, 23
Koran 3, 5, 28, 31, 39, 43
KPD (Communist Party of Germany) 10, 98
Krishnachandra, Maharaja 4
kuṛiñcippāṭṭu 23

labour 8, 32–3, 61, 81, 84, 87–8, 110
  agricultural 8
  contractors 8
  exploited 8
  human 8
  indentured 8
  lowly-paid 32
  manual 32
  plantation 8
langar 4, 35, 120
languages/literatures 1–3, 5–6, 8–14, 17–19, 24–5, 38–9, 41, 49–51, 53, 55–6, 59–60, 63–5, 67, 83,

88, 99, 102, 109–37, 140, 142–7,
    152–60
ancient 2
  susceptibility of 2
Anglo-Indian 124
Bhasha 13–14, 153–60
British 124–5
Bengali 9, 12–13, 34, 43, 49, 53–5,
    59–61, 64–7, 95, 112–13, 123,
    127, 133, 139–44, 146–7, 151,
    155, 159, 162
Brajabhasha 5, 38
caṅkam 2, 19
cosmopolitan 14
English 10, 12–13, 65, 110, 112–14,
    116–19, 123–5, 128–30, 132–3,
    137, 153, 155–6, 158–9
  Asian 12
  Indian 13, 110, 112–13, 116,
    123–5, 129
evolution of 14
Hindawi 5, 38
Hinglish 12, 120–2
historical 12
Indian 14, 17, 39, 109, 122, 124–5,
    128, 137, 155
Indo-Anglian 11, 14, 117, 124
Indo-English 124
intermingling of 5
  process of 5
Islamic 3, 6
  medieval 6
Latin 6, 43, 120, 158
modern day 3
nationalist 6, 49–51, 55, 59, 63, 67
Persian 3, 5–6, 14, 27–9, 38–43,
    112, 124
Persian Sufi 14
preservation of 24
pre-Sufi 3
Punjabi 5, 38, 125, 127
Russian 9
Sanskrit 6, 39, 42, 63–4, 111–12,
    114–15, 129, 137, 162
Sufi 3, 5–6, 14, 41
  medieval 6

mystical 3
Tamil 1, 3
  classical 1, 3
  vernacular 109–10, 156
  vernacularization of 5
Lenin 98–9, 104
Lev Karakhan 9, 96, 106
literacy 10
Lodi, Sultan Sikandar 5, 39
Lukacs, Georg 10
  Rote Fahne (Red Flag) 10, 98
Lunacharsky, Anatoly 9, 97, 99, 106
Luzzatti, Luigi 143, 145

Macaulay 10, 112, 156
Mahabharata, the 5, 7, 51, 136
Mahadevan, I. 21–2
Mahmud of Ghazni 5
Majma-ul-Zabanat 5
Majumdar, Harinath 60
Maktabkhanas 5
malfuzat 4, 32
Manchester Guardian 9, 103
manuscripts 19–20, 41
marriage 30, 33, 67, 88, 128
Marxism 104
  German 104
Masters, John 124
materialism 7, 84, 87
  Western 7, 87
Maulana Ala'u'd-din Usuli 31
mentality 1–2, 17
  historical 17
Meyerhold 9, 97, 99, 106
meykkīrtti 20
Mirza Mazhar Jan-i-Janan, a Naqsh-
    bandi Sufi poet 5
misery 2, 8, 19, 23, 51
missionaries 10, 111
modernity 14, 62, 67, 114, 119, 128
Modern Review 8, 96, 105
monasteries 5, 37
  sufi 5, 37
monasticism 27
  christian 27
  medieval 27

monotheism 6, 42–3
　Koranic 6
　Upanishadic 6, 42
monuments 17, 55
motherland 52, 56–8, 64
Muhammad-bin-Tughluq, Sultan 4
Muhammad of Ghur 5
Muharram 4, 35
Mukherjee, Meenakshi 114, 125, 129–30, 159–60
Mukherjee, Sujit 105
Mukhopadhyay, Bhudev 7, 51
　Adhibharati 7, 51
　Pushpanjali 7
Mulla Daud 5, 39
Mulla Shah 4, 36–7
multiculturalism 5, 37, 43
Muslims 3, 5, 7, 27–8, 34–5, 37, 39–43, 52, 58, 64, 66–7, 82–3
　cultivators 82
　men 3, 28
　rulers 5, 39
　women 3, 28
mysticism 4–5, 37, 42
　Indian 5
mystic revelations 4

Nadia 4
Naik, M.K. 124, 129
　A History of Indian English Literature 124
Naivedya 82
namazes 4, 32
Nandini 8, 83–5, 88
　red flowers 8
Nandy, Ashis 82, 86
Narayan, R.K. 11, 114, 125, 130, 157
　Swami and Friends 11
narrative 1, 18, 68, 113–17
　statist 18
narratologies 18
Nasir-ud-din 4–5
nation 6–7, 14, 43, 49–50, 53–4, 56, 58, 60, 67–8, 82, 86–7, 89, 96, 102, 117, 119, 123, 160
　authenticating 53

　Bengali 53–4
　folk roots of the 60
　geographical identity of 53
　Hinduaryan 60
　human aspect of 53
　Indian 50, 54, 67, 119
　nature and 6
　pan-Indian 67
　romantic recovery of 67
nationalism 6, 14, 49–50, 53, 56, 60, 65–7, 69, 82, 86–7, 98
　literary 6
　romantic 6
nationhood 2, 60, 68
nation-states 82, 86
　Western 82
nature/natural 1, 6–7, 12, 14, 22–3, 29, 31, 38, 40, 49, 50–8, 60, 62–9, 85–6, 99, 102, 114, 116, 119, 127–8, 131, 133, 162
　nationalization of 6, 49, 56
Nava Yuga 6
nazms 32
Nehru, Jawaharlal 97, 104–5, 116, 118, 123
nihilism 9, 83, 96
　moral 9, 83, 96
Nilakantha Shastri, K.A. 1, 17, 24
Nizamu'd-din Auliya 29–32

Oldenburg 9, 97
orientalists 9, 10, 97–8, 112
orthodoxy 3, 28, 41, 112
　Islamic 3
Orutantai 24

painting 11, 23
Pandarattar, T.V. Sadasiva 20
Pāri 23
paricil 20
Pasternak, Boris 13, 140
pāṭān 22
Patanjali 5, 39
　Yogasutra 5
pāṭāntinai 2, 22
Pathak, Vishwambhar Sharan 2, 17–18

Ancient Historians of India: A Study in Historical Biographies 17
Path O Patheya 82
patikams 2, 20–1, 24
Patiṟṟuppattu 1–2, 17, 19, 21, 23
pattuppāṭṭu 19
Pavlovich 9, 97
Pearson, W.W. 85
peasants 10, 58–9, 89–90, 100, 102, 127
  upliftment of 10
perceptions 59, 127, 146
  non-Western 146
Permanent revolution 9
Persian sources 3, 27
phallic criticism 154
philosophy 10, 38, 40, 99
Pir 5, 33–4
Pir Hazrat Gorachand Razi 33–4
pizza effect 13, 146
poem 2, 7–8, 13, 19–20, 22–4, 50–3, 55–7, 59, 62, 65, 67, 87, 139–43
  colophons of 20
  decade 19–20, 22, 24
  laudatory 19
  realistic 8
poet 2–3, 5–8, 10, 12–13, 19–24, 27, 39–40, 50–7, 59, 62, 64–5, 83, 89, 97–9, 115, 139–44, 148
  Eastern 12
  Hungarian 10, 98
  Tamil 22–3
    classical 22–3
poetry 22, 61, 63, 89, 114, 124, 141–3, 147, 157
  court 22
  heroic 22
  Indian 124
Pollock, Sheldon 11, 14
Prakriti 7, 63
prasasti 24
prejudice 3, 145
Prem Chand 159
  Godan 159
Prince dara 4, 6, 27, 35–43
  Safinat-ul-Awaliya 6

Prophet Muhammad 3, 5, 27–9, 32, 36, 41, 43
  sympathy for women 3, 27
prose 18, 20, 24, 42, 61, 109, 112–14, 139, 141, 145
P_rP 19–22, 24
Punjab 4, 35, 127
puṟam 19, 22
Puṟānanuāṟu 19
Puranas 5, 39
purity 8, 58, 118, 123, 128

Qadiryya 4
Qaza'i Ilahi 31
Qilae Sipri 31
Qutbud-din Mubarak Shah, Sultan 3

Rājarāja 20
Rabi'a al-Adawiyya 3, 28
railways 6
Raman, C.V. 97
Ramayana, the 5, 7
Ramgiri 7, 63
Ranjan 83, 88
Ranke, German historian 1
rationalism 38
Raushan Ara (Raushan Bibi) 4, 33–4, 37
Ray, Gobinda Chandra 7
  Jamunalahari 7, 51
Ray, Kamini 7, 51
  Ashar Swapan 7, 51
Ray, Rajkrishna 8, 52
Ray, Satyajit 146, 159
  Pather Panchali 159
realism 61, 114, 116–17, 129, 145
recitation 20
  metrical 20
religions 3, 5–7, 27, 38, 40–3, 87, 100, 102, 111
religiosity 3
religious
  injections 28
  knowledge 5, 38
Reminiscences 82
repression 8, 10, 86

rebellion against 8
rhythm 20, 60, 85, 90, 141
rivalry 8, 60
  group 8
rivers 4, 7, 33, 50–1, 53–7, 61, 63, 68, 140
  Ganga 7, 50, 59, 160
  Ichamati 4, 33
  Jamuna 7, 50–1
  Kaveri 7, 50
  Narmada 7, 50–1, 53
Robinson, Andrew 105
Roerich, Nicholas 96
Rolland, Romain 104–5
romance 59–60, 62, 65, 113
  rural 59–60, 62
Romanticism 61–5
Roy, Arundhati 13, 125, 127, 129–30, 144, 157
  God of Small Things 13, 125, 127, 144–5
Roy, M.N. 10, 98
Roy, Rammohun 6, 40, 42–3, 112
Roy, Sabitri 13, 155
roza 32
rule of law 6
Rushdie, Salman 11–13, 109–10, 116–17, 119, 122–3, 127–31, 144–5, 156–8
Russia 8–10, 81, 83, 86, 88–9, 91, 95–8, 100–6
  conspiracy against the communist experiment in 9
  efforts to spread literacy 10
  negative image of 9
  political experiment in 9
  political situation in 9, 95
Russian Revolution 96–7, 104

Sahitya Akademi 124, 128
saints 3–6, 28–33, 35–9, 41–2
  female 4, 33
  sufi 4, 6, 29–30, 35, 38
Saiva Siddhanta Works Publishing Society (SSWPS) 2, 19–20
sajjada 5, 33, 37
sajjada nashins 5, 37

Santiniketan 7–8, 81–3
Sanyal, Sulekha 13, 155
Sardars 8
Sastri 17, 24
Scott, Paul 124
Scott, Sir Walter 1, 124
scriptures 6, 40, 88
security 8, 33, 58
Sen, Keshab Chandra 6, 43
Sen, Kshitimohan 81
Serebryanny, Sergei 103
Shadi Muqri 31
Shah Jehan 6
Shaikh Abdul-Haqq Muhaddis Dihlawi 3–4, 28, 30
  Akhbar'ul-Akhyar 3, 28–9, 31, 35
Shaikh Badru'd-Din Ishaq 30
Shaikh Fariduddin Ganj-i-Shakar 29
Shaikh Nasir-ud-din 4
  Chirag-i-Dihlawi 4
Shaikh Nizamu'd-din Auliya 3–4, 28–32
Shakespeare 13, 125, 148
Sind 5
Sinha, Sasadhar 9, 95
Sipri Fort 3
society
  outlook of 5
  reordering of 8
sociology 10, 99
songs 19, 60, 114, 128, 136, 140–1
Soviet Communist Party 98
Soviet Union 8–11, 83, 89–90, 95–106, 116, 140
  authorities 9–10, 95, 97–9, 101, 105–6
  ideals 9
  ideologues 9
  intellectuals 9
spiritualism 10, 96–8, 100
Spivak, Gayatri Chakravarty 13
Squalor 8
Stalin 98, 101, 103–4, 106
Stalinism 102, 104
Stanislavsky 9, 97, 99, 106
Sufi 3–6, 14, 27–33, 35, 37–41, 43
  belief 30

biographies 28
female 33, 35
hierarchy 31
hospices 5, 39
literature 3, 5, 14, 41
monasteries 5, 37
movement 28, 37
poet 5, 39
saint 4–6, 29–30, 35, 37–9
woman 4
Sufism 5, 27–8, 30–1, 38, 40
Indian 27
Sultan Qutbu'd-Din Mubarak Shah 31
superstitions 8, 89
religious 89
Swadeshi 114
Swaminathan Aiyar, Mahamahopadhyaya U.V. 2, 19

Tagore, Rabindranath 1, 7–10, 12–14, 17–19, 51, 56, 59–62, 64–5, 81–91, 95–106, 113–14, 139–48, 159–60
1930 letters 9
at the crossroads 8, 96
Creative Unity 7, 87
creative voice of 18
denunciation of Western materialism 7
Dui Bigha Jami 59
Ghare Baire (the Home and the World) 10, 159
Hindu Melay Upahar 51
letter of 25 September 1930 8
Letters from Russia 95, 100–1, 105–6
Paschim Yatrir Diary 83
Rakhibandhan Utsav 83
Rakta Karabi 8, 81, 83, 87–8
Russiar Chithi 9, 95
Sadhana: The Realization in Life 7
Santiniketan Essays 7
Sarat 61
visit to the Soviet Union 10
Tagore, Surendranath 82
Tagore syndrome 12, 139, 145–6
tales 1, 11, 27
Koranic 27
Talib, Abu 3
Qutal Qulub 3
tapovana 7
tarjuma 159
Tasawwur-i-Shaikh 5
Tauhid 6
texts 1–3, 8–10, 17–23, 99–100, 129, 131, 145–8, 151, 159, 161–2
ancient 2–3
canonical 159
literary 8–10, 17–19, 100
contents of 18
Indian 18
Tamil 1–3, 17, 19, 21, 23
classical 1–3, 17, 19, 21, 23
thoughts 5, 84, 100
Tinai 2, 22
Titu Mir 4
tolerance 3
Tolkāppiyar 22
Tolstoy 97
traditions 1, 3, 6, 23–4, 27, 31, 34, 37–8, 41, 43, 50, 58, 60, 63, 82, 96–7, 113–16, 124, 128, 135–7, 142, 144, 146, 152, 157–60, 163
eclectic 3, 27, 37, 41
folk 60
Greek 124
Kavya 1
liberal 6
literary 23–4, 63, 136, 146, 157
Tamil 23–4
mystical 3, 27, 31
pluralistic 82
Purana 1
Roman 124
tranquillity 8
translations 13–14, 17, 24, 39, 81, 95, 114, 122, 124–5, 127, 139, 141–3, 147, 151–6, 158–63
annotated 13
English 13, 141–2, 151, 155, 158
literal 124, 127
policies 14
norms of 14
translators 13, 111, 141, 153, 160–2

Trotsky 10, 98
tāukku 20
Turai 20
Turkomenistan 89

Ulema 31
unilinearity 9, 101
United States of America (USA) 86, 95–6, 100, 105, 114, 116, 123
Urs 34
USSR 96–8, 105–6
uttarupaniveshbad 162

vallal 23
Vedas 5, 7, 39, 63
Veltman 10, 98
veneration 28
vernaculars 5, 12, 111, 154
  Englishization of 12
verses 19, 32, 140
village 7–8, 11, 24, 33, 54–5, 58–62, 65, 68, 90–1, 127, 130
  economy 8
  life 8, 130
    evils of 8
  romanticization of 8
  Taragunia 33
virtue 3, 27, 87, 159
vivartanam 159
VOKS 9, 97, 103–4

wahdat-ul-wujud 5
West Bengal 33
womanhood 27
women 3–5, 13–14, 27–30, 32, 35–7, 41, 56, 84, 86, 114–15, 127–8, 151–6, 160, 162–3
  capability of 3

  intellectual 3
  moral 3
  elderly 29
  Muslim 3, 28
  pious 28
  position of 5
  Prophet's sympathy for 3, 27
  role of 3, 27
    in religious life 27
  Sufi 4
  virtuous 28
  writers 13, 153, 155, 160, 162
World War, First 7, 9, 62, 67, 88
writers 2, 7, 10–11, 13, 27–8, 51, 59, 61–2, 67, 99, 109–10, 114, 117, 119, 125, 127–31, 135–7, 140, 145, 152–60, 162
  creative 110
  women 13, 153, 155, 160, 162
writings 1, 6, 10–14, 18, 27, 35, 38, 49, 62, 65, 81, 83, 85, 98, 102, 109–10, 112, 116–17, 119, 124, 128–31, 135–6, 139, 141, 143–7, 151, 153–7, 159–60, 162–3
  academic 18
  historical 1
  Indian 109–10, 112, 116, 129–30, 135, 153, 156–7
    English 117, 124, 130
  non-Western 12

Yeats, William Butler 12–13, 139–40, 142–4, 148
Yogis 5

Zainul Abedin, Kashmir 5
zikr 29
ziyarat 4, 31